REFORMING WELFARE
Lessons, Limits, and Choices

REFORMING WELFARE

Lessons, Limits, and Choices

EDITED BY
Richard M. Coughlin

University of New Mexico
Public Policy Series
Fred R. Harris, Series Editor

UNIVERSITY OF NEW MEXICO
Albuquerque

Chapter 9 has been reprinted by permission of the
National Governors' Association.
Chapter 10 has been reprinted by permission of the
National Coalition on Women, Work, and Welfare.

Library of Congress Cataloging-in-Publication Data

Reforming welfare.

   (University of New Mexico public policy series)
   Includes bibliographies and index.
     1. Public welfare—United States. 2. Social policy—
United States. I. Coughlin, Richard M. II. Series.
HV91.R424 1989   361'.973   88-28044
ISBN 0-8263-1130-X
ISBN 0-8263-1131-8 (pbk.)

Design by Susan Gutnik

Contents

Foreword

It is my pleasure to introduce *Reforming Welfare: Lessons, Limits, and Choices* as the second volume in the University of New Mexico Public Policy Series. A primary goal of the series is to make available to a wide audience of scholars, students, policy makers, and the public at large recent research and scholarly perspectives on contemporary policy issues of importance to the nation and the Southwest region. A secondary goal of the series is to stimulate participation of scholars from different academic disciplines in the analysis of public policy issues. By their very nature public policies intersect with a variety of academic disciplines and research traditions, beginning with political science but extending to economics, sociology, and history, to name a few. In addition, no analysis or attempt to understand the development and impact of public policies can be complete without some account of the viewpoints and experience of policy makers and program administrators whose acquaintance with the subject is firsthand.

Reforming Welfare: Lessons, Limits, and Choices grew out of a regional symposium on welfare reform. All across the political spectrum, both within government and as advocated by citizen groups, there has been strong agitation for reform of America's welfare system. What are the purposes of welfare—and how well are we doing? How can we dispel persistent myths and misperceptions about welfare? How much poverty is there, and what is its nature? What is meant by the "feminization of poverty," and how should it be dealt with? What about medical care for the poor? How well do work programs work? What are the terms and merits of the various welfare reform proposals that have been put forward? These are some of the serious questions about welfare that were addressed in the regional symposium and that are, now, in a more refined and organized way, dealt with in this book.

The Public Policy Series is sponsored by the University of New Mexico's Institute for Public Policy as part of its mission to promote public policy research and analysis, seminars and symposia, and policy-related publications. The Institute gratefully acknowledges the financial support of the College of Arts and Sciences to help establish the series. With a grant from the University of New Mexico Foundation, the Institute has conducted seminars and symposia on the management of governmental budget cuts, Southwest energy policy, and welfare reform.

Fred R. Harris
Series Editor

Introduction

Richard M. Coughlin

Since the 1960s welfare reform has been a topic of perennial concern as well as a persistent sore point in American social policy. The welfare system—a term used principally to refer to Aid to Families with Dependent Children (AFDC) but at times embracing related public assistance programs such as food stamps and Medicaid—has been widely perceived as a failure. The "welfare crisis" that began nearly thirty years ago has stubbornly persisted despite repeated efforts to reform the system. Like Sisyphus, the mythical king of Corinth whose punishment was forever to roll a huge stone up a hill in Hades only to have it roll down again, those who sought to reform welfare in the 1980s seemingly found themselves once again at the base of the mountain.

In 1987 and 1988, however, the pace of activity picked up and the public debate took on a renewed sense of optimism and purpose. The deadlock that had long stalled legislation in Congress broke sufficiently to enable passage of the Family Support Act of 1988, which made significant changes in the AFDC program. The papers in this volume, most of which grew out of a symposium held at the University of New Mexico in April 1987, provide a background and critical assessment of the issues and questions central to welfare reform. While this volume owes its existence to the same spirit of constructive possibility that paved the way to passage of the 1988 legislation, it also serves as a caution that the controversies surrounding welfare have not been put to rest.

THEMES OF WELFARE REFORM

Like the national debate over welfare reform, the papers in this volume do not follow a single path or speak with one voice; never-

1

theless, they do converge on a few main themes. The first theme explores *developments in empirical research* concerning the characteristics of the welfare recipient population, the dynamics of dependency, the effectiveness of work requirement and job training programs, and a variety of other social and economic correlates of public assistance programs. Roughly half of the chapters in this volume address, wholly or in significant part, the relationship between welfare and dependency. It is clear that recent social science research has provided a much sounder base for the policy discussion and action than was available during previous periods. What is remarkable is that it has taken so long for social scientists to study many fundamental questions about welfare.

A second theme concerns what broadly speaking might be termed the *politics of welfare reform.* Several chapters deal with ideological currents found in the American political culture—including attitudes toward the role of government, dominant beliefs about the nature of inequality and dependency, and prevailing myths and misconceptions about welfare and poverty—and their implications for welfare reform. Other chapters cover the policy positions of significant actors and interest groups who have sought to influence the course of welfare reform. A final group of papers addresses aspects of the relationship between federal and state initiatives in reforming welfare and related assistance programs.

Taken together, these two broad themes—the nature of dependency and the politics of welfare reform—help to build a bridge between knowledge about welfare and poverty and what it is possible to do with this knowledge to guide and sustain reform initiatives within the constraints of political and economic reality.

ORGANIZATION OF THE VOLUME

The volume is organized into four parts. Part one, which provides some historical background, consists of Jane Cotter's chapter on the evolution of policy reforms in AFDC and other social welfare programs originating with the New Deal. Cotter's analysis illuminates some of the disparities that have crept into the nation's social programs over the years, particularly between AFDC (which Cotter reminds us is after all "the program for children") and programs for the elderly and disabled. She notes that of the major public assistance programs, AFDC has evolved the least since its inception (as evidenced, for example, in the wide variations still found among the states in need standards and benefit levels). Not only has AFDC fallen behind other programs in budgetary terms, it has been isolated for special negative treatment in public attitudes, in the stigma attached to recipients, and in the exaggerated emphasis on the question of fraud and abuse. Cotter's list of major reforms needed in AFDC include removal of the deprivation of parental support criterion, enactment of uniform national standards for eligibility and benefit levels, and, finally, fundamental changes in the public perception of the program.

Part two consists of analytical perspectives on welfare drawn from political science, sociology, and economics.

Edward Harpham and Richard Scotch critically review the welfare reform ideologies of contemporary radical, liberal, and conservative critics, concluding that the ideologies of all three camps have failed to provide a sound basis for reforming welfare in the United States. For example, they note that Charles Murray's proposal, set forth in *Losing Ground,* to dismantle the American welfare state is out of step with the long-standing public consensus in favor of maintaining a wide range of basic governmentally sponsored social and economic protections. Likewise, neither the current sentiment of the American people nor present economic realities are hospitable to left-liberal proposals to enact large increases in spending to fight poverty. Harpham and Scotch conclude that the only feasible approach to welfare reform is to forge a "pragmatist consensus" on a modest reform agenda—one that accepts as givens both the institutionalized nature of existing programs, which realistically cannot be done away with, and the stringent budgetary conditions that exist now and are likely to continue into the foreseeable future. The authors' conclusion presages the 1988 welfare reform legislation that emerged out of a compromise between liberals and conservatives in Congress, but it also serves as a warning that proposals to increase spending for public assistance programs will likely remain in jeopardy as policy makers seek to reduce the federal deficit.

The chapter by Charles Lockhart also begins with the assumption that to succeed, welfare reform must attempt to reconcile, or at least bridge, opposing ideological currents present in American politics. Lockhart's analysis goes well beyond the incremental reform measures found in recent legislation. He notes that social insurance programs such as Social Security have been successful in distributing benefits to broad segments of the population while at the same time maintaining high levels of public support. In contrast, public assistance programs have posed a much more difficult challenge: to be most effective benefits must be narrowly targeted, but targeting by means tests and related methods contributes to social stigma and conflict and undercuts the base of popular support. Lockhart's discussion of these issues underscores the point that the problems of the welfare poor are simply less tractable than those of other groups. As solutions he proposes gradually withdrawing most existing public assistance benefits from working age adults, restructuring of AFDC and related public assistance programs on a basis similar to successful social insurance programs, and facilitating welfare-recipient access to the labor market by increased provisions for child care and job training.

In the same section, my own paper explores the origins and consequences of myths and stereotypes related to welfare. I argue that common misconceptions about welfare represent more than simple lack of knowledge about poverty and economic dependency. These myths and stereotypes are deeply rooted in the dominant ideology of American society, and their existence owes much to enduring popular values and beliefs about the causes of poverty and the characteristics of the poor. I suggest that in the policy debate a variety of misconceptions borne of ideology has tended to divert the attention of the public and policy makers alike to problems of the welfare system that are blown out of proportion (e.g., the problem of fraud and abuse) or entirely unsubstantiated (e.g., the perceived overuse of social services by illegal immigrants). While recent social science research has provided the requisite "facts" to counter many of the prevailing welfare "myths," I conclude that knowledge alone is not enough; the reform of welfare programs needs to be accompanied by reforms in the terms of the welfare debate.

Chapters by Daniel Weinberg and Gary Burtless address the economics of welfare and speak directly to the issues of work requirements and program costs and benefits. In an exhaustive review of over 150 studies, Weinberg explores two contrasting views of welfare: one view holds that the poor have become mired in a state of dependency that welfare programs only exacerbate; the other view is that poverty is largely a short-term condition for which welfare programs provide essential temporary relief. He concludes that both views contain some truth, in large part reflecting a basic split within the welfare dependent population between short- and long-term recipients. Policies aimed at one group of welfare recipients may not work for the other group. While Weinberg does not offer specific prescriptions for reform, his analysis has important policy implications in several areas, including "workfare" programs, family structure, youth unemployment, intergenerational dependency, migration, and child support enforcement. Overall, Weinberg's analysis suggests that although our understanding of the dynamics of welfare dependency has improved there is still much we do not know.

The chapter by Burtless is more narrowly focused on the impact of work requirements and job training programs for welfare recipients. He notes an emerging consensus in American society in favor of work requirements in welfare—a basic attitudinal change growing out of the changing patterns of female labor force participation in the larger population. More and more middle-class women with dependent children are employed outside the home, and this has led to a reconsideration of the exemptions from work for welfare mothers with young children. At the same time Burtless sees only modest gains to be made from work and training programs in welfare: such programs may do some good in some cases, but overall he concludes that the prospects of eliminating or even significantly reducing public assistance through such means is illusory. Given the emphasis on work requirements in recent welfare reforms, Burtless' conclusions should serve as an important cautionary note.

Part three covers the welfare reform policy positions of important political actors and interest groups in the debate of the 1980s. These proposals span the political and ideological spectrum. Daeley's chapter, entitled "Up From Dependency," summarizes the position of the Reagan Administration set forth in a wide-ranging and lengthy series of studies published from 1986 to 1988. The central thesis of this position is that current welfare programs act to diminish personal choice and individual responsibility, they encourage the receipt of welfare benefits over work, and they undermine the traditional role of the local community. The proposed solution is to devolve responsibility for welfare from the federal government to the states. While it is unlikely that the call for a radical decentralization of welfare will carry over to the new administration, the underlying support for such changes continues to be strong among American conservatives.

The following chapter by A. Sidney Johnson, III, outlines the position of the American Public Welfare Association, reflecting an "emerging consensus" over welfare reform. The elements of this consensus include the idea of reciprocal obligations between individuals and society; the importance of work as the alternative to welfare; the responsibility of government to provide training and education required for employment; the need to link increased support services (such as child care, transportation, and medical care) to efforts to employ welfare mothers; enforcement of child support payments; and finally increases in welfare benefits. In addition, Johnson's chapter charts the progress of recent Congressional initiatives leading up to the passage of the legislation worked out by House and Senate negotiators in the summer and fall of 1988.

The bipartisan willingness to reach compromise on welfare reform is suggested in the following chapter presenting the welfare reform policy of the National Governors' Association (NGA). The NGA proposal calls for a job-oriented reform program emphasizing prevention of dependency. The purpose of such a program would be to transform welfare from a payment system with a minor work component into a jobs program backed by income assistance. This aspiration, however bipartisan and moderate, may not be realistic. Although recent changes in AFDC place increased emphasis on employment training for welfare recipients, it is doubtful that we are close to seeing the kind of reversal in the perception or reality of public assistance programs that the NGA proposes.

The last of the position papers describes the welfare reform proposal of the National Coalition on Women, Work, and Welfare. The coalition stresses many of the same elements (e.g., child support, expanded services) as the other reform proposals, but departs from the "emerging consensus" mainstream on the question of mandatory work requirements. The coalition proposal argues pointedly that poverty, not welfare, is the problem that needs to be redressed. As the solution, the coalition proposes federally supported income maintenance benefits equal to at least 100 percent of the established poverty level, with universal eligibility for all needy families based only on income that is actually available to the families seeking assistance. In addition, the coalition supports new federal and state initiatives in education, training, and employment for welfare recipients, but only if participation in such program is *voluntary*. A key premise of the coalition's position is that no welfare family should be placed at risk of having benefits punitively withdrawn as a result of failure to participate in training or employment programs, or by refusal to accept a job. While a minority position in the recent debate, strong resistance to mandatory work requirements was voiced by Representative Augustus Hawkins (D-Ca.) and nine other members of the joint House and Senate committee who opposed such measures on the grounds that they were "slavefare," conjuring images of Victorian work houses.

Part four of the volume consists of two case studies of welfare or welfare-related reform initiatives in states of the American Southwest. These chapters each provide insights into how the unique political, economic, and cultural contexts of Texas and New Mexico have influenced the development of government programs for the poor. Both are states that, for different reasons, have historically lagged in developing social welfare programs.

Tomás Atencio describes the history and current prospects of welfare reform in relation to the traditional, rural Hispanic communities of northern New Mexico. His thesis is that welfare programs based on a model of urban-industrial society have from the very start been incongruent with the "social and cultural antecedents" of these communities, and that current proposals at the state level for welfare reform are similarly misguided. As an alternative to conventional welfare policies Atencio suggests a reform strategy that builds on traditional elements of the rural region's culture and social relations, an approach he sees as the only way to improve the "post industrial" economic circumstances of a people who were for the most part bypassed by the development of urban-industrial society.

The chapter by Philip Armour describes the recent enactment of indigent health care legislation in Texas. Although its focus is on health care rather than AFDC, Armour's analysis is nonetheless valuable in helping to understand the dynamics of policy reform at the state level. His discussion sheds light on the interaction of policies at the national and state levels, and while the focus of his attention is health care, the policy making setting he describes shares many common features with state efforts nationwide to reform welfare. Specifically, Armour's discussion of policy reform in Texas is suggestive of what states may be able or forced to do in the absence of uniform national policies. Equally important, Armour provides a detailed account of how such efforts at the state level can be made to succeed despite adverse political conditions.

PROSPECTS FOR CONTINUING REFORM

Passage of the Family Support Act of 1988 marked a significant milestone in American solical politics, but it did not mark the end of the road of welfare reform. The 1988 legislation has raised expectations that will be difficult—some would say impossible—to fulfil. Heralded as the first major overhaul of the welfare system in fifty years, in many respects the 1988 law is a modest initiative: it includes new requirements for job training or education for AFDC recipients, provisions for one year of day care assistance and continuation of Medicaid eligibility to ease the transition from welfare to work, stepped up enforcement of child support payments, and limited expansion of benefits to two-parent families. While these changes are not inconsequential, they leave many problems and issues unresolved. To illustrate this point, I will conclude by addressing two questions: Why has welfare proved so hard to reform? What can be expected (and not expected) as a result of recent reforms?

Partial answers to these questions can be found in the two main themes of this volume. One explanation of the widely perceived failure in previous attempts at welfare reform has to do with the sheer magnitude and complexity of the social and economic problems afflicting the welfare dependent population. The simple fact is that there is still much that we do not know about the dynamics of dependency. Although access to cash and in-kind benefits is essential to improving the lives of welfare recipients, in many cases such aid leaves the root causes of dependency untouched. In both its origins and effects welfare is inherently more complex than income maintenance programs targeted at other groups at risk of being poor, such as the elderly or the disabled, and so it has been more difficult to arrive at acceptable, much less ideal, solutions.

Another major factor inhibiting effective welfare reform has been the political vulnerability of the AFDC program and the clientele it serves. AFDC has scant support among the general public: time and again public opinion surveys have identified "welfare" as an area in which Americans would like to see government expenditures trimmed. The constituents of AFDC (single mothers and their dependent children) are (correctly) perceived to have little political clout. Compared to the elderly and many other social program constituencies the welfare poor are not strategically positioned or very well-equipped to compete in the struggle for their share of governmental budgets. They have suffered as a result, with welfare benefits eroding over the past decade and welfare programs, unlike Social Security, most definitely "on the table" in political discussions of how to cut government spending.

Finally, there are the unrealistic expectations with which welfare programs have been burdened. Poverty and social problems do not begin with public assistance programs, nor will they end with welfare reform. Nonetheless, welfare programs have often shouldered the blame for the persistence of poverty and dependency. The fact is that welfare is only one part—and a relatively small one at that—of a social and economic system that generates a large amount of inequality, material deprivation, and social pathology. Welfare has often served as the whipping boy for endemic failures of the American political economy.

What, then, is the significance of the recent reform measures? Clearly, the strategy that has been singled out for emphasis is to increase job training, education, and work opportunities for welfare recipients. The broad agreement on the need to link work and welfare reveals little, however, about how the two will actually be combined and, more importantly, what effect such measures will have on welfare dependency. At its worst, such "reform" amounts to little more than enforcing rigid work and training requirements, no matter what the circumstances of the individual or local economic conditions. At best, increased emphasis on education and job training may encourage development of real employment opportunities—meaning stable, full-time employment at a living wage—for those who move off welfare by getting a job. It remains to be seen which variant actually emerges at the state level as a result of the 1988 federal legislation. Barring some major change in the economy, providing meaningful employment opportunities will entail higher levels of government spending than is currently planned. Equally important, if past experience is any guide, such schemes will have only a modest impact on reducing welfare dependency.

Similarly, providing expanded child care services for welfare mothers poses difficult challenges of implementation. Nearly everyone accepts the idea that child care needs to be more widely available, but in practice services of even minimally acceptable quality are extremely expensive to provide. How much are we willing to pay for child care so that single mothers of young children can move off the welfare rolls? Is what we are willing to pay enough?

The same argument applies to raising welfare benefits to a level approaching adequacy. While few would be willing to defend the existing benefit structure, improving benefits will cost money: how much depends on whether the benefits in "low" states are brought up to some minimum national standard, or, costlier still, if welfare and other public assistance programs are redesigned to be effective in lifting recipients out of poverty. Generating political support for increased welfare benefits has always been difficult—and the prospects for any improvement are bleak. For example, although the Family Support Act of 1988 calls for increased welfare spending of some $3.3 billion over five years (less than half of the $7 billion the original House bill provided), it makes no provision for increased benefit levels. Moreover, the continuing problem of the federal budget deficit may place even these modest gains at risk.

How much the nation is willing to pay for welfare reform is, of course, important. But perhaps even more important is the question of what expectations are attached to reforms at the outset. One danger is that relatively limited changes will be oversold, encouraging a false sense of confidence that the problems of welfare dependency and poverty have been resolved. If it is miracles we are seeking, experience teaches that they may be hard to come by at any price— and that disappointment is not necessarily inexpensive.

I

Background

1

Twenty Years of Welfare Reform: An Insider's View

Jane Hoyt Cotter

Reform of welfare is an "in" subject. There are many perspectives and seemingly near unanimous agreement that reform is needed, although what the current round of reform will mean is not yet decided. There is little satisfaction with welfare and no lobby for the status quo. Now may be the best opportunity in many years to restructure governmental aid to poor children, who represent an ever increasing proportion of the poor.[1]

My perspective is that of a bureaucrat, someone who over a period of twenty years has had bottom to top personal experience working with the public in programs that are intended to aid those who lack essential income. My career has included working as a caseworker interviewing people in their own homes; as a supervisor overseeing and directing other staff; as a manager of a large office; and as a state director of income supplement programs. These tasks have given me a wide range of experiences, from first hand observation of how people with limited income cope to helping to formulate state policy. My interaction with other human services employees enhanced my sense of the client's perspective as well as how staff are affected by the rules and regulations governing public assistance programs. In later years I had an opportunity to share perceptions with federal administrative personnel and to experience state government budget and policy-making processes. My experience in New Mexico should be reasonably representative of the situation in other states. I believe that my insights on welfare and reform will add to the usual economic and political considerations of the social policy debate.

In this paper, I will first discuss the changes—the reforms—that have been enacted in the Aid to Families with Dependent Children program and related social programs, with emphasis on the years 1960 through 1987. The second part of the discussion will focus on the impact of these reforms on the operation and administration of welfare at the state level.

WELFARE POLICY

There is no uniform, national welfare policy, if by welfare the impressively entitled Aid to Families with Dependent Children Program (AFDC) is meant.[2] AFDC policy is a mix of federal and state regulation, which results in fifty-one programs in the various states and the District of Columbia, plus others in Puerto Rico and other island jurisdictions. The often heard comment, "If I didn't have this job, I'd have to go on welfare," may represent the normal public expectation that AFDC offers a fall back position, but depending upon the state of residence, it may or may not represent any kind of reality for financial aid.[3]

Not all governmental aid programs are addressed to those normally thought of as the poor. Many programs are intended to prevent poverty or to help individuals rise higher on the economic ladder. Governments spend money to bolster the well-being of their citizens. Some of this spending is intended to meet common objectives; public education and road building are obvious examples. Other programs are more narrowly targeted but are defended as having a positive aspect for society in general. Agricultural subsidies are governmental aid, just as much as food programs targeted to the aged in their own homes or in community centers, to children in school, or to families with limited income through the food stamp program or WIC.[4] Medicare and Medicaid are welfare programs, as is Social Security, to the extent that benefits eventually exceed personal contributions for most recipients. Supplemental Security Income and housing subsidies are means-tested government aid programs. AFDC and food stamps are means-tested as well. Some veterans' benefits are means-tested, and some are awarded as continuing compensation for service. Aid to higher education, day care subsidies, unemployment and workers' compensation are likewise programs designated to aid certain populations. Even tariffs, tax breaks, government "bailouts," and import quotas are forms of aid that benefit specified industries and their work forces. It is a premise of my argument that welfare, meaning AFDC, serves as important and necessary a function as any of the above programs and deserves more general support than it has lately received.

BEGINNINGS

AFDC, originally Aid to Dependent Children (ADC), has its origin in the Social Security Act of 1935. Prior to 1935 governmental aid to needy individuals had been the responsibility of state and local governments with significant contributions from churches and other private organizations. The acute suffering of large numbers of persons, due to lack of employment during the Depression years, had conditioned the country to welcome federal government involvement in relief efforts. The original Social Security legislation created only five income programs: a retirement program for workers (initially called and limited to Old Age Insurance), an unemployment insurance program, and three public assistance programs for the aged, for the blind, and for dependent children. The two insurance programs were designed for federal administration with the public assistance programs under state administration with federal matching funds.[5] Over the intervening years a large array of social programs has been legislated; many programs have been added as amendments to the Social Security Act. Thus, aid to children was one of the earliest social programs to have public endorsement; in fact, most states were already giving limited help to families with deceased fathers under state programs called "widow's" or "mother's" aid. ADC was similarly envisioned as a small program for children whose fathers were deceased.

Created simultaneously with ADC were large-scale work programs for the unemployed, primarily for male heads of households and young single men. These programs were conceived of as temporary (i.e., until employment returned to normal) and were in fact phased out as industry recovered.[6] It is important to remember that there were never enough openings in the programs for all the unemployed at any given time. People were rotated through the jobs, and restrictions were placed on multiple family members. Many were left to shift for themselves, helped only by donations of food and private charity. When the economy improved and the work programs ended with World War II mobilization, the expanded job openings were not evenly distributed throughout the country.

A distinctive aspect of ADC was the requirement that the father be dead, absent, or unable to work.[7] This restriction was intended to channel those families with an employable male parent through the work programs. In 1938 the Social Security Act was amended to add survivors and dependent coverage to the retirement provisions; and an aid program for disabled workers was added in 1950. Both of these expansions enhanced family unity and were intended, in part, to reduce need for ADC. This ADC requirement for "deprivation of parental support" (defined as absence, disability, or death) remained in place with the ending of the work programs. This restriction prohibited aid to families with two able-bodied parents present in the household, a direct contradiction of the societal value placed on complete families.[8]

FEDERAL/STATE STRUCTURE

In the creation of public assistance categories, a federal presence was added to what the states individually already had set up to provide for needy citizens. For some states, the Social Security Act created public programs that had not existed before, while in other states it helped in sharing the fiscal burden and extending participation to more of the needy. The programs were to be jointly funded.

At the federal level, the Social Security insurance programs, need based public assistance, child support enforcement, and medical aid programs, plus much more, are all directed by the U. S. Department of Health and Human Services (previously Health, Education and Welfare, and before that Health and Welfare). This is a very large, cabinet-level organization with multiple planning, audit, and rule-making divisions and a huge budget. Most states have adopted derivative administrative structures that include multiple social welfare related programs under a single administrator.

While states may, and most do to varying degrees, create their own complementary programs with state resources, in general the direction and creation of new AFDC reform measures flows from Washington. States may be given some discretion in the implementation of new programs, or they may not. Many new initiatives are introduced with either total federal funding or an enhanced federal funding level intended to facilitate state implementation. In time the federal funding for special initiatives can be reduced if reform emphasis changes, with states required to absorb more of the total cost or scale back previously offered benefits. With states having the responsibility for the actual operation of programs, their stance is often one of reaction to the federal design.

Programmatic and fiscal audits ensure that federal regulations are adhered to under threat of the withholding of federal funding. The arrangement, sometimes called a federal-state partnership, is in practice more a superordinate/subordinate hierarchy. In the 1960s federal reform measures were responsible for broadening public assistance programs, particularly AFDC in concert with the War on Poverty effort. In the 1980s, in contrast, federal reforms have restricted the aid program for children with differential impact among state populations because of the variation in state provisions. These latter changes were accomplished through new statutory provisions in federal budget legislation.

In AFDC the single factor most under state control is the amount of the actual grant payment. The grant payment, and thereby who is eligible for aid, is determined by a formula called the "standard of need," which is different in every state. The standard, by family size, is naturally expected to represent (but frequently does not) a realistic cost of living basis; furthermore, there is no formal requirement for any periodic readjustment of these formulas, and provisions exist to reduce the actual payment level below the standard to meet fiscal restraints. Only eighteen states equate the payment to the standard of need. Sometimes the difference is slight; sometimes it is less than half. The adequacy of the standard of need and the actual amount of aid being provided constitutes the most obvious disparity between the programs for children from one state to another.

This means that the federal government's contribution to poor children as individuals varies greatly from one state to another. The formula for "federal financial participation" is pegged to the state per capita income. Today these federal contributions range between a low of 50 percent to a high of about 70 percent of direct payments. States with higher per capita incomes receive smaller percentage payments than do the states with lower per capita incomes. The actual amount being paid into a given state depends upon the number of qualified persons, which in turn depends upon the incidence of unemployment and the standard of need. The states with low standards make a lesser commitment to the needs of poor children than do higher standard states, and the low standard states also forego federal dollars that would otherwise be available to give those children a higher standard of living. One state may dispense two or three times as much money as another, and the federal portion may also differ greatly. In general, the higher the standard the greater the federal funding (i.e., 70 percent of $100 is less than 50 percent of $200.) Twenty states provide maximum grants between $300 and $400 to a family of three persons, while the range is between $118 in Alabama to $617 in California and $740 in Alaska. The highest standard is $859 in Vermont and the lowest is $197 in Kentucky.[9]

Table 1.1   Variation in Federal Funding On Per Case Basis*

Grant Amount	Federal Formula (%)	Federal Funding	State Funding
$600	50	$300	$300
$400	50	$200	$200
$400	70	$280	$120
$200	70	$140	$ 60

*Unit of three persons; approximately eighteen states receive 50 percent funding

CHANGE IN THE 1960S

Many new programs of governmental aid were established in the 1960s and 1970s as part of the War on Poverty. This period saw expansions in program funding and a vast amount of new legislation intended to give the disadvantaged a better economic opportunity. Newly legislated programs increased access to medical care, better housing, better nutrition, greater education and training opportunities and resulted in increased income for many.

In 1961, prior to the War on Poverty, an increase in unemployment prompted an intended temporary change in the ADC program, renamed Aid to Families with Dependent Children. The Social Security Act was amended to permit states to provide help to families with unemployed male parents. The new provision required the unemployed parent to have a work history and to continue efforts to locate work. The AFDC-UP program was primarily intended to give aid to those families where unemployment benefits had been exhausted. The enhancement did not eliminate the requirement for deprivation of parental support, but added unemployment to the definition along with death, disability, and absence. This optional expansion was adopted in twenty-six states, including most of those with large industrialized labor forces. It was a method to help families lacking work or unemployment benefits; the benefit level and the formula for federal financial participation was consistent with funding for the basic AFDC program in each state. Today twenty-six programs, mostly the same twenty-six as in earlier years, including the District of Columbia, offer this limited aid to keep families together. The Children's Defense Fund, in an early 1980s survey, reported that caseload for the AFDC-UP program constituted on average 7 percent of the basic AFDC program, where it is offered. The remaining states—about half—have opted not to provide help to families if the father is present.[10]

The 1960s brought more visibility to AFDC as case loads increased. This visibility led to louder criticism of the program, especially allegations of misrepresentation and fraud, and some change in philosophy about the exclusion of mothers from having to work. To address these concerns, President Kennedy in 1962 proposed legislation to establish community work and training programs for adult recipients, establish day care facilities, increase incentives to work, provide rehabilitating social services, expand efforts to locate absent fathers, and intensify efforts to prevent fraud.

TRAINING AND EMPLOYMENT

Despite criticism that more welfare mothers were not working, employment of female adults had certainly not been effectively encouraged up to this time by the regulations within AFDC, which required reduction in the amount of assistance on a dollar for dollar basis of any other available money.[11] Because there are always costs associated with employment, working sometimes meant an actual reduction in income compared to not working. The first in a series of reforms began by allowing a "work related expense" deduction from earned income and subsequently a provision was added to "disregard" or exempt from countable income the first thirty dollars of earnings and one-third of remaining earned income. These reforms resulted in an increase in the number of working mothers receiving some supplementation to their earnings from AFDC.[12]

These reforms in the treatment of earned income were applicable to all who worked. To assist those who were not employed work experience programs were created; two of the first were designated for welfare agency administration. A Community Work and Training Program was formed by amendment to the Social Security Act, while Title V of the Economic Opportunity Act of 1964 authorized a broader range of projects for all categories of public assistance under the title Work Experience and Training. Multiple state training programs were organized, some of which were focused on training for men. This training constituted a mandatory obligation for those selected. The training included incentive payments and was well received by those who were enrolled. However, only a relative few were accommodated and even fewer found ongoing employment in the field in which they had been trained. Further Social Security amendments in 1967 created the Work Incentive Program (WIN), which replaced both of the earlier programs. The WIN legislation set up a jointly administered program between the Department of Labor at the national level and state employment agencies locally, and federal and state welfare administrations. This reform legislation made participation in WIN mandatory in 1971 for all persons over sixteen years of age and not enrolled in school, but there were exemptions from participation primarily for the care of children under the age of six and for those who live in areas lacking employment opportunities. Although conceived to provide employment and training services to all, the funding for WIN was never sufficient to mount an effort large enough for all AFDC recipients.

In the later 1970s emphasis in WIN changed from training to job finding, which meant that persons living in those geographical areas with high unemployment and/or very limited paid employment were exempted from inclusion in the state programs. Uncertainty about program continuation and reductions in funding have reduced the effectiveness of WIN during the 1980s. In the later years many states opted to return to running programs themselves as WIN Demonstration Projects. Relaxed federal regulation for WIN demonstrations permitted greater flexibility. The success of WIN is measured in the amount of reduction to welfare grant cost, called "WIN savings." This measure is distorted somewhat by the inclusion in WIN savings of all employment related grant reductions, whether or not the individual was enrolled in the WIN component. The WIN program has been characterized by its detractors as excessively costly to provide in relation to the results achieved.

Other reforms dating from the mid-1960s included the provision of social services to recipients, the establishment of a quality control component to measure effectiveness of administration and detect any incidence of fraud, and the placement of more emphasis on contacting absent fathers for support. Finally, a limited quantity of day care subsidies for working women also became available.

HEALTH CARE

In the early 1960s public assistance recipients and some of the elderly were granted access to payment of medical treatment. Medical assistance for the aged, a limited means-tested program, originated as the Kerr-Mills Bill and was passed as an amendment to the Social Security Act in 1960; but most of the lower income elderly had no coverage. A major reform to provide access to medical care for all of the elderly led to the creation of the federally administered Medicare program in July 1965. Medicare provided universal coverage for persons sixty-five years and older for hospital based services, and upon payment of a premium (usually deducted from the retirement benefit) for physician care and other medical services. To improve the comprehensiveness of medical care for public assistance recipients, Medicaid was established at the same time. As with other grant-in-aid programs Medicaid was adopted as state administered with federal oversight, and the federal monetary contributions followed a formula similar to AFDC. Federal funding ratios in the AFDC and Medicaid programs are now consistent, inasmuch as states can elect the sometimes more generous Medicaid reimbursement formula for both programs. From the start Medicaid programs have varied between states due to state selection of the services to cover beyond a mandatory core and the standard of need. Initially the larger numbers of children and parents receiving AFDC welfare than Aid to the Aged, Blind and Disabled (AABD) meant that more Medicaid funds benefited families than individual adults. The reverse has long since been true, for reasons discussed below, although that may not yet be the public perception.

FOOD PROGRAMS

During the decade of the 1960s and into the mid-1970s other programs for the poor, including the working poor, proliferated. Writing in *Income Support Policy: Where We've Come From and Where We Should Be Going,* Irwin Garfinkel (1978, 51) identified over forty separate programs that together constitute the income support system in the U.S.

This list includes various food programs, such as school lunch and breakfast subsidies, feeding programs for the aged and homeless, WIC, and commodities for nonprofit organizations including the schools. The largest and most expensive is the food stamp program. Enacted in 1964 on a small scale and available in almost all states by the beginning of the 1970s, food stamps replaced the distribution of surplus foods to families. The use of stamps exchangeable for food was intended to provide for a more nutritionally balanced diet and allow for personalization of diet according to custom and preference, as well as bolstering the retail food industry.[13]

Even though it is an in-kind program, food stamps really provide an expansion of spendable income and, because of the supplementary nature of the program serve to reduce inequities in income between low-grant and high-grant states and between low and higher per capita incomes. The early programs contained a purchase requirement for recipients to receive a greater "bonus" value of stamps. However, the purchase requirement for public assistance households was so minimal or absent that the purchase was not a substantial burden. In all cases, the purchase requirement had to be made "up front," which discouraged some enrollment, but the bonus provided a month's worth of food if care was exercised in how the stamps were spent. The purchase requirement was dropped in the mid-1970s with the result that individuals and families now receive a value intended to supplement existing income. The maximum value is issued only to those with little or no money, although there are some income disregards which reduce income to a net amount before benefits are calculated. Persons receiving only a supplementary amount, which can be ten dollars or less, cannot expect to purchase an adequate supply of food only with stamps.

The food stamp program has been characterized by frequent changes in regulations. It has seen one reform after another. The program is not as generous as it was originally and is now restricted to households at or below 130 percent of the poverty level for a given family size. Federally funded (except for half of actual program administration costs) and state directed, the program has national standards. This has led to minute examination and interpretation of the ever increasing regulations. The program tends to have an urban bias and a deliberate provision of higher benefits for the aged and disabled. Nonetheless, the food stamp program boosts total public assistance awards as well as helping the working poor—and it is popular. Participants have told me that the in-kind basis that restricts use of stamps to food is actually preferred by many recipients who experience multiple demands on the expenditure of the cash that they have at their disposal.

SUPPLEMENTAL SECURITY INCOME

Another major reform, and a missed opportunity for reforming programs for children, dates to the latter 1960s. A presidential Commission on Income Maintenance had been created in 1968 to make recommendations for changes to public assistance programs. The commission quickly recommended a complete overhaul of public assistance, noting that existing welfare programs were inadequate, inequitable, and inefficient. The commission suggested that a single program be designed, without categories of recipients, that would assist all persons on the basis of income and family size, including families with employed members who could not earn enough to provide adequate support.

Based on the findings of this report, President Nixon proposed the creation of a Family Assistance Program. This proposed reform would transfer administration and funding of public assistance to the federal government. It would create a national income standard, with states required to supplement in those jurisdictions where benefit levels were already higher than this new standard. (In most states the proposed standard was much higher than the existing benefit levels.) In arriving at a national income standard consideration would be given to the value of food stamps and Medicaid benefits, and work would be required of the able bodied. Disagreements over the work issues, including disincentives and the value placed on Medicaid, contributed to the defeat of the proposed welfare reform for children. Nevertheless, assistance programs for the aged, the blind, and the permanently and totally disabled were approved for restructuring and renamed the Supplemental Security Income program, coming under federal administration effective January 1, 1974. The program most changed was that for the disabled, as eligibility changed from persons over eighteen years of age with "total and permanent disability" to a finding that disability had lasted, or could be expected to last, for a minimum of one year. The minimum age restriction was dropped. A higher national payment level was established that included a disregard of twenty dollars in other income, with some state supplementation.

THE SEVENTIES

Other reforms of the 1970s were largely work oriented. The Comprehensive Employment and Training Act (CETA) channeled many into work experience and skills training. The food stamp program added a job search requirement for less than fully employed participants. The availability of educational aid increased. In AFDC, states were enticed to offer work experience wherein there would be no pay for work, but the hours of work would be equated to the amount of the aid received at the minimum wage. Such programs provided or reimbursed the cost of child care, transportation, and incidental out-of-pocket costs. Participation was required for those enrolled. Work experience fits the definition of workfare, the compulsory nature of which has been criticized by many, although much of the early concern has been relaxed. Most programs offer an appeal procedure and exemptions in exceptional cases. The early programs set up by states were generally less than statewide, in fact many were limited to a single geographical district. Usually the program components are somewhat tailored to the individual, ranging from instruction in how to apply for a job to on-the-job training or even classroom training. Some states have successfully enrolled large-scale employers in providing training opportunities, and provisions today include grant diversions in which the grant amount is payable to an employer who offers an actual salary. Ultimately the success of such efforts depends upon the availability of reasonable numbers of unsubsidized job openings. Studies of the effectiveness of these programs indicate that the recipients who receive the most lasting benefit from such training are those who have the least employment credentials and the most difficulty in finding employment on their own.

During this period equal rights legislation for women at the state level and a national dialogue resulted in the removal of gender distinctions in deprivation of parental support. Now children could be eligible for AFDC if the mother was absent or disabled. Men would no longer have disparate work requirements although either parent had to comply with WIN if ineligible for exemption.

As a further inducement to employment in AFDC, rules were changed to permit the receipt of Medicaid for four months after financial aid ended, providing employment continued.

The 1970s also saw an increased emphasis on efforts to collect child support from absent parents, very few of whom were voluntarily contributing any money to support their children. New statutes required states to designate separate entities to focus on the establishment of paternity and the collection of child support for all families owed such support, whether in receipt of AFDC or not.

Largely because of rising program costs, federal government concern intensified over reported increases in errors in calculating benefits in AFDC and food stamps and plans were announced that a sanction process, to include the withholding of federal funds, could commence in states whose error rates exceeded federally specified levels.[14]

THE EIGHTIES

Reform in the 1960s and 1970s brought expansions of programs in the areas of health care, food and nutrition, education, and housing, as well as cash assistance increases. Throughout this period Social Security benefits were increased several times to raise the living standards of elderly beneficiaries. Lesser and more sporadic benefit increases were enacted in public assistance.

Reform in the 1980s has meant considerable trimming of AFDC and more rigid eligibility in the food stamp program but also expansions of medical care benefits and a new Labor Department employment program called Job Training Partnership Act (JTPA), which is intended to involve the private sector in the creation of jobs and give job finding/training priority to welfare recipients.

The Omnibus Budget Reconciliation Act of 1981 (OBRA) introduced the first of the retrenchments to the welfare program for children. This reform legislation placed a cap on the amount of income from employment, child support, Social Security, or other sources that a family could possess and still remain eligible for supplementary financial aid. Disregards and deductions from earned income could no longer be used to reduce gross income if the gross exceeded 150 percent of the need standard. This new cap eliminated families with an employed adult, with the exception of minimal part-time employment. The new rules also cancelled eligibility for many other families with some child support or Social Security, but far more poor families in low-standard states were affected than in high-standard states. Criticism of this restriction resulted in a revision one year later to cap income at 185 percent of the standard, rather than 150 percent; but the impact remained great in low-standard states and exacerbated the differences among states regarding which children could benefit from AFDC. OBRA also reduced the maximum age for child participation from twenty-one to eighteen years, eliminating assistance to those continuing with some higher education or training.[15] There were a number of other changes; the most significant mandated that income of other siblings, a step-parent or the parents of a minor mother (i.e., the grandparents of the child) all had to be counted as available to the child. Considerable numbers of families were terminated from assistance as a result of this reform.[16] Another major change was in restricting the payment to a pregnant woman without other children both in amount and the onset of eligibility, although medical care was potentially made available earlier. A further medical care expansion permitted the continuation of Medicaid up to nine months for persons made ineligible due to employment. The Tax Equity and Fiscal Responsibility Act of 1982 (TEFRA) added certain other minor changes, but again expanded Medicaid (at state option) to pregnant women and infants where household income did not exceed the state's AFDC standard of need.

This rather significant change to separate medical care from financial aid and the canceling of the deprivation of parental support feature represents a real reform, although the change was intended more as a medical advance than as any change to AFDC. Its impact is limited by the low level of the standard of need in many locations, but is an important benefit for the unemployed. The Comprehensive Omnibus Budget Reconciliation Act of 1985 (COBRA) went even further in permitting states to offer (with federal financial participation) prenatal care and infant and child care, up to age five, to all families with income below the poverty line. About this same time a reinterpretation of Medicaid legislation determined that children living with step-parents and ineligible for AFDC because of deemed income could not be denied Medicaid. Prior to these extensions in Medicaid, deprivation of parental support governed the provision of any federally funded medical assistance to families, even in states that offered medical indigent aid, unless an unemployed parent option was in effect. Extending Medicaid coverage for prenatal, infant, and child care to families with income somewhat above the poverty line is under discussion. At present there is considerable variation among the states in what is actually offered.

The Child Support Enforcement Amendments of 1985 represent a new initiative for a public role in the establishment of child support orders and the collection of child support for all families in which a parent is absent. The legislation primarily facilitates legal procedures for obtaining a court order for support and putting into place effective measures for collection, including wage or other income garnishments. The legislation reemphasizes efforts to establish paternity for children. AFDC families now receive the first fifty dollars in support collected, and if the regular receipt of child support closes an AFDC case Medicaid benefits continue for four months. Attempts to obtain court ordered medical coverage in the support stipulation is also emphasized, as is more effective reciprocity between states and added services to non-AFDC families. When implemented, only about 12 percent of AFDC families received any acknowledged child support, either assigned to the child support enforcement entity or sent directly to the custodial parent.

Job training, job search, and work experience remain top agenda items for reform in both AFDC and the food stamp programs. Work requirements in the food stamp program, formerly handled through contracts with state employment offices, are now a state welfare agency responsibility. Most reform proposals now in circulation include further procedures intended to strengthen a commitment to work.

The remaining activity in the 1980s that could be considered policy reform in AFDC and the food stamp program includes a strong federal emphasis on reducing fraud and abuse, and strengthened requirements for reimbursement of benefits erroneously received. There has been considerable state resistance, including law suits and lobbying, to the federal agenda in using quality control results (from fifty-one quality control sections) as a common denominator, to form a basis for fiscal sanctions. As a result collection of money penalties has been suspended pending further analysis of how to achieve an equitable system. The sanction process and the publication of state error rates applies only to AFDC, food stamps, and Medicaid for recipients whose eligibility is state determined. There is no comparable publication nor concern voiced over eligibility errors in other need based programs including SSI and SSI-related Medicaid which the states cofund, other food programs, housing programs, or many other programs with income and asset restrictions.

REFORM EVALUATED

Aid to Families with Dependent Children does not deserve its negative reputation. A program intended to prevent destitution of young children is a necessary and deserving social policy. At the same time, AFDC does not reflect strongly accepted values of contemporary society. We believe in the obligation to pay ones way, that parents are responsible for caring for their children, and that the two-parent family is the best environment for raising productive citizens. AFDC represents none of these values.

How has this come to be? There is no simple explanation or single culprit, but rather a series of interrelated factors and events. Chief among them, in my view, is the continuing requirement for deprivation of parental support. This restriction no longer serves any useful purpose; it is merely a detriment. No other need based aid has such a restriction, limiting financial help to one-parent families only. Other income support programs for the poor, including housing aid, energy assistance, food programs, and aid to children with handicaps or disabilities, do not specify the composition of the household. Head Start and day care do not eliminate children with resident fathers.

When the AFDC program was established 92 percent of all children enrolled had a deceased father. Today, only 2 percent of AFDC children have a deceased parent, including mothers and cases in which paternity has not been established for Social Security survivor's benefits. Currently, 6 percent of children are eligible because a parent is disabled, and 92 percent live without one parent.

Children are needy today for reasons other than the death of a parent, yet the program remains structured as if that were still the most important factor. When death of a parent does occur, Social Security survivor's benefits meet the financial needs of most families. Likewise, Social Security disability benefits, SSI, or workers' compensation provide income to families in need because of injury or illness, and unemployment compensation benefits (UCB) may help to carry families through brief spells of joblessness. When UCB ends, the intact needy family is left to deplete all its resources or split up to allow some members, most often the mother and children, to qualify for aid.[17]

It is a matter of conjecture how many families actually split up for the explicit purpose of gaining access to AFDC. But certainly the number is large even in some states with the unemployed parent (UP) option, and including families where the father has some income from employment, but not enough to support the family. In addition, there is the problem of families that are not formed in the first place (i.e., out-of-wedlock pregnancies that might otherwise be followed by marriage) because of the deprivation of parental support requirement. Without this restriction more young couples facing early parenthood would create intact families. A public policy that encourages, even demands, that prospective parents not marry and live apart is antisocial.

Removal of the parental support deprivation restriction would give more dignity to AFDC and enhance public support, but it would hardly mean that all children would be returned to two-parent households. The majority would continue to live with only one parent, and the other parent would remain "absent." Absence in itself, however, is not the crucial element; children are needy not just because a parent is absent but because the absent parent is not providing support.

REFORM FOR ADULT CATEGORIES

It is useful at this point to examine the gains in public assistance—welfare—for the aged, blind, and disabled in comparison to AFDC. It is important to recall that a significant part of the agenda in creating SSI was to eradicate the stigma attached to welfare for the elderly, so that more eligible recipients would enroll in benefit programs. The name change in the programs and the change in administration (to well-regarded Social Security offices) were calculated to improve the image of the aid programs serving the elderly. The plan worked; hardly anyone now considers SSI as "welfare." No such

29

campaign has been undertaken to redeem AFDC. On the contrary, the apparent redefinition of the term "welfare" to mean only AFDC has even increased the opprobrium.[18]

Fifty years after the creation of Social Security, public assistance programs for the aged and disabled have neither been phased out nor remained small. In fact, on a per person basis, expenditure for cash assistance for the disabled and aged has increased manifold; and the attendant expense for medical care is more costly still. Conversion to SSI raised income standards for virtually all beneficiaries and broadened coverage to include mentally and physically disabled children. It reduced restrictions on disability aid from a requirement of "permanent and total" disability to disability expected to exist for at least one year. SSI established a national payment standard, higher than the former state average, which is supplemented with state contributions in some states. With effective political influence centralized on Congress, provision has been made for annual upward adjustments to SSI grants. Additionally, reform has meant that Medicaid eligibility is not lost when increases to Social Security benefits, which many SSI beneficiaries also receive, raise the total benefit level beyond the SSI maximum for income. SSI recipients now have automatic eligibility for food stamps and are further helped by certain provisions that increase food benefits, without which their income would be above the maximums imposed for younger families.[19]

The relationship of Medicaid to financial aid and of Medicaid to Medicare requires some special comment. Although there is much present concern over the cost of all health care programs and current reform efforts designed to reduce expenditures, the creation of Medicaid and Medicare has made medical care more available, prolonging life and benefiting the entire health industry. The increases in cost of medical care have come not just from more expensive procedures, but also from an expansion in coverage. Medicare was expanded in the 1970s to include the disabled (after a two-year waiting period following approval for Social Security disability payments), as well as persons needing renal dialysis; and recent legislation will soon provide catastrophic expense coverage and coverage of drugs. Although usually described as a program for the poor, Medicaid expenditures go mostly to support the low-income aged and disabled. Medicaid provides nursing home care, payment for mentally retarded services, organ transplants, and continuing drug treatment under special income standards applicable to this exceptional treatment. Usage of

Medicaid by some aged and disabled individuals can be weekly or even daily, as opposed to more episodic usage by persons in better health; this accounts for the disproportionate cost for these populations. Medicaid coverage now extends to hospitalized children of self-supporting parents and to in-home care for such children and certain adults under income waivers. The majority of expansions to Medicaid have been incremental, in response to political pressure to provide public help for one serious medical crisis or another. In this way, the medical aid programs have become as much oriented toward the middle class as they are toward the poor.

Medicaid is also an attendant benefit for AFDC recipients and has been a significant factor in the rise in enrollment in the program. Separate payment for medical services for all welfare recipients was necessitated historically by the low level of cash payments. When costly medical treatment is needed, the value of the medical care can greatly exceed the value of financial aid. In fact, it is possible to see most of the important expansion of public assistance over the past twenty years as medically driven: the lobby supporting expanded medical benefits is larger and more effective than any advocacy of general support for poor families. The expansion of Medicaid, most recently for prenatal and infant care is typically defended on grounds of prevention. What is usually not articulated is that in many cases the availability of such care negates having to choose between AFDC eligibility and doing without medical care altogether.

The distinction between Medicaid coverage for SSI recipients (who by definition are either over 65 or disabled) and those receiving AFDC is that the former also have Medicare, which provides universal coverage to everyone in those classifications. There is nothing comparable to Medicare for families. While most have medical insurance through employment, large numbers of mid to low income families have none. Consequently, Medicaid in AFDC is considered by some to have a value equatable to real money. This assumption expresses itself in the defense of low cash payment levels and in opposition to AFDC for intact families. (The presence of the father in the home would not increase Medicaid cost for services to children and mothers. Unemployed fathers are usually in reasonable health, if not they need care as much as anyone else and if truly disabled they are already Medicaid eligible.)[20]

In many ways the reforms that have benefited those over sixty-five or disabled have been achieved at the detriment to comparable needs of young families and children. This is especially true in the allocation of funding. The transfer of programs (now constituting SSI) from state administration eliminated any state financial participation in their costs, except for supplementary payments continued in a minority of states. State responsibility for partial funding of Medicaid remains, however, for SSI recipients as well as for AFDC households and children in foster care. At the state level, Medicaid funding constitutes one of the largest budgetary outlays, and it is increasing at about 15 percent per year. This ever increasing expenditure squeezes all other state funded activities, but has hit hardest on other social programs—child welfare services (including foster care, adoption programs, child abuse prevention, and day care), adult services, multiple behavioral and developmental health programs, and juvenile correction programs. AFDC has become sort of an odd man (woman) out. Active public advocacy, which is characteristic of all of the above, is either completely lacking or much less effective in the case of AFDC. The consequences of this situation are predictable: in contrast to other benefit programs, AFDC payments have changed little over the years, and the buying power of the grants has undergone a dramatic decline.[21]

AFDC REFORMS

Some very recent reforms have great potential for improving children's welfare, although their impact is not yet great. The first of these is the strengthening of emphasis on and actual procedures to make a public effort in the collection of child support more effective. There is a tremendous backlog of delinquent support cases to handle and insufficient staff to accomplish it. Collection of support for some families will make greater income available to children, and it will likely also strengthen ties to the absent parent. Nonpayment of support leads to resentment and guilt for the adults and generally estranges the child from one parent. For families also requiring public financial aid, the emphasis on child support makes it more obvious that two parents owe support to a child, not just one.

The other recent important change is the extension of medical care to pregnant women and young children. While states will implement these optional enhancements differently, it is the first opportunity for some states to offer medical coverage without the attendant need to qualify for financial aid and meet the deprivation of support requirement.

While the availability of training and job-experience activities can be helpful to many, the effort and money spent have produced mostly disappointing results. These training and job-search efforts are expensive to administer because child care and transportation are usually required and add to the total cost of the program. Recipients are not reluctant to work, as some would suggest, rather they lack the opportunity. The incidence of working mothers (before the standard of need caps were put in place) as well as the reuniting of families when Title V was operative indicate that there is incentive to work when employment opportunities exist and living standard is improved. Unemployment represents the major route to welfare need, if not the unemployment of the female parent then the unemployment of the male parent, or both.

This is not to suggest that all efforts toward help in locating jobs or in providing subsidized day care are unwarranted. Such help is definitely needed, but why assign a role that rightly belongs to the education and labor departments to welfare? Welfare budgets can accomplish more by providing more adequately for everyday needs. Individuals are better able to aspire to improving their circumstances when there is some lessening of the perception of total disadvantage.

REFORMS BADLY NEEDED

As discussed above, removal of the deprivation of parental support criterion is overdue and critically needed. This rule prevents any assistance to families with two parents in the home—a situation which is antifamily and ultimately antisocial. The traditional family is a core value that should be supported by social policy, not the reverse. Work requirements associated with receipt of such aid could easily be imposed. This reform would be a tremendous plus for children compared to having a father who is somewhere else.

Some current reform proposals call for the mandatory adoption in all state jurisdictions of the unemployed parent policy, but that solution is not as good as removal of the criterion altogether. The present unemployed parent policy does not accommodate parents who have not worked or who have been attending school, for instance. While it is conceivable that a modification could be made to equate schooling with work, it makes no sense to retain this restriction. Children need the assurance that their government cares enough about them and their family to help out when needed, but not at the cost of a lost parent.

A national income standard is overdue. There is no justification for continuing the variation in the amount of the federal commitment to children from state to state. The cost of the basic essentials of life do not vary greatly from one area to another, with the possible exception of housing in some urban areas. It should be in the national interest to treat children comparably. The location of the home should not render some children less in need of governmental protection than others. In fact taxpayers in states with low standards are actually helping to support children in higher standard states more adequately than children in the home state. A new national standard needs to be higher than it currently is in many states. When parents require help to support their children, the income level has to be adequate.

With the creation of SSI, greater support levels have been established for mentally and physically disabled children. It is twisted social policy to deprive potentially more productive members of society over those who are, and will be, less productive. The support should at least be equal.

Finally, an equally important reform needed is to modify the public perception of the acceptability of this category of public assistance. Financial aid for young families should be viewed as temporary, but appropriate at certain times. The scorn attached to welfare does no good but harms the self-image of both children and parents. Children are owed support from both parents. If it is not forthcoming from the parent no longer present, the remaining parent needs positive, not negative assistance.

Emphasis on self-support by women as well as men is reasonable if recognition is also present that there must be job opportunities. The commitment to work is strong for all Americans, including the poor. Beyond being a source of livelihood, work also provides a sense of accomplishment, belonging, and activity that everyone craves. The poor are no different.

Reform proposals strongly charging that welfare recipients must be prepared to work in return for aid are generally misleading. Work requirements already exist; there is no evidence that participants are allowed to refuse jobs. We also need to consider that asking a single parent to parent alone, maintain a household without help, and work full time out of the home may sometimes be inappropriate. Generally, the current receipt of welfare for children is an indication that little or no child support is being received. Many working mothers also receive no child support, but are ineligible for welfare aid because of the standard of need maximums. This points out an essential inequity in welfare policy. The absent parent is only expected to provide a portion of income, usually a minor portion, in child support. The parent providing a home for the child, however, has her (or his) entire income counted in determining the child's eligibility, with only minor disregards from earnings. While this policy dilemma is not easily solved, it suggests that the provision of a child benefit, not necessarily tied to need and provided on demand, might be a good idea. This is done in many industrialized European countries with presumably good results. It acknowledges the interest of government in the healthy development of children and recognizes that young families with limited incomes need some help in meeting the expenses of childbirth and child rearing. For those families with better than average or improving financial circumstances the aid would be recaptured through the tax system.

Such an approach would encourage family creation and continuation. It would facilitate a family environment for the children containing the complementary interaction of two parents. We would have a social policy that supports the role of the father and the complete family, not the reverse.

CONCLUSION

The social safety net for older and disabled citizens has grown quite comprehensive, perhaps even consuming a disproportionate share of resources, much of which benefits middle-income persons. Supplementary aid for poor families is more restricted. The unavailability of resources to pay for prenatal and childbirth care for many low-income women has stimulated the use of the welfare program (AFDC) often to the detriment of long-range interests of women and children. This shortcoming has been partially corrected by recent legislation, but the problem remains in existence.

Real reform in the AFDC must include more than a heightened

demand for work. The failure of the marketplace to create enough employment opportunity is mostly responsible for dependency on public programs, as has been demonstrated (in obverse) during past wartime economies. The greatest need in reform is to remove the impediment from providing help to intact families, for the well-being of children in these families. While it is not possible to restore a father who has died, good social policy can keep some fathers from being missing.

Reform needs to result in a change of public attitude about the need for, and desirability of, helping young families with the financial burden of raising children. Welfare assistance for children should be available readily on a need basis, without unnecessary restrictions, pending employment availability. Aid to *Families* with Dependent Children should fully merit its name.

NOTES

1. *One Child in Four,* a 1986 study of poverty with recommendations for reforms in public assistance, concluded that one child in every four in the United States today is born into poverty and one in five lives below the poverty line. Prigmore and Atherton (1986, 91) state, "Approximately 40 percent of the poor are children under eighteen!"

2. The term *welfare* has several levels of meaning. In its broadest definition, welfare means general well-being. When we say we are concerned about the welfare of our families, our country, our enterprises, we refer to prosperity, happiness, and a positive environment. In a secondary, more restricted sense, welfare means financial aid from government. In current usage, the term is very frequently employed to mean only AFDC, and often carries a pejorative connotation.

3. Other welfare programs such as food stamps and unemployment compensation would possibly be available.

4. Women, Infants, and Children Nutrition Program offers, through Maternal and Infant Care Projects, food vouchers and associated preventive health care.

5. Unemployment Insurance is funded by tax offsets from employers against federal tax obligations. The basic programs are state based with no matching state revenues.

6. The largest of these programs are best remembered by their acronyms, WPA, PWA, and CCC. The Civilian Conservation Corps for young men performed conservation work. The Work Projects Administration,

which evolved into the Work Progress Administration and then the Public Works Administration undertook multiple activities including building construction and road building. The programs were in effect from 1935 to 1943.

7. The social mores of the period did not endorse the paid employment of mothers. Most of the jobs for women were filled by single women, while mothers handled all manner of tasks in the home. While some mothers did find jobs, such as taking in laundry or cleaning offices at night, these employment opportunities were generally limited to urban areas.

8. An optional program for unemployed parents is discussed below.

9. The comparison is between basic grants for housing, food, clothing, and household supplies. Further variation exists, however, with the provision of special allotments. The majority of states provide few or no such supplements, but in others there are multiple special circumstances including different allocations for housing within a given state. The New York City program provides minimal accommodations to families unable to locate private housing in welfare hotels at enormous expense, cofunded with federal funds. For a descriptive discussion of welfare hotels, refer to Kozol (1988).

10. Most popularly publicized accounts of AFDC tend to reflect the programs in the biggest population states. Because these states generally have provision for aiding families with an unemployed breadwinner, there is little public awareness of the limited nature of aid programs in many other (smaller, poorer) states.

11. A need based system is the opposite of an insurance program that pays benefits regardless of the presence or absence of another source of income. In a need based system there is a cap on the amount of total income permitted for participation, according to the program standard (called standard payment amount in SSI). In a need based system the availability of other money reduces the amount of the grant: the more other income available the less the welfare payment. Even gifts of money from family, if received regularly, reduce the grant further.

12. This provision allowed gross earned income to be reduced by the disregards and deductions to net income before assessing eligibility to the standard. The process was reversed in the 1980s with the establishment of a gross income test.

13. Distribution of surplus foods in a much wider variety was reintroduced in the early 1980s only for persons living on Indian reservations as an electable alternative to food stamps, which can only be exchanged for food at sometimes far removed stores. Additionally, the Temporary Emergency Food Assistance Program (TEFAP) was instituted to permit the distribution of large governmental supplies of surplus cheese and butter. Rice and powdered milk are also sometimes available. Eligibility for TEFAP is consistent with the eligibility provisions of the food stamp program and is considered a supplementation to the latter program.

14.   An error does not always imply that the amount of aid received is incorrect. See the chapter by Coughlin in this volume for an explanation of the differences between "fraud" and "error" in AFDC and other programs.

15.   At state option, AFDC can be continued for an eighteen-year-old who will complete a course of education before reaching nineteen.

16.   Program participation is limited not only by income maximums but also by asset value, which may not exceed $1700, excluding the value of a home and a low-value car. Poor rural families are sometimes ineligible due to the value of land owned, which is not contiguous to the home. This has been a particular issue in New Mexico where subsistence farming was (is) practiced on tracts on the periphery of the community. More recent changes to regulations may permit participation if the land is offered for sale, but many cash poor families resist selling land which may have been owned by ancestors for multiple generations and may have no ready market as small individual tracts except at unfairly low values. Recent escalations in the cost of vehicles may also exclude rural participants, who need dependable transportation in the absence of any public transportation system over distances too far to walk. Whereas horses and other farm animals can be excluded from the asset maximum, the value of a truck cannot; yet trucks have mostly replaced horses and wagons for travel.

17.   Another solution is the voluntary placement of children into foster care. Ironically, if this extreme measure is taken, the foster family will receive several times the amount of aid to care for the child than the natural family could receive under either AFDC or AFDC-UP.

18.   From the earliest days of the program, recourse to AFDC has resulted from a need for income and medical care not otherwise available and has often required a choice between the usual family configuration and public aid. Women generally do not make this decision alone but after consultation with the father, with parents and perhaps others. While the short term need may make AFDC the rational choice, the program is obviously divisive to relationships, demeaning, and entrapping. Alone among all the myriad government aid programs, AFDC carries a stigma of something for nothing. The stigma is intensified by the need to demonstrate absence of the male parent. Many women have been convinced that it is in their self interest not to reveal the location of the absent parent, in some instances even his identity is concealed. Such data create a perception that the women are undeserving and solely responsible for their circumstances. Officially, then, children are registered as illegitimate and with no father listed, and they often grow up with a sense of rejection. Moralists justify meager financial aid as adequate, but the lack of normal childhood experiences that require more income than is available, plus this stigma, lead to dropping out of school, another negative social consequence.

19. Additional benefits are provided under the Older Americans Act and other service programs for the elderly.

20. Myers (1985, 16) and other experts think differently, stating "... Medicare benefits or food stamps ... in fact have the same value to the individual as actual cash income." While I agree regarding food purchases, I disagree concerning Medicaid. To be considered the equivalent of income, expensive medical procedures would have to fall within the optional ability of the individual to pay to consider Medicaid the same as cash. No AFDC family with income as low as one hundred dollars or two hundred dollars a month has the ability to pay for any medical treatment; and co-payments for drugs, which are sometimes imposed, represent a hardship. Without Medicaid AFDC clients would be charity cases or medically unserved, but income is unaffected.

21. In 1987 an SSI eligible individual living in New Mexico, including children, would have a monthly income of $340 (or $360 if some Social Security payment were involved) while a family of four on AFDC could qualify for a maximum grant of $313. Even though the value of food stamps would be considerably greater for the family, the discrepancy in income is large. The need standard in New Mexico ranks forty-ninth in the nation. However, the payment level is representative of more than one-third of all states. The average AFDC family size, both in New Mexico and nationwide, is three persons—generally one adult and two children. The benefit for all three would be $258. The most frequent case size is only two persons, typically a young child and a mother in her twenties, who could qualify for a cash payment of up to $210 per month or $2,520 on an annual basis.

BIBLIOGRAPHY

Achenbaum, W. Andrew. 1986. *Social Security: Visions and Revisions.* New York: Cambridge University Press.

American Public Welfare Association. 1986. *One Child in Four.* Washington, D.C.: American Public Welfare Association.

Garfinkel, Irwin. 1978. *Income Support Policy: Where We've Come From And Where We Should Be Going.* Institution for Research on Poverty. Madison: University of Wisconsin.

Kozol, Jonathan. 1988. "The Homeless." Parts 1 & 2, *The New Yorker,* January 25 and February 1.

Myers, Robert J. 1985. *Social Security.* 3rd ed. McCahan Foundation. Homewood, Ill.: Richard D. Irwin, Inc.

Prigmore, Charles S., and Charles R. Atherton. 1986. *Social Welfare Policy, Analysis and Formulation.* 2nd ed. Lexington: D. C. Heath and Co.

Spindler, Arthur. 1979. *Public Welfare.* New York: Human Services Press.

Turnbull, John G., C. Arthur Williams, Jr., and Earl F. Cheit. 1968. *Economic and Social Security.* 3rd ed. New York: Ronald Press Co.

U.S. Department of Health and Human Services. 1986. *Characteristics of State Plans For Aid To Families With Dependent Children Under The Social Security Act, Title IV-A.* 1987 ed. Washington, D.C.: Family Support Administration, Office of Family Assistance, U.S. Department of Health and Human Services.

II
Analytical Perspectives

2

Ideology and Welfare Reform in the 1980s

Edward J. Harpham and
Richard K. Scotch

INTRODUCTION

Along with the poor, proposals for changing government poverty programs seem always to be with us. In the past quarter century in the United States, we have had periodic public discussions and debates over the nature of our public assistance system, leading to a number of attempts at reform; some of these have been successful, other have simply fueled public dissatisfaction with "welfare."

In the 1960s eligibility for benefits was vastly expanded, and supplements including social services, medical care, housing subsidies, and food assistance were added to cash payments. With demographic, economic, and program changes the number of families on the welfare rolls increased dramatically. In the 1970s a series of unsuccessful proposals were made to scrap the AFDC program and replace it with simpler systems of graduated cash payments based on income and family size. The number of beneficiaries continued to increase, while benefit levels eroded with inflation. In the early 1980s eligibility for AFDC and other federal social welfare programs was tightened to exclude many of the working poor.

Accompanying each set of reform proposals were periodic calls for incentives, sanctions, and supportive programs to encourage welfare recipients to become self-supporting through paid employment. In the late 1980s, we are again experiencing attempts to "reform" welfare. A variety of proposals have been made, many of which have focused on making benefits less open ended in duration and on providing supportive services such as child care, job training, and transportation, which would facilitate a transition to work.

As we experience yet another round of reform proposals, some may be tempted to ask, why can't we get it right? That is, why have reform attempts shifted from one direction to another, sometimes the opposite, in a relatively short period of time? There are a variety of reasons for the peripatetic nature of reform. Demographic trends and structural changes in the economy have affected the composition of the low-income population as well as the employment opportunities available to them. Ideas such as "workfare" and the "negative income tax" which seemed plausible in the abstract (and on the campaign trail) have often had serious budgetary and structural limitations in practice and frequently have been based on naive assumptions about poor people and their potential participation in the labor market.

The evolving debate over welfare reform has also been shaped in fundamental ways by ideology. In the past twenty-five years there have been important changes in the underlying ideological assumptions made by politicians and policy experts about the goals of public assistance. These assumptions serve to define the range of acceptable choices for reform and are rooted in broader systems of understandings about the nature of poverty and the appropriate response to poverty by government.

In this chapter we will explore the ideological basis for the current debate over welfare and the implications for welfare policy making of the dissension among policy intellectuals. We will examine several of the leading contributions to the ideological debate over public welfare in the 1980s and assess their implications for welfare reform. We will conclude that a pragmatist consensus among policy makers is emerging, which has been shaped in response to ideological critiques but reflects the existing nature of the institutionalized American welfare state.

IDEOLOGY AND WELFARE POLICY

Most public policies are rooted in collective understandings about the causes and consequences of societal problems, and about the capacity and appropriateness of governmental action in dealing with them. These understandings come from many sources. They may reflect a social consensus, but they often express the interests and beliefs of elites who dominate the policy process. In the modern state such collective understandings are typically articulated through the work of policy intellectuals.

Such ideological underpinnings have been particularly evident in government policies concerning poverty. From laissez-faire liberalism to democratic socialism, changing assumptions made about why people are poor and the appropriate response of government to the conditions of poverty have led to dramatic shifts in public policy, most notably in the New Deal of the 1930s and in the Great Society and its aftermath in the 1960s and 1970s.

Three broad ideological perspectives—conservative, liberal, and radical—have dominated American policy debates since the 1960s. The modern conservative perspective has typically characterized poverty in terms of individual moral inadequacy—people are seen to be poor because they lack the motivation to undergo the rigors of the labor market. Such moral laxness is sometimes believed to be innate, but frequently conservatives see it as being promoted by public programs that assist the poor, negating the discipline of the marketplace. The resulting policy response, conservatives say, ought to be some combination of moral inculcation and a reduction in government assistance; this would make poor people more willing to accept work and would shift incentives making it more difficult for them to turn down any job which might be offered. The conservative critique of government welfare policy as argued by New Right intellectuals such as Charles Murray, will be discussed at greater length below.

Conversely, radicals see the source of poverty as systematic rather than individual, an inherent characteristic of a capitalist economy. Poor individuals are portrayed as victims of an economic and political system that has too few jobs, many of which provide inadequate income. Government policies reinforce the disadvantaged position of poor people, while protecting capitalism from the social disorder that results from its own excesses by providing a minimum of benefits to the poor. While a wholesale restructuring of society is ultimately sought, radicals advocate policy changes which are the opposite of those favored by conservatives—major benefit increases that enhance the living conditions of the poor, but which also strengthen their bargaining position in the labor market.

Perhaps the most articulate presentation of the contemporary radical position on welfare policy may be found in *The Mean Season: The Attack on the Welfare State*, a collection of essays by Fred Block,

Richard A. Cloward, Barbara Ehrenreich, and Frances Fox Piven (1987). While many on the left had previously criticized the American welfare state as essentially a mechanism of social control (Piven and Cloward 1971), the authors of *The Mean Season* defend welfare programs as important protections for the poor and the working class during a time of transition to a post-industrial economy. Welfare is characterized as a necessary means of guaranteeing that minimal human needs be satisfied, but also as a hedge against the pressures of an exploitative labor market. Benefits, they argue, should be kept as high as possible so that workers will not be forced to accept whatever undesirable and poorly paid jobs the capitalist economy offers. The authors go on to assert the social value of child rearing and to contend that forcing single mothers to work is a punitive attempt to resurrect the traditional patriarchal family. Social justice, they claim, demands that the welfare state be expanded and not be used as an instrument to discipline and control its beneficiaries.

The value assumptions of *The Mean Season* are certainly consistent with the tradition of American socialism, but they are completely at odds with both conservative and liberal policy makers. Radicals reject the notion that welfare should only be a last resort and should not be considered a legitimate alternative to paid employment. Moreover, they refuse to accept the basic legitimacy of the economic institutions of capitalism. In their eyes, capitalism represents a system of class exploitation directly at odds with the values of democratic life.

The left had some influence on welfare policy in the 1960s and 1970s by calling for broader program participation, more humane benefit levels, and enhanced rights for beneficiaries. In the welfare reform debate of the late 1980s their resistance to the gospel of work and the legitimacy of capitalism has left them out of the immediate policy debate.

The contemporary liberal perspective characteristically stands between the conservatives and the radicals. As the ideological persuasion of those who have created the American welfare state, liberalism rejects major structural change while supporting incremental reforms. Like the radicals, liberals see poverty as fundamentally caused by societal inequalities; but they are ambivalent about whether structural inequality is a bad thing. Liberals are uncomfortable with the "blame the victim" mentality they associate with conservatism, but they also support the American system of capitalism. They seek to humanize and protect capitalism by both enhancing the living conditions of the poor and promoting their participation in the labor market.

Since the New Deal liberalism has been the dominant ideology of American governance, with all of the accompanying baggage. While successful in incrementally building a welfare state in the United States, liberalism has been chastised by the left and the right for the welfare state's failures. In the 1960s and early 1970s liberalism faced a critique from radicals who questioned the efficacy and legitimacy of programs which did not challenge the institutions of capitalism. Since the late 1970s the more threatening critique has come from the right. While neither radicals nor conservatives have been able to supplant the dominance of the liberal perspective, the authority of liberalism's voice has been undermined both within and outside of government.

Disenchantment with liberalism and the social welfare policies it has produced intensified in the 1980s with the election of Ronald Reagan. With an inflationary economy that appeared out of control and a number of well-publicized policy failures ranging from a scandal-ridden CETA to the botched attempt to rescue American hostages in Iran, widespread pessimism prevailed about the efficacy of government policy. Many Americans came to believe that the War on Poverty and the Great Society were well-intentioned failures in the face of persistent poverty, which the optimistic advocates of the 1960s had claimed was eradicable. This disaffection was reinforced within the government and academic communities by the proliferation of public policy studies in which explanations for program failures far outnumbered accounts of program successes. Even political liberals have distanced themselves from past optimism by re-christening themselves "progressives."

In the first two years of the Reagan presidency federal policy came under assault from conservatives in Congress and the administration. While social insurance programs geared to the middle class have continued to grow throughout the Reagan years, poverty programs were cut in 1981 and 1982. Many categorical programs were consolidated into block grants with fewer mandated services and lowered overall budgets, while others were completely eliminated. Since the 1982 elections, which reestablished liberal and moderate influence in Congress, budgets have remained essentially level for non-health means-tested programs; and Congress consistently has rebuffed Reagan administration proposals for further budgetary reductions in social welfare. Only proposals with wide bipartisan support have received approval from both Congress and the president, and the few major domestic policy changes have not included social welfare.

Despite this stalemate, in recent years policy makers have undertaken a reexamination of federal poverty policies, particularly the long standing and unpopular Aid to Families with Dependent Children (AFDC). In 1986 and 1987 proposals for welfare reform became a virtual policy fad, emanating from the White House, the Congress, and numerous state governments. Demands for reform have been fueled, in part, by the continuing debate over the merits of the past quarter century of social policy. A full appreciation of these reforms demands an understanding of the role that ideology has come to play in shaping debates over welfare in the 1980s.

THE DEFENSE OF THE WAR ON POVERTY

Many of the problems confronting liberalism as an ideology in the 1980s can be attributed ironically to its very success. Since the early 1960s, a liberal perspective has tended to dominate policy discussions of the "poverty problem." While both conservative and radical perspectives have had some influence, as in the debate over the negative income tax in the early 1970s, neither has had enough support within government to displace the liberal hegemony. While liberals have been able to develop programs consonant with their world view, however, they have also been held accountable for perceived program failures.

By the late 1970s liberals were forced to address the outcomes of the policies they had created. In the face of neo-conservatism and the "Reagan Revolution," traditional liberals have had to defend social programs that had well recognized problems. For most of the twentieth century American liberals had defined themselves in terms of a progressive view of the future. In the debate of the 1980s, however, they were forced into thinking of themselves in terms of the past. The defining characteristic for a 1980s liberal was no longer a belief in the future possibilities of benevolent state action; it was rather a commitment to the institutions and policies of the New Deal and the War on Poverty.

Creating a useable past has become an important concern for

liberals who want to go beyond the short-term defense of welfare programs and budgets in order to chart a new course for the welfare state into the twenty-first century. Throughout the 1980s liberals have defended their social policies by developing a body of evidence that demonstrated success, both in terms of specific programs and of aggregate outcomes. Perhaps the best example of the more broadly conceived defense of social programs is John Schwarz's *America's Hidden Success* (1988, revised edition).

Responding to conservative critics, who claim that government became overgrown and out of control by the early 1980s, Schwarz provides a positive sense of the nation's immediate past and articulates a revived ideological perspective from which liberals might act in the future. For Schwarz, the current debate over welfare reform is as much about conflicting world views as about welfare policy itself. In the epilogue to the revised edition of *America's Hidden Success*, revealingly subtitled "Looking Back to the Future," he notes:

> For nearly a decade, a spell of antigovernment rhetoric has taken hold. Evolving from a myriad of misunderstandings of the past, the spell has beckoned us to reject the twenty years of the post-Eisenhower era and the accomplishments that we as a nation, through government, achieved in those years. Only if we recognize the negative spell that has been cast can we draw renewed confidence from the knowledge that in the past we accomplished much through governmental activism to improve Americans' lives. Only then can we realize our capacity as a nation to do so again in the future. To continue to hold a falsely diminished view of the past, and to compare what the nation does today with that diminished view, is dangerous. It causes us to elect our leaders and to construct our policies on faulty premises. As important, it prompts us to ask less of ourselves as a nation—and thereby to advance less—even while we imagine that we are asking and advancing more. (1988, 186–87)

In the first edition to his book, Schwarz sought to document governmental accomplishments of the 1960s and 1970s, which he claimed had been underestimated and distorted by conservative critics. He noted that as the result of government action the proportion of Americans with income below the poverty line had decreased from 20 percent in 1960 to between 6 percent and 8 percent in 1980, and that advances had also been made in nutrition, health, infant mortality, housing, employment, and pollution control. In sharp contrast to conservative critics, he concluded that what he calls the post-Eisenhower era was "an age of distinguished public achievement" (1983, 57).

In building a useable past from which liberals in the 1980s could draw inspiration and direction, Schwarz looked beyond poverty programs per se. He noted productivity gains among government workers and the creation of massive numbers of new jobs to accommodate the entry of the baby boom generation and large numbers of women into the workforce. In so doing, Schwarz articulated a general ideological position defending the legitimacy and efficacy of government domestic policies, arguing against privatized solutions to social problems. Through the development of this useable past, Schwarz has given an informed liberal response to conservative naysayers.

In his 1988 revised edition of *America's Hidden Success*, Schwarz goes on to offer a wholesale indictment of the conventional wisdom of the Reagan years. Right wing apologists to the contrary, Schwarz rejects the idea that the prosperity of the Reagan years can be attributed to the triumph of conservative views, attributing it more to circumstance than to successful policies. Declining oil prices, an evolving Keynesian policy of huge government deficits, and an easing of pressure from the entry of the baby boom generation into the workforce—not the translation of conservative ideology into public policy—lay behind the Reagan success story, in Schwarz's view.

Schwarz charges that not everyone shared equally in this prosperity, and that the poor, particularly, have suffered. He cites a massive increase in the poor population, from fifteen million in 1979 to twenty-five million in 1985, which constituted "the first sharp rise in net poverty in America for any extended period since prior to 1950" (1988, 153).

Schwarz concludes the recently revised edition of his book by calling for major reforms of public assistance based on his assessment of the successes and failures of social policy since 1960. He proposes increases in benefits, the implementation of reasonable workfare requirements, and the establishment of income grants to the working poor in order to provide more incentives for taking low-wage jobs. Conceding that such reforms might cost $40 or $50 billion, he argues that the ensuing eradication of poverty would justify such an expenditure. Schwarz thus calls for a new war on poverty, one grounded not simply in dreams of the future, but also in a firm understanding of the past. He argues that liberals should be proud of past accomplishments and build on them rather than distancing themselves from past efforts by apologetically redefining themselves as "neo-conservatives" or "neo-liberals."

Schwarz's proposals identify him with the leading intellectuals of the Democratic Party's left wing, although his defense of the policies of the 1960s and 1970s could be embraced by a variety of critics unhappy with Reagan program cuts. Schwarz goes beyond defending past efforts, however, to urge substantial new efforts, in contrast to those fallen liberals who have preached caution and limits since the Carter years.[1]

The scope of such ambitious proposals suggest the political limits of Schwarz's book and of the brand of liberalism he espouses. Even in good economic times, programs costing $40 billion would be greeted with caution by Washington policy makers. With the massive federal deficits incurred under the Reagan administration, coupled with jittery financial markets touched off by the stock market crash of 1987, such proposals appear virtually utopian, and for the foreseeable future outside of the range of political feasibility. While Schwarz does acknowledge the deficit problem at the end of his 1988 edition, his comments are more an afterthought than a rigorous inquiry into the problems of welfare reform in an era of limits.

Beyond Schwarz's failure to adequately address problems of political feasibility, in his broad stroke approach to poverty he does not seriously consider another major concern of the 1980s—the so-called underclass. For conservatives and for many without a clear ideological position, a major problem facing government antipoverty policy is that a segment of the poor may have become culturally as well as economically isolated from the American mainstream, with dangerous implications for participation in family life and in work. It is this concern which lies at the heart of the contemporary conservative critique of welfare policy.

CONSERVATIVE CONCEPTIONS OF WELFARE REFORM[2]

Liberals such as Schwarz are not the only ones rethinking America's immediate past. In *Losing Ground* (1984), Charles Murray constructs a conservative vision of the past that challenges many of the fundamental assumptions which guided the growth of the American welfare state throughout the twentieth century. Echoing the themes developed by New Right scholars such as George Gilder and Walter Williams, Murray indicts the massive expansion of the state's role in social welfare in the 1960s. According to Murray, the War on Poverty was a failure based on a misguided understanding of what motivates people in a market society. Far from eliminating poverty in America, these programs are said to have made matters worse by promoting dependency on government and making it profitable for poor people to behave in socially destructive ways. In trying to help people escape poverty, Murray believes that liberal policy makers inadvertently built a trap that kept people poor.

Much like Schwarz's work, Murray's attempt to forge a conservative past is supported by demographic and economic data. But in contrast to Schwarz, Murray claims that the lot of the poor actually got worse during the 1960s and 1970s. For example, "latent poverty" (a term used by Murray for income excluding government transfer payments) had declined from almost one-third of the population in 1950 to 18.2 percent in 1968, but then leveled off between 1968 and 1970 and increased to 21 percent by 1976 and 22 percent by 1980 (64–65). Murray goes on to describe what he believes to be negative trends in black youth unemployment, the status of low-income earners, the quality of public education, the threat of crime, and the proportion of illegitimate births among the poor.

For each of these trends Murray blames the misguided actions of the well-intentioned liberal "elites" responsible for social policy making. He charges that beginning in the 1960s, these elites failed to heed the popular ideology that people react to incentives and, if possible, will avoid work and be amoral. By assisting those who were not independent, self-sufficiency was discouraged and sacrifice was replaced by welfare rights. Further, Murray charges, poor people were not held responsible for their actions, and failure and antisocial behavior were excused as a result of victimization. Thus irresponsible behavior was condoned and expectations of failure were promoted, morally isolating the poor from the rest of society. In short, Murray claims that liberal social programs actually helped to create a culture of poverty in America.

Murray calls for increased accountability through elimination of all federal programs of assistance to low-income individuals and families, including AFDC, food stamps, housing subsidies, Medicaid, SSDI, and workers compensation. Private charity would replace some of the deleted benefits; others would be provided by local governments willing to fund and administer programs. For many of the poor, however, help would not be available—those unable or unwilling to earn enough to live would presumably be forced into the underground economy or would perish. The salutary effects of making people dependent on their own efforts and on the voluntary assistance of their immediate neighbors would, Murray believes, remove the perverse incentives which reward amoral behavior and would reinforce the value of work and self-sufficiency.

Murray denies that his intention is simply to free the government of responsibility for the poor. He claims a moral imperative for government assistance, but not in the form of services and benefits. Rather, by freeing the poor from the perverse incentives of current policies, Murray maintains that government will be helping to create hard working and independent citizens. Murray has taken the traditional ideological agenda, called conservative in the twentieth century and liberal in the nineteenth, and provided a mass of statistics to justify it.

THE RESPONSE TO MURRAY

Losing Ground received considerable attention from the popular and business press upon its publication. Conservative periodicals such as *Business Week* and *The Wall Street Journal* predictably applauded Murray's analysis, but the broad and often positive popular response to the book led many liberals and those on the left to respond to Murray's thesis. By contrast, Schwarz's work did not garner much attention beyond academic journals and liberal leaning publications.

One line of criticism addressed Murray's disregard for the effect of those economic and demographic trends discussed by Schwarz, which may provide a more persuasive explanation than social policy changes for the deteriorating status of the poor since the late 1960s. Another critical point stated that Murray did not acknowledge positive program outcomes, such as reduced infant mortality or increased life expectancy, which are not reflected in poverty rates.

Further, Murray's analysis of perverse incentives has been rejected by many critics as simply wrong. AFDC benefits, for example, have declined in real terms since the early 1970s, and even minimum wage jobs were more profitable than welfare in most parts of the country (Greenstein 1985; Jencks 1985). Empirical analysis of state

AFDC programs also suggests that the level of welfare benefits has no impact on childbearing by unmarried women (Ellwood and Bane 1985).

Murray has been unwilling to make any concessions to his critics and defends his use of empirical data (see Harpham and Scotch 1988). Nevertheless, he seems increasingly hostile to quantitative studies of welfare policy. The seeds of such hostility can be found in *Losing Ground* itself, where Murray notes, "Data are not essential to certain arguments about social policy and indeed can get in the way. The terms of debate can be grounded wholly in preferences about how the world ought to be, not how it is" (53). More recently (1986), Murray rejects empirically based critiques, stating:

> [It is not] necessary to treat the hypotheses raised here as ones to be abruptly tested or discarded. . . . These hypotheses, rather, are more useful for the perspectives they provide. When ways to shrink the underclass are found, they will grow from a strategic under-standing of how social policy shapes behavior. To get leverage, analysts of social policy badly need a place to stand. (11)

Murray's goal, then, is not to change our understanding of specific social programs, but rather the ideological perspective from which we view government action as it affects human behavior. This is the source of Murray's appeal to conservatives critical of the welfare state; but it is also its liability as a political call to action. Most policy makers are suspicious of the antigovernment brand of conservatism espoused by Murray. Even throughout the Reagan presidency, Americans from Wall Street to Main Street have looked to government for solutions to their problems.

Moreover, there is no indication that the public at large wants a fundamental dismantling of existing welfare state programs. Polling data and electoral results suggest that there is popular support for most social programs. Since 1982 there has been little Congressional support among Democrats or Republicans for Reagan administration proposals for major cuts in social program spending. As David Stockman discovered to his dismay, by the 1980s most of us have become social democrats of one sort of another in heart, if not in mind.

Much of the popularity of *Losing Ground* can be attributed to the fact that it has put old wine into a new bottle. The idea that public welfare promotes dependency and is thus injurious to the poor has been around for centuries. Many of the themes articulated by Murray about the underclass were propounded in the 1960s by many liberals as well as conservatives. Similarly, reformers well before the time of Jeremy Bentham argued that relief for the poor undercut public morality. In many ways, Murray's policy agenda is a modern version of the English New Poor Law of 1834.

But the traditional popularity of the idea of an underclass living off of our good intentions does not alone account for the wide hearing that Murray's work has received. Whatever truth *Losing Ground* contained, the time was right in the mid-1980s for a book that questioned governmental programs and justified their elimination on moral as well as economic grounds. An ongoing federal budget crisis and continuing demand for programs from various constituencies has imposed on Washington policy makers the difficult task of choosing among programs. Murray's book spoke directly to people confronting difficult policy choices, providing a conservative strategy for dealing with poverty in an age of fiscal limits. While the changes advocated by Murray have little chance of being adopted, Murray's ideological challenge has forced policy makers and policy intellectuals to justify existing policies, and thus may have stimulated a needed reassessment. That reassessment may lead to significant reforms in social welfare programs, although not in the direction Murray would choose.

TRIUMPHANT INCREMENTALISM

Both Schwarz and Murray have called for broad programmatic and budgetary changes in social welfare policy, but few public officials are likely to accept either Schwarz's call for large program expansions or Murray's blanket condemnation. The reform proposals being considered in the 100th Congress involve adding new work requirements and supportive services to aid the transition to work, and making the long-term receipt of benefits more difficult. They also reflect a willingness to allow the states more discretion in program innovation and implementation. Ultimately, however, these proposals would mean much less substantive change than one would expect, given the rhetoric that accompanies them. Most do not involve elimination of significant programs, and they typically propose incremental spending increases.

There is little doubt that the new national debate over welfare, poverty, and the underclass has been stimulated by ideologically based analyses of the problems of welfare. These ideological critiques, however, have been incorporated into essentially incremental reform proposals that will please neither the left nor the right.

Current reform proposals reflect an evolving consensus that takes into account the conservative concern with the underclass. It treats that group, however, as a subclass among the poor worthy of special attention but not representative of the majority of program beneficiaries. Reform proposals also incorporate liberal and radical concerns about the obligation of government to assist the poor, and beliefs that locate the roots of poverty in the structure of post-industrial capitalism rather than in the moral failings of individuals. Structural changes are eschewed, however, in favor of targeted categorical programs which have been gaining renewed favor among the social welfare establishment, in recognition of the political limitations inherent in the broad stroke approaches favored by the left and the right.

Such programs are reminiscent of the initiatives from the 1960s designed for people then called the "hard-core unemployed," and it is not surprising that a central actor in the contemporary debate was a participant in the development of the earlier programs, Daniel Patrick Moynihan. Moynihan, currently a United States senator representing New York, had been a major contributor to debates over welfare policy as a Harvard professor and official in the Johnson and Nixon administrations. Moynihan's once controversial views on the decay of the black family have become part of the newly conventional wisdom about the underclass, and he is the author of perhaps the most heralded legislative proposals to once again reform public welfare. The growing influence of his ideas, more than those of anyone else, speak to the triumph of incrementalism in the debate over welfare reform in the late 1980s.

Moynihan's diagnosis of the problem of poverty was presented in the Godkin lectures, which were published in 1986 as a book, *Family and Nation*. Moynihan expresses skepticism about the impact of the War on Poverty, pointing out that while its programs were legitimated by grandiose rhetoric, in fact they were rather modest efforts. The real expansion in the size of government and the amount of social spending took place in social insurance programs, such as Old Age and Survivors Insurance, Medicare, Disability Insurance, and Unemployment Insurance, not in Great Society programs per se (79).

Moynihan reaffirms his concern about the rise of single-parent

families, particularly among blacks, and about the ensuing feminization of poverty over the past two decades; but he flatly rejects Murray's contention that this trend is the result of government programs.
He agrees with Murray that the incentive effects of government
policies must be recognized, but asserts that we actually know little
about the true causes of poverty. Moynihan concludes by calling on
government to adopt sensible policies that reinforce intact families
and responsible parenting; but he stops far short of advocating broad
reforms.

Such an incrementalist approach is also advocated in another
recent and widely noted discussion of poverty, Ken Auletta's *The
Underclass* (1982), based on his study of several programs operated
by the Manpower Demonstration Research Corporation. Auletta
shares conservatives' concerns about the psychologically and socially destructive behavior of some individuals among the poor, but
he rejects the laissez-faire solutions favored by Murray. Because of
what he perceives as deeply rooted behavioral pathologies, however,
Auletta doubts that the large-scale economic interventions favored
on the left will adequately address the problems of those he labels the
underclass.

Auletta favors the establishment of many small-scale programs
based in local communities that encourage self-reliance within the
context of supportive services, such as work programs which include
training and counseling, child care, family planning, strict law enforcement, and sensible affirmative action. Auletta does not claim
that such programs would eliminate poverty, but contends that they
would concretely improve the quality of life and moral climate that
many poor people experience. As with Moynihan, Auletta's incrementalist call for local initiatives and self-help, supported by federal
financial and technical assistance, is clearly in tune with the political and fiscal constraints facing welfare policy.

IDEOLOGY AND REFORM IN THE AMERICAN
WELFARE STATE

In the last decade we have experienced a full blown polemical
attack on liberal social welfare policy from the right. With Ronald
Reagan in the White House and members of the public who had
become more likely to identify themselves as conservatives, it would
not have been unreasonable to expect the elimination or major alter-

ation of social programs. Instead, what we have experienced are changes on the margin—incremental restrictions on program eligibility, budgetary increases which have not kept pace with inflation, and the elimination of a few of the smaller categorical programs. How can we account for such modest results from so much sound and fury?

We believe that the answer lies in the institutionalized nature of the American welfare state. It is axiomatic that established programs develop political constituencies who seek to protect their interests, but the base of support for existing welfare programs goes far beyond the poor families who benefit from them and their liberal allies. The New Deal and the War on Poverty helped to construct state institutions with the administrative capacity to insulate public policies from ideological rhetoric. The War on Poverty also stimulated the creation and expansion of institutions in the private sector to deal with aspects of the poverty problem. Such public and private institutions have tended to blunt the edge of the conservative attack on the American welfare state.

Moreover, there appears to be a general social consensus that, however much we distrust public welfare, the scope and nature of existing programs is just about right. Most voters and most public officials appear to be unwilling to accept either the economic costs of significantly expanded programs or the social costs of program elimination. Since our complex governmental system of checks and balances makes the adoption and implementation of major reform a difficult and slow process even with strong political support, it should not be surprising that so little has happened and that the actual reform proposals being suggested are so minimal.

An institutionalized welfare state is not the only factor undercutting significant reform. In coming years the ability of the government to engage in dramatic action will probably be seriously circumscribed by the ongoing budgetary crisis. The choices made in the early 1980s to increase defense spending rapidly while limiting the growth of taxes may have precluded any significant welfare initiatives for the foreseeable future. This constraint may not have been a significant limitation for the Reagan administration, but it will certainly affect the ability of liberals to pursue new programs in the 1990s, unless they can build political support for major new taxes.

In certain respects, these developments raise questions about the importance of the current ideologically driven controversy over welfare reform. The constant tinkering with incentive systems, supplementary support programs, and ways of ensuring parental financial support has been and will continue to be motivated and informed by ideologically based critiques, from both the right and the left. Such critiques shape the way that policy makers and the public perceive the "problem" of welfare and the need for reform.

Even if no substantial changes take place, the basis of legitimacy for the status quo appears to have shifted as the result of the recent debate, and this shift will influence the terms of future debates and proposals. In the late twentieth century, the important issue involving welfare reform is not simply which ideology has the most insight into the problems of poverty, but also how the concerns embodied in contending ideologies filter their way into a welfare state whose policy processes have become increasingly incremental in nature.

NOTES

1.   Similar proposals have been made recently by Michael Harrington in *The New American Poverty* (1984) and by William Julius Wilson in *The Truly Disadvantaged: The Inner City, the Underclass, and Public Policy* (1987).

2.   Some of the discussion presented in this and subsequent sections is based on an earlier review essay by the authors (Harpham and Scotch 1988).

BIBLIOGRAPHY

Auletta, Ken. 1982. *The Underclass.* New York: Random House.

Block, Fred, Richard A. Cloward, Barbara Ehrenreich, and Frances Fox Piven. 1987. *The Mean Season: The Attack on the Welfare State.* New York: Pantheon.

Ellwood, David T., and Mary J. Bane. 1985. "The Impact of AFDC on Family Structure and Living Arrangements." *Research in Labor Economics* 7:137–207.

Greenstein, Robert. 1985. "Losing Faith in *Losing Ground.*" *The New Republic* (March 25):12– 17.

Harpham, Edward J., and Richard K. Scotch. 1988. "Rethinking the War on Poverty: Ideologies of Welfare Reform." *Western Political Quarterly* 41:193–207.

Harrington, Michael. 1984. *The New American Poverty.* New York: Penguin.

Jencks, Christopher. 1985. "Comment on Murray." *The New York Review of Books* (May 9):41–49.

Moynihan, Daniel Patrick. 1986. *Family and Nation.* New York: Harcourt, Brace, Jovanovich.

Murray, Charles. 1984. *Losing Ground: American Social Policy 1950–1980.* New York: Basic.

———. 1986. "No, Welfare Really Isn't the Problem." *The Public Interest* 83:3–11.

Piven, Frances Fox, and Richard A. Cloward. 1971. *Regulating the Poor: The Functions of Public Welfare.* New York: Vintage.

Schwarz, John E. 1983. *America's Hidden Success: A Reassessment of Twenty Years of Public Policy.* New York: Norton.

———. 1988. *America's Hidden Success: A Reassessment of Public Policy from Kennedy to Reagan,* rev. ed. New York: Norton.

Wilson, William Julius. 1987. *The Truly Disadvantaged: The Inner City, the Underclass, and Public Policy.* Chicago: University of Chicago Press.

3

The Contradictions of Public Assistance and the Prospect of Social Merging

Charles Lockhart

American social provision comes in forms that can be differentiated in numerous ways. One basic distinction is captured by the terms social insurance and public assistance. Social insurance—for example, social security benefits—characteristically serves to keep people who have generally provided adequately for themselves from falling into poverty when they are confronted with various episodic social hazards such as, aging, disability, or unemployment. Further, social insurance benefits are generally earned through some form of prior contribution. While some social insurance programs are clearly more popular than others (Coughlin 1980, 117–20), social insurance has been fairly well accepted in the United States.

In contrast, public assistance is focused on people whose needs are not so clearly episodic. These persons include the disadvantaged, who may use public assistance episodically but spend much of their lives near poverty levels, as well as an underclass exhibiting not only cultural deprivation but systematic problems of functioning in family, school, and work environments (Mead 1985, 21–25). Public assistance is characteristically distributed on the basis of need rather than on prior contributions; so these benefits are unearned, in contrast to social insurance. Americans have never been enthusiastic about public assistance programs. The connotations of public assistance or "welfare" differ sharply from those of social insurance, particularly social security. We have engaged in public assistance at a roughly constant proportion of GNP for a long time (Lebergott 1976), but we have done so grudgingly (Katz 1986, Patterson 1981). My purpose in this paper is to examine the promises and problems of public assistance and to propound a means, suggested by this analysis, for ameliorating some of the problems.

PROMISES AND PROBLEMS OF PUBLIC ASSISTANCE

The promises (or objectives) and the problems of public assistance are closely intertwined. This is so in part because the objectives are multiple and frequently conflicting, and some are extremely demanding. I will take these distinct problems up in turn and focus on Aid to Families with Dependent Children (AFDC) as a prominent example of public assistance.

Conflicting Objectives. Public assistance serves multiple objectives, some more manifest than others. Most obviously, it serves some needs of vulnerable, frequently desperate, people. Program benefits have included limited efforts to brighten the future prospects of recipients through the inculcation of job skills or moral reforms. But the central focus of benefits directed at these persons has involved money and other material resources designed to mitigate some pains of immediate destitution. AFDC, for instance, provides limited financial support to approximately eleven million destitute, or nearly so, single mothers and their children.[1] Since these benefits are technically unearned, they are widely considered a form of charity. Indeed, the status of these benefits as formal entitlements is undercut by numerous aspects of their provision, most notably the wide variation in benefit levels from state to state (K. Friedman 1981). But we should not conclude from the frequent characterization of these benefits as charity that society receives nothing but a sense of having donated to the needy. Even the most ardent critics of government intervention such as Milton Friedman (1962, 190–91) are unwilling to contemplate widespread starvation in urban centers, and benefits to the poor have long been maintained with an eye toward avoiding increases in crime that might follow in their demise.

More particularly, public officials benefit from public social provision. Many authors have associated social insurance with electoral competition (Tufte 1978; Wilensky, Luebbert, Hahn, and Jamieson 1985), although others have been more hesitant about labeling support for social programs as a viable strategy for electoral victory (Heclo 1974). The votes to be won from supporting public assistance in the contemporary United States are few, and public assistance serves public officials in a different sense. Piven and Cloward (1971) characterize this service as regulating the poor, although this phrase fails to reveal much of what they have in mind. In essence, public assistance holds the poor who receive it in a politically quiescent mode. It is difficult for them to receive their benefits and also virulently attack the state and society that provide them. Public assistance thus contributes to social order; and to the degree that benefits carry a stigma, or the procedures entailed in applying for benefits are used to deter applicants, or benefits are low in comparison to wages, public assistance reinforces labor market discipline. These contributions to social order and labor market discipline are relatively inexpensive. A more creative and less punitive method of dealing with vulnerable people would be more expensive.

Public assistance also benefits those who sell to the poor by expanding the effective market demand for goods and services among its explicitly targeted recipients. Katz (1986, 36) relates that merchants such as local grocers were major supporters of relief outside of poorhouses in the nineteenth century. And more recently, physicians and various economic groups associated with the housing industry have been noted for their interest in public assistance (Califano 1981, 331).

So the benefits that mean food, shelter, clothing, or perhaps a more encouraging future to the disadvantaged mean various forms of social control to societal elites and income or profits to other well-developed economic interests. It is clear that these interests are not merely distinct but frequently conflicting. It is convenient for social elites to have exceptionally disadvantaged people sidetracked from disrupting the economic and political practices of a society that doom them to extremely limited lives by modest offers of aid. It is icing on the cake that processes associated with acceptance of this aid tend to reinforce among recipients a vision of personal failure rather than underscoring limitations of social structure. But these results neither hold a monopoly on truth nor reflect the interests of vulnerable citizens. And physicians and urban realtors frequently have incentives (unnecessary or unperformed diagnostic testing or urban "renewal") that mesh poorly with the interests of public assistance recipients.

Inherent Difficulty of the Task. Additionally, public assistance confronts tough tasks; its objectives are simply more demanding than are those of social insurance. Generally social insurance facilitates the accomplishment of some respected activity by members of mainstream society—receiving medical care, educating children, maintaining incomes through problematic episodes. Public assistance faces more difficult challenges in several respects.

For instance, public assistance generally serves people in the lower ranges of the socioeconomic spectrum; and we can make several generalizations about characteristics that distinguish these people from more advantaged strata. First, being disadvantaged frequently means having poorer information (Coe 1981, 32; Auletta 1982). Poor people are commonly less well informed about how public assistance programs might aid them than are wealthy people about how to take advantage of tax codes. Second, efficacy among the impoverished (particularly for dealing with middle-class bureaucrats who serve as gatekeepers for public programs) is generally lower than among upper-middle-class citizens (Almond and Verba 1963; Beeghley 1983). A third and closely related generalization is that, as the socioeconomic status of public program recipients falls, the social distance between them and the professionals who deliver medical care and other sophisticated services grows, and the interaction entailed by the delivery of services removes each party progressively from customary and comfortable social interaction. Such gaps may inhibit an unfettered two-way flow of information and support (Sennett and Cobb 1973, 83). Fourth, as we work down the socioeconomic ladder, we are apt to encounter with increasing frequency social norms that make using social programs in a fashion similar to the societal mainstream less feasible (Beeghley 1983, Townsend 1979, Mead 1985). This will be the case regardless of whether these norms arise from flawed personalities, as some maintain (Banfield 1974), or represent reasonable adaptations to limiting social circumstances, as others argue (Gans 1962). Finally, when social programs attempt to work with seriously disadvantaged people, they must work with persons whose freedom of action is much more narrowly constrained than is the case for people in more advantaged positions in the socioeconomic hierarchy. Limitations of both material (income) and intangible (education) resources place narrow constraints on such things as job opportunities, housing options, and associates.

We can capture some of the more important consequences these generalizations hold for public policy by considering them in light of four common sense guidelines.[2] First, we can reasonably expect the consequences of public policy to be more encouraging when we minimize the changes we ask people to make in their customary activity. We can reasonably expect that, when we extend a pension to a worker and spouse who have supported themselves modestly across a working life of nearly five decades, the pension will facilitate their supporting themselves responsibly in retirement. We can be far less certain about the results of a new educational program on an adolescent whose home and peers have to-date provided little effective support for doing well in school.

Second and relatedly, the more public policy asks for in the way of complicated cooperation, the more problematic the consequences are apt to be. When we extend transfer payments to the elderly, we require that they get on the distribution list and that the public officials whom they contact in this regard do their regular jobs. Characteristically, this process goes fairly well. When we try to intrigue a previously disinterested adolescent with school, turn an adult smoker away from tobacco, or ask a physician to treat a public program patient through practices that deviate from her or his normal routines, we are requiring that these people engage in complicated forms of cooperation over lengthy periods of time, and we cannot be certain that this cooperation will be forthcoming.

Two more guidelines form another related pair. Third, the consequences of social programs are more constructive and involve fewer unanticipated, disturbing consequences when association with the program (as either a recipient or provider) creates no injury to an individual's social status or personal dignity. Injuries arise both from specifics of program design and the general character of program targeting and visibility. For instance, participating in a program such as AFDC that penalizes efforts at self-support in a cultural environment that creates expectations of both self-support and material success is bound to damage social status and personal dignity. Targeting programs on narrow groups of particularly disadvantaged people stigmatizes as well. And American concerns for the target efficiency of public assistance demand efficiency only in terms of reducing annual program expenditures. The visibility of programs, particularly their visibility as social programs, is relevant here as well. Neither suburban commuters who make daily use of interstate highways explicitly constructed for defense purposes, nor wealthy citizens whose tax breaks are presented as necessary prerequisites to economic recovery are perceived, by themselves or generally, as recipients of welfare.

Fourth, social program consequences are apt to be more encouraging when programs require that those associated with them are linked to responsible activity. For recipients this translates roughly into earning benefit rights from prior or concurrent contributions. For providers the interpretation is apt to involve delivering services professionally.

Some programs pose fewer problems for abiding by these guidelines than others. Social security pensions for the elderly fit nicely, and social insurance programs in general do fairly well in terms of these criteria. Public assistance programs fare less well. Characteristically, these programs have difficulty meshing with both the first pair of guidelines and the second pair or vice versa. That is, if these programs require little in the way of activity changes or complicated cooperation from recipients, they are apt to stigmatize, and recipients are apt to have only limited association with constructive activity. If, on the other hand, these programs seek to avoid damage to participants' social status and personal dignity and to create linkages between program use and constructive activity, they are apt to require changes in participants' activity and complicated cooperation efforts.

The thoroughness and effectiveness with which people use social programs may vary directly with socioeconomic status. Life is stacked against the disadvantaged in a variety of disturbing ways, and I want to make two comments about this distressing fact. First, modern polities like the United States that necessarily rely primarily on the impersonal operations of bureaucracies are better suited to working with people's aspirations, fears, and capacities (as social insurance objectives generally allow) than for changing these factors (as working with particularly disadvantaged recipients sometimes requires). It is meritorious for the state to improve the lives of people in disadvantaged circumstances, but it is a demanding task. Public assistance, in other words, has extremely demanding objectives and limited capacities for achieving them. Second, allowing for some residual program for people who are effectively disabled through psychological or physiological afflictions,[3] state programs aimed at helping the disadvantaged should work with whatever desires the disadvantaged have to merge with the socioeconomic mainstream by supplementing and facilitating their efforts. Unfortunately, current public assistance efforts tend to block such aspirations.

AFDC AS A CASE IN POINT

AFDC is a prominent example of public assistance,[4] and it has frequently served as a focus for criticism of public assistance in general. There are good reasons for this. AFDC does not meet the needs of its explicitly targeted beneficiaries well. And in the process its practices fly in the face of some prominent American values, so the contributions the program makes to the interests of others also are limited.

Distinct Patterns of Use and AFDC Program Design. AFDC serves two distinct clienteles. The first of these (and the vast majority over time) uses the program episodically (Duncan, Coe, Corcoran, Hill, Hoffman, and Morgan 1984). In effect, the program helps these recipients cope with "spells of poverty" (Bane 1984) that are brought on by changes in household composition or separation from the labor market (Duncan et al. 1984). Many of these people hover close to the boundaries of poverty even in the best of times, and AFDC deals poorly with their intermittent needs for an infusion of external resources.

For instance, AFDC eligibility does not characteristically commence when a problematic episode begins; instead households must use up some of the resources they possess until a specific degree of indigency is reached. This is a significant savings disincentive for people whose attachment to the labor market is generally precarious. The underlying policy concern is one of target efficiency, but this focus limits household financial stability among women whose labor market potential is modest. Modest potential stems from market discrimination, the characteristics of these women as workers (low skill levels), and from the competing demands of child rearing as single parents. Many of these women cannot reasonably expect that conscientious effort on their part will return steady wages sufficient to lift their households out of poverty or the fringe benefits necessary to meet their households' medical care needs.

For people already receiving AFDC benefits the incentives for work or other forms of capacity-enhancing activity have always been mixed, and since 1981 they have been virtually nonexistent. High rates of taxation on earnings are a central problem (Aaron 1973). People in this category gain independence from the program not because the program design features facilitate this process, but in spite of them. It is easy to imagine that they seek independence from the program in part to regain a sense of personal dignity and societal membership that program use—in a work ethic, personal development culture—assaults (Goodwin 1983).

Another category of program recipients (a small minority across time but over half at any given point in time) use the program in a more lengthy fashion (Duncan et al. 1984). These people are disproportionately urban, black single mothers. For this group the program represents a way of coping with various facets of a generally hostile culture. These recipients are exceptionally disadvantaged; they bear a heavy load of racial, sexual, and moral discrimination and have far fewer opportunities for utilizing the major means—changes in household composition—that recipients in the first category use to gain independence from the program. For black single mothers, adding a male adult to their household represents a risky step from the standpoint of improving their overall economic position. And for this and other reasons (Guttentag and Secord 1983), these women have markedly lower rates of marriage and remarriage than do their white counterparts. AFDC does little to facilitate labor market participation through child care and skill improvement for this population. Nor does AFDC any longer significantly supplement efforts at self-support across any but a brief (four-month) initial period.

In short, against the standard I introduced earlier—working with whatever desires the disadvantaged have to gain self-respect and become full-fledged members of society—AFDC has little to offer.

AFDC and Prominent Values of the American Political Culture. Inevitably then AFDC practices create problems for some prominent American values. First and probably most important, AFDC lacks any feature that legitimizes or certifies adult recipients. Benefits are distributed on the basis of need, and American reactions to distributing according to this norm are ambivalent (Anderson 1978, Feagin 1975, and Jaffe 1978). On the one hand, support for "true need" is strong; and the needs of children, who cannot reasonably be held responsible for their predicaments, explain the origins of the program as well as its major current rationale (Bell 1965). On the other hand, Americans tend to be skeptical about the needs of adults associated with the program. In contrast to social security beneficiaries, whose pensions are linked to dignified efforts at self-help, adult AFDC recipients are viewed suspiciously by their fellow citizens as exhibiting a distressing dependence.

Additionally, the program's response to need is loose. Equal need will not produce equal program support. This is partly true because of considerable interstate variation in program benefits, but even more basically because of the program's categorical character. AFDC exists to serve one category of need—that appearing in households led by single women with children.[5]

Also, the dependence among recipients that the program is alleged to foster is widely perceived to discourage economic efficiency. AFDC's consequences for work incentives have been widely studied and are hotly disputed among experts (Danziger, Haveman, and Plotnick 1981). There are, nonetheless, widespread perceptions among mass (Feagin 1975) and elite (Mead 1985) publics that the program destroys work incentives. Growing interest in various workfare proposals in the 1980s has developed in large measure as a result of such perceptions.

By virtue of these perceptions AFDC is isolated from effective political support. The program's explicitly targeted beneficiaries are rarely politically active. The same public officials who have worked long and effectively to support social security and its middle-class beneficiaries have been far less willing to exert similar efforts on behalf of AFDC and its more disadvantaged clientele (Cates 1983). Apart from specific groups who sell goods and services to this population, the general public has shown little supportive interest in the program. In a society dominated by a success ideology, a program focused narrowly on the weakest and most vulnerable has an extremely difficult time winning strong political allies.

These weaknesses in program design do not mean that AFDC does nothing constructive. The program helps roughly eleven million people—most of them children—cope with economic desperation. We should not overlook this contribution, but neither should we associate it with a program whose design features merit emulation. AFDC's manner of helping these people reinforces the theme that their predicaments arise from personal failure. And the rather limited resources devoted to the program—less than $13 billion in 1983 in contrast to $170 billion for social security the same year— (Sugarman, Bass, and Bader 1983) denote not only the limits of the general public's willingness to subsidize what is perceived as failure, but assures that a good portion of the true costs of the program involve a substantial price in terms of personal dignity and societal membership among recipients.

SOCIAL MERGING

I want to introduce briefly a means of dealing with the problems of disadvantage that I call social merging. Social merging is one aspect of a larger enterprise that I refer to as an investments approach to public social provision. This approach rests on three basic principles that—at least in the abstract—find support within the American political culture. The first of these is *reciprocity*. By this principle those who make constructive contributions to society may reasonably expect nurturing assistance from society with respect to basic needs when social hazards afflict their lives. Second, this assistance should be *supplementary*. That is, it should augment household efforts at self-help, rather than replace such efforts. What this means precisely will vary from one program to another. The third principle is *inclusivity*. The programs through which this assistance is provided should be accessible to citizens generally rather than targeted on narrow and particularly disadvantaged segments of the population. Social insurance programs—social security in particular—already realize these principles. Social merging would apply new programs that embody these principles to populations now served by public assistance. The practical keys to these new applications involve relying on concurrent as well as prior contributions, supplementing the concurrent efforts at self-help of disadvantaged households through lengthy problematic episodes such as child rearing, and building political allies for such help by drawing these households into programs that serve broad swaths of the public.

I will begin my explanation of this approach by attacking a theme that has tinged American public assistance to the poor for over a century (Katz 1986, Patterson 1981)—the notion of the "withering away of the poor." From this perspective poverty arises from personal aberrations that social programs ought ideally to eliminate over time. By this view the bottom line measure for poverty program effectiveness is whether the rate of "latent poverty" falls.[6] This concern has been a recurring theme of welfare reform in America. It has appeared in a variety of specific forms. The AFDC reforms of the early 1960s shared the sentiments of this theme. Lawrence Mead (1985) presents a sophisticated, interesting argument for this approach, carrying the contemporary label of workfare. His suggestions form a recent incarnation of the withering away thesis. Mead does not imagine that all poverty will wither away through coercively imposed work, but he is optimistic that a good deal of it will. Asking for more acceptable actions from many among the impoverished is reasonable, but supposing that poverty rests on personal actions alone ignores characteristics of the labor market that limit its utility for household support for many workers. Low wages and limited skills combine to keep a large proportion of households hovering barely above various poverty demarcation lines. The position of these households is tenuous, and any social hazard is apt to plunge them into poverty. Many recover through their own efforts, so turnover among the impoverished is high if we study it longitudinally. But the pool of households likely to experience poverty episodically is so large and the persistence of their collective problems so great that eliminating or even dramatically reducing such poverty through work alone seems unlikely. The overall problem is less one of changing the attitudes of a distressing subculture (although this may be a factor among persistent AFDC users) than of overcoming a variety of obstacles that reduce the ability of people to use labor market participation to support their household.

The 1967 AFDC reforms represent nascent examples of an alternative second approach, offering a more adequate recognition of the limitations of the existing labor market. Until 1981 these changes extended to a category of the poor a minimal level of economic support (a guarantee), which could be enhanced by work. The Family Assistance Plan (FAP) and Program for Better Jobs and Income (PBJI) proposals expanded this approach (Moynihan 1973, Shapiro 1978). In doing so they offered both advantages and drawbacks in comparison to AFDC. They covered more people, thus reducing horizontal or support inequities. But they also brought a much larger population into prospective programs that offered their recipients economic support insulated from requirements for working. And the imagery of guarantees as developed from WIN through PBJI is simply wrong for the American political culture. Americans consistently express beliefs in work, self-sacrifice, and deriving dignity through exertion (Hochschild 1981). Perhaps it is time for us to consider a realistic approach centered on these beliefs. Our efforts over the last quarter-century have either tried to alter the capacities of people ill-suited for the existing labor market or to insulate these people from the rigors of this market. My proposal is that we help these people to merge with the socioeconomic mainstream by supplementing their ability to participate in the labor market, and by facilitating their participation.

In the renewed debate over workfare conservatives have tended to argue that it is necessary to reduce the public assistance rolls by putting people to work, and liberals have tended to argue that jobs are needed. My position lies in some senses between these views. We need public programs that enable people to support their households through the labor market. My proposal shares with conservatives the view that working age adults should participate in the paid labor force. Accordingly, single adults and childless couples can generally be expected to look out for themselves in income maintenance terms (although probably not in terms of housing), just as public policy expects them to do today. But this approach is not sufficient to cope with the problems of households with children, particularly single-parent households. Family incomes based on regular full-time work at low wages will not cover basic needs or raise a household out of poverty in these instances. And especially in single-parent households, regular full-time employment is extremely difficult in the absence of additional assistance such as child care.

AFDC, as we have seen, has dealt miserably with this situation. Its eligibility rules require that a household sink into indigence before assistance begins, and the earnings of program beneficiaries are taxed at extremely high rates. Neither of these features provides powerful incentives among recipients for working or achieving independence from the program. But the outlines of a vastly improved system that would use public social provision to supplement and facilitate the efforts of individuals to act in responsible, socially approved ways can be discerned. I will present a three-step outline of the ideas involved in this suggestion.[7]

Efforts across the last quarter century to achieve greater self-sufficiency among AFDC recipients, and concomitantly to guide these people to better lives and reduce the recipient population, have foundered on three central problems: program design features creating only weak work incentives, inadequate labor market opportunities, and limitations of program recipients. Accordingly, we need three measures—one designed to counter each of these problems.

First, allowing exceptions for legitimate disability and counting on help in times of episodic social hazards from an expanded social security system, we must gradually withdraw current public assistance from working age adults. This places these adults progressively in a position of having to rely on the labor market. The limited and largely toothless work incentives associated with AFDC are replaced by a simple work-to-survive principle for most adults. But I am not recommending Murray's (1984) solution. I am interested in creating a structure of opportunities as well as incentives far stronger than any that has characterized AFDC to date. I wish to hold out the hope that those who try have reasonable chances of succeeding.

So second, we must have some means of supplementing the income of low-wage workers with children. It is crucial to the supplementary character of this aid that it be relatively modest and that earnings up to certain levels not threaten these benefits. I have in mind among other things a social insurance program—distinct from social security—that treats child rearing as a social hazard. This program would provide child allowances—varying inversely with income—to all households with children. I think a reasonable initial goal here is to supplement household earnings in a way that allows households with children and an adult working full time at the minimum wage to achieve poverty level income and group medical insurance, assuring feasible maximum out-of-pocket annual expenses. This step is designed to counter the limitations many positions in the existing labor market pose for household support.

Third, we need to facilitate use of the existing labor market, especially for groups who have particular disadvantages. Providing child care is one example of a facilitating action that is particularly important for single parents. Additionally, against the background of the first step—withdrawing current public assistance—a variety of measures that use public programs to expand the number of work positions and to train people for these positions would be appropriate and also have somewhat better prospects than similar measures have had in the past.

Let me contrast the general structure of these steps with the alternatives mentioned previously. These measures share with Mead's a concern that people be engaged in constructive activities, most importantly work. But in contrast to an approach that would enlarge existing public assistance bureaucracies with what would amount to a police force, these steps simply provide measures that supplement and facilitate the activities we want to encourage.

These measures share with the WIN and related guaranteed income proposals an acknowledgment that low-wage income—all that a significant portion of the population can expect at any given point in time—is frequently insufficient to support a household at levels even close to the officially recognized poverty lines. But in contrast to guarantee proposals, these measures work from the initiatives of people in the labor market. In this approach public social provision merely supplements and facilitates these initiatives, so that they have a reasonable chance of realizing household support.

CONCLUSION

I have admittedly been vague about the details of social merging. My purpose instead has been to focus on the central contrast between programs that assist fairly widespread desires of people for personal dignity (as their society understands it), and societal membership and programs—such as most of current public assistance—that inhibit such desires. It is, I think, appropriate to ask whether the measures I propose will work. The response depends on what "work" entails. If work means saving all the members of each disadvantaged American family from current destitution and extremely limited futures, the answer is no. But no program will achieve this objective.

If by work we focus instead on what happens to those who can and wish to use these measures, what we see is far more encouraging. These proposals do not assure a citizen of support. Rather, extensions of help require a quid pro quo, some form—generally but not always participation in the paid labor force—of constructive activity. In this regard, these proposals have more in common with the market than with a system of distributive justice based on need. These similarities are intentional and designed to give social merging efforts more appeal among both elite and mass audiences. But these proposals are also more forgiving than the market. The market represents a results oriented survival of the most capable (Hochschild 1981). These proposals, while not including everyone, define capability far more broadly. They operate on the basis of effort. People who apply themselves to support their households have a much better chance of realizing the provision of basic goods in culturally approved and thus dignified ways.

NOTES

1. A small proportion of the beneficiaries in some states is composed of two-parent families with unemployed fathers—AFDC-UP.

2. These guidelines draw on background provided by Salamon (1981) and Chase (1979).

3. This residual program might take the form of an expanded Supplementary Security Income (SSI). The expansion I have in mind would involve providing more thorough treatment for the conditions afflicting these individuals. It might be that private charities, working within public guidelines and perhaps with public financial assistance, could bring humane service to this task, which would otherwise be impossible for the modern state to achieve.

4. AFDC was once the largest public assistance program in budgetary terms. Medicaid now holds this position, and for a portion of the 1970s the food stamp program rivaled AFDC for second place.

5. Once again, there is a limited AFDC-UP option.

6. The level of latent poverty is the proportion of the population that is impoverished before public policy transfers are taken into account.

7. This proposal fits into a larger one (Lockhart, forthcoming) that includes both a social security system that deals with an expanded array of social hazards and a system of widespread national health insurance meeting minimal national guidelines that assures coverage to all households with children.

BIBLIOGRAPHY

Aaron, Henry J. 1973. *Why Is Welfare So Hard to Reform?* Washington, D.C.: Brookings Institution.

Almond, Gabriel A., and Sidney Verba. 1963. *The Civic Culture: Political Attitudes and Democracy in Five Nations.* Boston: Little, Brown.

Anderson, Martin. 1978. *Welfare: The Political Economy of Welfare Reform in the United States.* Stanford: Hoover Institution.

Auletta, Ken. 1982. *The Underclass.* New York: Random House.

Bane, Mary Jo. 1984. "The Poor in Massachusetts." In *The State and the Poor in the 1980s,* edited by M. Carbello and M. J. Bane, 1–13. Boston: Auburn House.

Banfield, Edward C. 1974. *The Unheavenly City Revisited.* Boston: Little, Brown.

Beeghley, Leonard. 1983. *Living Poorly in America.* New York: Praeger.

Bell, Winifred. 1965. *Aid to Dependent Children.* New York: Columbia University Press.

Califano, Joseph A., Jr. 1981. *Governing America: An Insider's Report from the White House and the Cabinet.* New York: Simon and Schuster.

Cates, Jerry R. 1983. *Insuring Inequality: Administrative Leadership in Social Security, 1935–54.* Ann Arbor: University of Michigan Press.

Chase, Gordon. 1979. "Implementing a Human Service Program: How Hard Will It Be? *Public Policy* 27:385–435.

Coe, Richard D. 1981. "A Preliminary Empirical Examination of the Dynamics of Welfare Use." In *Five Thousand American Families: Patterns of Economic Progress,* Vol. 9. Edited by M. S. Hill, D. Hill, and J. N. Morgan, 121–68. Ann Arbor: Survey Research Center, Institute for Social Research, University of Michigan.

Coughlin, Richard M. 1980. *Ideology, Public Opinion, and Welfare Policy: Attitudes Toward Taxes and Spending in Industrialized Societies.* Berkeley: Institute of International Studies, University of California.

Danziger, Sheldon, Robert Haveman, and Robert Plotnick. 1981. "How Income Transfer Programs Affect Work, Savings, and Income Distribution: A Critical Review." *Journal of Economic Literature* 19:975–1028.

Duncan, Greg J., Richard D. Coe, Mary E. Corcoran, Martha S. Hill, Saul Hoffman, and James N. Morgan. 1984. *Years of Poverty, Years of Plenty: The Changing Economic Fortunes of American Workers and Families.* Ann Arbor: Survey Research Center, Institute for Social Research, University of Michigan.

Feagin, Joe R. 1975. *Subordinating the Poor: Welfare and American Beliefs.* Englewood Cliffs: Prentice-Hall.

Friedman, Kathi V. 1981. *Legitimation of Social Rights and the Western Welfare State: A Weberian Perspective.* Chapel Hill: University of North Carolina Press.

Friedman, Milton. 1962. *Capitalism and Freedom.* Chicago: University of Chicago Press.

Gans, Herbert J. 1962. *The Urban Villagers: Group and Class in the Life of Italian Americans.* New York: Free Press.

Goodwin, Leonard. 1983. *Causes and Cures of Welfare: New Evidence on the Social Psychology of the Poor.* Lexington: D. C. Heath.

Guttentag, Marcia, and Paul F. Secord. 1983. *Too Many Women? The Sex Ratio Question.* Beverly Hills: Sage.

Hochschild, Jennifer L. 1981. *What's Fair? American Beliefs About Distributive Justice.* Cambridge: Harvard University Press.

Heclo, Hugh. 1974. *Modern Social Politics in Britain and Sweden: From Relief to Income Maintenance.* New Haven: Yale University Press.

Jaffe, Natalie. 1978. "A Review of Public Opinion Surveys, 1935–76." In

Welfare: The Elusive Consensus, L. M. Salamon, 221–28. New York: Praeger.

Katz, Michael B. 1986. *In the Shadow of the Poorhouse: A Social History of Welfare in America.* New York: Basic.

Lebergott, Stanley. 1976. *The American Economy: Income, Wealth, and Want.* Princeton: Princeton University Press.

Lockhart, Charles. Forthcoming. *Gaining Ground: Tailoring Social Programs to American Values.* Berkeley: University of California Press.

Mead, Lawrence M. 1985. *Beyond Entitlement: The Social Obligations of Citizenship.* New York: Free Press.

Moynihan, Daniel P. 1973. *The Politics of a Guaranteed Income: The Nixon Administration and the Family Assistance Plan.* New York: Random House.

Murray, Charles. 1984. *Losing Ground: American Social Policy, 1950–1980.* New York: Basic.

Patterson, James T. 1981. *America's Struggle Against Poverty, 1900–1980.* Cambridge: Harvard University Press.

Piven, Frances Fox, and Richard A. Cloward. 1971. *Regulating the Poor: The Functions of Public Welfare.* New York: Random House.

Salamon, Lester M. 1981. "Rethinking Public Management: Third-Party Government and the Changing Forms of Government Action." *Public Policy* 29:255–75.

Sennett, Richard, and Jonathan Cobb. 1973. *The Hidden Injuries of Class.* New York: Knopf.

Shapiro, Harvey D. 1978. "Welfare Reform Revisited: President Jimmy Carter's Program for Better Jobs and Income." In *Welfare: The Elusive Consensus,* L. M. Salamon, 173–218. New York: Praeger.

Sugarman, Jule M., Gary D. Bass, and Matthew J. Bader. 1983. "Human Services in the 1980s: President Reagan's 1983 Budget Proposals." Washington, D.C.: Human Services Information Center.

Townsend, Peter. 1979. *Poverty in the United Kingdom: A Survey of Household Resources and Standards of Living.* Berkeley: University of California Press.

Tufte, Edward R. 1978. *Political Control of the Economy.* Princeton: Princeton University Press.

Wilensky, Harold L., Gregory M. Luebbert, Susan Reed Hahn, and Adrienne M. Jamieson. 1985. *Comparative Social Policy: Theories, Methods, Findings.* Berkeley: Institute of International Studies, University of California.

4

Welfare Myths and Stereotypes

Richard M. Coughlin

"Welfare Mother Begets 3 Welfare Daughters, Perpetuating Life Style"
"Controversial Mother of 14 Won't Stop"
"Suspect May Dethrone Current 'Welfare Queen'"
                                        —Newspaper headlines[1]

WELFARE IN AMERICAN PERSPECTIVE

American attitudes toward welfare are ambivalent to the point of paradox.[2] Positive indicators of the public's concern about the plight of the poor are not hard to find. For at least the past twenty-five years, public opinion surveys have charted substantial and fairly consistent majority support for governmentally sponsored efforts to help the poor and other disadvantaged segments of the population.[3] Moreover, nothing strikes a responsive chord of public sympathy (and brings in an outpouring of cash donations) as much as a news media report of some beleaguered family in need of food and shelter, or a child in need of an expensive, life saving operation that the parents cannot afford.

At the same time, surveys conducted over the years also testify to the strong majority belief that many among the poor—especially those who are able-bodied adults—are to blame for their condition. Nowhere does this ambivalence toward poverty and the poor find clearer expression than in attitudes toward public assistance programs, or as they are more commonly known, "welfare."[4] As the above quoted newspaper headlines suggest, where welfare is concerned Americans seem generally prepared to believe the worst.

One program in particular, Aid to Families with Dependent Children (AFDC) historically has borne the brunt of public opprobrium. Ironically, AFDC is by no means the largest of the United States' social programs, having long since been eclipsed in budgetary importance by the old age pension and disability programs of Social Security, as well as by its Medicare component. AFDC is no longer even the largest of the nation's public assistance programs; it ranks far behind Medicaid and only slightly ahead of the food stamp program in terms of its total yearly cost to taxpayers. But in the public's mind AFDC and the clientele it serves remain the focus of what is perceived to be a "welfare mess" that seemingly defies all efforts to clean up.

The first part of this paper is devoted to the analysis of how widely shared negative perceptions and beliefs about welfare have developed, and how they have persisted over time in a variety of welfare myths and stereotypes. The second part of the discussion examines these myths and stereotypes in light of the evidence available from recent social science research into poverty and welfare dependency. The third and concluding section briefly considers the consequences that welfare myths and stereotypes have wrought in efforts to reform policy.

CONVENTIONAL WISDOM ABOUT WELFARE

Public mistrust of welfare runs deep. It forms the core of prevailing attitudes and beliefs that have dominated the public debate over welfare reform for at least the past decade. It has forged a widely shared set of perceptions that identify "welfare" as the cause, or at least a major contributing factor, in a host of vexing social ailments. And it has been instrumental in defining the conventional wisdom, "what everyone knows about welfare": that it is plagued by fraud and abuse; that it is to blame for rising rates of illegitimacy and a host of other antisocial behaviors; that it fosters habits of dependency which are transmitted from one generation to the next; that its costs are spiraling out of control; and so on.

Given the broad—one might even say, universal—acceptance accorded these and a number of related propositions, it is perhaps not surprising that recent radical critiques of the welfare system, typified by Murray's *Losing Ground* (1984), have gained such wide and positive recognition. Indeed, for anyone who adheres to all of these beliefs, Murray's draconian proposal to eliminate public assistance programs altogether and force welfare recipients to find other sources of support must seem eminently reasonable.

What is surprising, or at least ought to be, is that these popular conceptions about welfare are for the most part *demonstrably wrong*, or, at the very minimum, *not borne out by evidence* from systematic studies.

ETIOLOGY OF MYTHS AND STEREOTYPES

Although the existence of welfare myths has been recognized for some time, the subject has been addressed only sporadically and in a piecemeal fashion in the social science literature.[5] Where do misconceptions come from and how do they persist? There appears to be no single all encompassing answer to these questions. However, there are at least four significant (and, to some extent, interrelated) factors that come into play: 1) use of unrepresentative case studies from which general conclusions are drawn; 2) inappropriate inferences drawn from systematic, large-scale studies; 3) gaps in the research literature; and 4) the role of ideology in providing fertile ground in which myths and stereotypes take root.

A common avenue by which welfare myths have entered the public debate is through the use, or more accurately *misuse*, of the individual case study methodology. Such case studies often are linked to some highly publicized journalistic account of the welfare system based on the situation of a single welfare family (or at most a few families) whose experience is then allowed to speak for the whole of the recipient population. Of course, the main problem with this approach centers on the representativeness and generalizability of the case or cases selected for investigation.[6] Social scientists have long accepted that the best way to capture accurate trends in a large and diverse population is through the use of statistical samples. Sample survey methodology enables very accurate estimates of the characteristics of a large population to be inferred from a relatively small number of cases. But *relatively small* here means hundreds or even thousands of cases, not one or two individuals or families. Case studies have their place in social research; they can be used to achieve a more vivid and more finely grained picture of social life than is possible with larger scale studies. Case studies decidedly cannot be relied upon to provide an accurate representation of the characteristics of the whole.

A second route by which welfare myths enter the debate is through the various limitations present in the use of even the most reliable systematic data to unravel the complexities of the social world. Beyond the inherent constraints of the scientific method— where all conclusions must be regarded as tentative and where there is no such thing as absolute proof—there are many ways in which social research can go awry, whether by accident or design. One potential problem is the use of aggregated statistical data to describe conditions or forces operating at the individual level; such an approach can lead to the "ecological fallacy" in which true conditions and relationships at the individual level are misrepresented.[7] Another sort of methodological problem arises from the use of cross-sectional data to infer conclusions about social and economic trends over time—conclusions that can be misleading or plainly wrong.[8]

Yet another source of welfare myths and stereotypes is the absence of good data on a particular question or problem. Given all the attention focused on welfare over the past two-and-a-half decades, it is surprising how many important questions have *not* been systematically studied and are still not well understood. Under such conditions, hypothesizing—sometimes plausible, sometimes not—and political posturing have often taken the place of knowledge.[9]

Finally, there is the role played by ideology, which is a *sine qua non* of the process by which myths and stereotypes are created and sustained. The dominant conceptions of welfare and poverty that I describe below are not made up of simple ignorance or randomly generated misinformation. They have developed in relation to enduring traditional American values and beliefs—values which hold that the individual bears chief responsibility for his or her own success or failure; that work is a virtue in and of itself and idleness a vice; that the appropriate role of government is to allow individuals to get ahead on their own; and that provision of social and economic protection is apt to dull initiative and encroach on individual freedom. For the most part, these traditional elements are not easily reconciled with the idea of providing benefits to able-bodied nonworkers. This underlying tension creates a set of conditions predisposed to the development of "social constructs" that help to sustain a variety of negative beliefs about welfare.[10]

THE WELFARE MOTHER

The stereotype of the welfare mother is a touchstone of many myths surrounding welfare. The stereotype is a familiar one, and lest we forget what it is all about there is no shortage of news reports on the intractable plight of the underclass to help fill in the details. Indeed, one remarkable feature of the newspaper headlines appearing at the beginning of this paper is their sheer ubiquity; they represent information that the average person might pick up on a routine basis from sources as diverse as the *Wall Street Journal,* the *National Enquirer,* and everything in between. Welfare mythology, like other myths, is an integral and pervasive part of the wider culture.[11]

The first and in many ways most significant example of the stereotype comes from Susan Sheehan's article, "A Welfare Mother," which first appeared in the *New Yorker* magazine in 1976 and was later published as a book (Sheehan 1977). Sheehan's work was influential in setting the tone for a number of subsequent popular accounts of the American underclass. Although over ten years have passed since its publication, "A Welfare Mother" could just as well have been dated 1987 or for that matter 1967; another characteristic of myth is its timelessness.

Sheehan tells the story of one Mrs. Carmen Santana (a pseudonym, Sheehan informs, us of an actual person). Mrs. Santana is of Puerto Rican descent, living in New York City. She receives benefits under a variety of programs, including AFDC, Medicaid, and housing assistance. Although at a point in the distant past she had a job, Mrs. Santana has been on welfare for many years, and there is little doubt that she will ever be able to move off the public assistance rolls. She has little formal education, virtually no job skills, and she suffers from a myriad of health problems associated with her extreme obesity:

> Mrs. Santana loves to dance; otherwise she avoids all physical exercise. She sits even while she is cooking, and she would rather leave the TV on when she isn't watching it than bother to get up and turn it off. Her obesity appears to cause her no distress. . . . She

makes no effort to conceal her thick neck, her big breasts, her big belly, and her enormous thighs; on the contrary, she favors tight-fitting, scoop-necked body shirts with Bermuda shorts or slacks. Because of her weight, she is unable to take off her fashionable platform shoes unaided. Dancing, she quickly loses breath, but she goes on dancing. She is generous and lazy. Nothing lasts long in her apartment; it passes from being brand-new to being either broken or lost or stolen or given away. (3)

The preceding paragraph, which appears early in the story, not only offers a vivid description of Mrs. Santana as an individual; it simultaneously weaves together most of the elements allegedly present in the "culture of poverty" (cf. Lewis 1966). We subsequently learn that Mrs. Santana has ten or eleven children by at least three different men.[12] Her oldest daughter is herself a welfare mother, and two of Mrs. Santana's sons who live at home with her are drug addicts constantly in trouble with the law.

Mrs. Santana by her own admission "cheats on the welfare" in various ways: by concealing income derived from the numbers game, lying about her assistance check being stolen, and by failing to inform her caseworker when one of her children moves out of her home. Sheehan tells us that Mrs. Santana has "no qualms" about cheating, and that, "Almost everyone she knows cheats on the welfare. Most of her friends are cheating by continuing to live with men—who in most cases hold jobs and have fathered some of their children—after claiming that the men have deserted them" (41).

In short, Mrs. Santana fits the stereotype of what "everyone knows" is a welfare mother. More to the point, Sheehan gives the impression, without ever quite saying so, that Mrs. Santana is a *typical* welfare mother.

My second example is a welfare mother named Louise Lowman, who is the subject of a lengthy article that appeared in the *Los Angeles Times* (Treadwell and Shaw 1981).[13] The article opens with a description of a trip to the welfare office that, in another century, might have been written by Charles Dickens:

On a slate-grey morning in late May, Louise Lowman stepped through the discarded newspapers blown along the sidewalk by the wind from the lake, entered a grime-streaked office building and climbed the worn marble staircase to the second-floor waiting room of the state Public Aid Department.

Beside her, matching her mother's measured tread, was her

19-year-old unmarried daughter, Teresa. Cradled in Teresa's arms, wrapped snugly in a sparkling white blanket against the morning chill, was the teenager's month-old baby, John. . . .

Louise Lowman, 57, had been on welfare for *35 consecutive years,* so the trip to the welfare office was nothing new to her. But this morning was different—this morning the process would begin to place baby John's name on America's welfare rolls. He would represent the *third successive generation* in the Lowman family to receive welfare. (20406–07; emphasis added)

The article goes on to tell how Louise, who is black, has *ten children—seven who were born out of wedlock—fathered by six different men.* She depends on a variety of public assistance benefits for her livelihood—AFDC, food stamps, and Supplemental Security Income (the latter for her handicapped son)—which together total $808 per month. In addition, she receives another $100 a month from one of her grown sons, income that she does not report to the welfare department ("practicing the decept" is Louise's term for petty welfare fraud). She is part of the "permanent underclass" whose costs "to the nation as a whole are enormous. . . . The most visible price paid is the estimated $20 billion a year in taxes for the basic welfare programs that support members of the underclass who don't, won't or can't work" (20407).

Only later in the article do we learn that five of Louise Lowman's children "have reached, or seem headed for, the middle class—they have become a policeman, a teacher, a cabdriver, a restaurant manager, and a service station cashier." For Louise Lowman and the five younger children, however, the "American tradition of upward mobility has become a dream deferred, or cancelled outright" (20407).

My third and final example of the welfare mother stereotype, although by no means the last one that has been the subject of media coverage in recent years, is Juanita.[14] Her story is told in a front page article in the *Wall Street Journal* (Salamon 1982) under the provocative headline, "Welfare Mother Begets 3 Welfare Daughters, Perpetuating Life Style."[15] The text of the article begins as follows:

Life has disappointed Juanita, and she hadn't asked for much. As a child, growing up in North Carolina, she had modest dreams: "I imagined a home. I imagined me and my kids out working together to make ends meet."

At age 16, she was pregnant. At 22, she had five children. At 28, she began to collect welfare. Her three daughters, Juanita hoped, would do better than she had done.

They haven't. Two gave birth before they were 18; her youngest daughter, 16, is pregnant. They are all unmarried. "I had so much I wanted them to have, even knowing I couldn't get it for them," says Juanita, now 38, as she pulls her granddaughter to her lap. "I wanted them to try to get ahead. Now there are the babies to take care of. *Welfare has gone to my daughters from me.*" (1; emphasis added)

Teenage mothers like Juanita's daughters, the article goes on to say, ". . . seem most vulnerable to the snare of dependence. . . . Their children are likely to know only the life of welfare recipients. . . . Many of these women and their children are likely to live on public assistance *indefinitely*" (1; emphasis added). The next paragraph quotes a researcher at the Ford Foundation as saying, "The likelihood of being in a welfare family and begetting a welfare family is *very strong.*" Further on, the article notes that "Some teenagers *have babies to increase the money they get from welfare,*" although it qualifies this statement by adding that "sociologists say . . . far more have babies for other reasons."[16]

Each of these portrayals—Mrs. Santana, Louise Lowman, and Juanita—neatly reinforces what "everyone knows" about welfare mothers: they come from minority group backgrounds; they have suspect morals, prodigious fertility, and hopeless futures.

There is no cause to doubt the accuracy of the reports on the lives of these three women or others like them whose stories are standard fare in newspaper, magazine, and television depictions of the welfare system. Nor is my purpose here to question whether or not welfare families with eight, ten, or fourteen children, or multiple generations on welfare, or lifetime recipients actually exist—they do, to be sure, although their numbers are few. I have introduced these individual case studies to ask how well they represent the condition of welfare recipients in general. In other words, *how accurate is the stereotype?* For an answer to this question we must look to systematic studies of AFDC recipients, the nonwelfare poor, and the general population that have been conducted, beginning during the 1960s, using reliable sample survey methodologies. As we shall see in the next section, research over the past twenty years tells a story that is quite different from the accounts of welfare mothers and their children that most people have grown accustomed to hearing.

TWO DECADES OF RESEARCH ON WELFARE AND POVERTY

The past two decades have produced a wealth of social science data on poverty and welfare dependency.[17] This literature is vast and variegated, and it is well beyond the scope of this paper to attempt any comprehensive analysis. Instead, in this section I focus on those parts of the research literature that speak directly to the myths that have dominated public discussion of welfare in recent years, beginning with the stereotype of the welfare mother, and extending into related questions such as intergenerational welfare dependency, fertility and illegitimacy, welfare fraud, and welfare-induced migration.

Poor Families, On Welfare and Off. The poor in America are a diverse group of which families receiving AFDC represent only one segment of a larger population living below or near the official poverty line. Census data collected over the past twenty-plus years provide a series of snapshots of the absolute and relative numbers of the poor.[18] A similar cross-sectional survey methodology has been used to gather detailed information on the characteristics of AFDC recipients at various points in time during the 1970s.

While they help to shed light on the incidence of poverty and the characteristics of AFDC families these successive snapshots of the poor, both on welfare and off, can also mislead since they reveal little or nothing about the actual condition of individuals and families over time. Indeed, as Duncan (1983) has noted, implicit in such cross-sectional data is an assumption of relative stasis; that is, that individuals falling below (or above) the poverty line in one year will continue to be below (or above) poverty the next year, and that any movement in or out of poverty is gradual and permanent. Results of the University of Michigan's Panel Study of Income Dynamics (PSID), which followed the economic and social circumstances of a sample of over five thousand families on an annual basis beginning in 1968, indicate that there is a large amount of movement in both directions across the poverty line. Moreover, data from the income dynamics study also reveal that there is a similar fluidity on the part of families receiving welfare assistance; fully one quarter of the United States population lived in families that received some form of public assistance between 1969 and 1978, while only one in fifty individuals were persistently dependent on welfare benefits for most of their income during the same period (Duncan 1983, 72).

Race and Ethnicity. As a group, American blacks are at greater risk of falling below the poverty line and of being on welfare. To a lesser degree, the same is true of the Hispanic population in the United States. Data from the 1970s reveal that the stereotype of the welfare mother as black has some basis in reality. Census data for 1979 indicate that blacks made up 43.1 percent of all AFDC families, although they constituted just over 10 percent of the total United States population. Although continuing to be overrepresented as a proportion of all AFDC families, however, blacks actually *declined slightly* through the 1970s.[19] Meanwhile, non-Hispanic white families increased slightly as a proportion of AFDC families, from 38.0 percent in 1973 to 40.4 percent in 1979. The proportion of AFDC families classified as Hispanic remained essentially constant over the same period.[20]

Household Composition. The popular image of the welfare family consisting of a single woman and her children is also substantiated by fact. In 1979 nearly three-fourths (72 percent) of AFDC families consisted of a mother and her child or children (U.S. DHHS, 1982, 20). In part this figure is simply a function of the eligibility criteria of the AFDC program, but it also mirrors a more general trend in poverty in the larger population. Indeed, of all segments of the population, female headed households in which there are dependent children are at the highest risk of poverty. As Duncan (1983) notes, "Almost three-fifths (59 percent) of all individuals poor in 1978 lived in families headed by women. Of the entire population in 1978, less than one-fifth (19 percent) lived in families headed by women" (49).

However, it should also be noted that the composition of AFDC households is more varied than is commonly assumed. For example, in 1979 about 15 percent of all AFDC families had a grandparent present in the household; 9 percent had a nonrecipient brother or sister present; 9 percent had a natural or adoptive father present; and 15 percent had "other relatives" living in the household (U.S. DHHS, 1982, 1). One largely ignored implication of this variation in household composition is that all AFDC families do not have the same resources upon which to draw in areas such as child care, shopping, and housework—factors that bear directly on the ability of the head of household to work, enter a job training program, or attend school.

Length of Time on Welfare. Popular mythology holds that welfare is a kind of addictive drug; once started, the receipt of public aid quickly grows into an unbreakable habit that dooms the individual to a lifetime of dependency.[21] Recent studies, while not discounting the problem of long-term dependency, paint a much more varied picture of individual use of welfare assistance over time.

Studies of AFDC caseloads over the past fifteen years have consistently found a pattern of high turnover. Across the entire caseload, the length of time AFDC cases remain open (that is to say, the time the recipient has been receiving benefits on an uninterrupted basis) is heavily skewed toward the low end; typically, a majority (56.7 percent in 1979) of AFDC cases remain open less than three years, and only a small fraction of cases are continuously open for more than ten years (7.1 percent in 1979).[22]

But current duration data on caseloads do not tell the entire story. The fact is that at any one time a large proportion of the total AFDC caseload is made up of medium (four to seven years) and long term (eight years and over) recipients (U.S. Executive Office of the President 1986, 35). The apparent discrepancy between annual data on all AFDC cases, where short-term use predominates, and time-point data where medium- to long-term cases figure heavily, is not as contradictory as it appears to be. Part of this pattern can be explained by the fact that individual cases may open, close, and then reopen over the course of a few years or even a few months. As an individual recipient moves on and off the welfare rolls, a pattern of long-term welfare use can thus be pieced together out of many short spells. But an even more significant factor in explaining "length of time on welfare" data is the balance between short- and long-term cases at any one point versus the relationship between these categories over time. Bane and Ellwood (quoted in U.S. Executive Office of the President 1986) use the analogy of the hospital to illustrate how this works:

> Consider a 13-bed hospital in which 12 beds are occupied for an entire year by 12 chronically ill patients, while the other bed is used by 52 patients, each of whom stays exactly one week. On any given day, a hospital census would find that about 85 percent of patients (12 of the 13) were in the midst of long spells of hospitalization. Yet viewed over the course of a year, short-term patients still dominate: Out of the 64 patients using hospital services, about 80 percent (52 of the 64) would spend only one week in the hospital. (34)

Analysis of the patterns of welfare use among members of the PSID sample helps to round out the picture sketched above. Duncan (1983) reports that less than 5 percent of the PSID sample received any benefits from AFDC and other assistance programs in eight or more of the years from 1969 to 1978, and as noted above, less than half of these (only 2 percent of the sample) were dependent on welfare for more than 50 percent the family's income. Duncan (1983) further concludes that as many as half of all welfare cases represent a temporary process of "digging out following some major crisis" (72) such as a divorce, loss of a job, or death of a spouse. The remaining half are divided into roughly equal groups:

> ... one—about a quarter of all welfare recipients—is made up of those who appear to be using welfare income as part of a more permanent income-packaging strategy; the other quarter is made up of those who appear to be in very serious economic straits, cut off from all other sources of help and very much in need of the resources that welfare provides. (72)

Fertility and Illegitimacy. In contrast to the stereotype of the large welfare family, every piece of reliable research indicates that the welfare mother with six, eight, ten or more children is a statistical rarity. Indeed, in 1979 the median number of children in AFDC families stood at 2.1, a figure only slightly higher than that for the rest of the United States population.[23] Moreover, between 1969 and 1979 fertility rates among AFDC mothers nationwide declined at about the same rate (roughly 30 percent) as for other women in the total population. For at least the past fifteen years, the modal—that is, the most frequently observed—AFDC family has consisted of a mother with *one dependent child* (42.5 percent of total cases in 1979), followed by families with two dependent children (28.0 percent), three children (15.5 percent), and so on. AFDC families with seven or more children make up *less than one percent* (0.9) of all cases.

Equally widespread and no less controversial is the posited link between welfare and out-of-wedlock births. The stereotype of the unmarried welfare mother producing offspring to increase the size of her welfare check has long been a hallmark of popular mythology and a focal point of intense public criticism of the welfare system. A common version of this story depicts the welfare mother thus engaged in irresponsible procreation as a teenager.

The fact is that the out-of-wedlock births *have* increased as a proportion of all live births since 1960. The rise, moreover, has been steepest among blacks, and among black teenagers in particular. Without minimizing the severity of the handicap that becoming a parent imposes on unwed teenage mothers, particularly those who are poor to begin with, the question at issue here is the extent to which the observed increase can be linked to the availability of welfare benefits.

Given the publicity that has surrounded this question (e.g., the television documentary on "The Vanishing Black Family," in which welfare was depicted as a direct cause of black teenage pregnancy), this question has been the focus of relatively little systematic research.[24] Results of several studies indicate that the provision of welfare benefits cannot be consistently tied to unmarried women's decisions to have children. For example, recent work by Ellwood and Bane (1985) comparing fertility rates across states with widely varying AFDC benefit levels concluded that welfare does not positively affect the decision to have a child: in fact, the birthrate is actually higher in low-benefit states.[25]

Intergenerational Welfare Families. The debate over what is wrong with the welfare system often begins and ends by invoking the image of the intergenerational welfare family—a mother whose children and even grandchildren are locked into an unbreakable cycle of dependency. It is not hard to understand why this is the case; the intergenerational welfare family offers an image that is both potent and disturbing. For the most part, recent research indicates that it is also *wrong;* but, as we have seen embodied in the accounts of the lives of stereotypical welfare mothers—Carmen Santana, Louise Lowman, and Juanita—and their children, the idea remains very much alive in media reports and, not surprisingly, in the public's mind.

The best available data on intergenerational welfare experience come from the University of Michigan PSID. Among the more than five thousand families in the sample, Morgan et al. (1974) looked at the welfare experience of children who "split off" from welfare and nonwelfare families between 1967 and 1971, and concluded that, "Whether or not the main family was on welfare in 1967 has only a slight effect on the splitoff's probability of being on welfare in 1971, and the variation in this pattern is so great that we cannot say with certainty there is any effect at all" (269). Subsequent studies have found some evidence for an intergenerational effect. A 1980 study (Levy, cited in Duncan, 1983) also based on the PSID sample found that about 3 percent of all women who split off from their parental homes between 1968 and 1976 became unmarried heads of their own families with children, receiving some welfare benefits in 1976. Among these, women who came from families that were receiving some welfare in 1968 were about 40 percent more likely to be on welfare in 1978 compared to women from nonwelfare families. Holden (1987) summarizes the findings of still another longitudinal study done by University of Michigan researchers:

> Although welfare has come to be perceived as an intergenerational phenomenon, the situation is not as bad as some think. The [Center for the Study of Poverty] did a longitudinal study of 1085 girls, at ages 13 and 15, and compared their welfare status at that time with the 3-year period when they were aged 21 and 23. Of those whose families were 'heavily' dependent (on welfare all 3 years), they found that 20% also became heavily dependent. . . . In contrast, 3% of those from nondependent families became heavily dependent in their 20s. (609)

However, while arriving at different estimates of the magnitude of the intergenerational effect, it is important to note that all these studies found that a large majority of "welfare children" do not go on to become welfare recipients as adults. In other words, contrary to stereotype and popular mythology, they are not locked into the "lifetime on the dole."

Level of Welfare Benefits. Another persistent idea is that welfare benefits are lush—much better than low-wage work and even approaching the income level of middle-class families. Under such conditions, it is often asserted, there are powerful incentives for individuals to select welfare over work.[26] This argument it should be noted is not new; it has its origins in the nineteenth-century concept of "least eligibility," which held that relief payments must not exceed the wage of lowest paid workers in the labor force.

But the fact is that average benefits are low—in some states, pitiably so. Although most welfare families receive benefits from two or more public assistance programs, their standard of living remains low by comparison to the general population. Several factors impede any precise characterization of the total benefit package actually delivered to eligible families; chief among these obstacles is the problematic valuation of Medicaid benefits and the low take-up rates in food stamps and some of the smaller, miscellaneous public assistance programs. It is theoretically possible to achieve a total income through multiple public assistance benefits that is higher than one gained from working at a decent paying job (as opposed to minimum wage employment), but this outcome presumes the confluence of a number of factors. It is possible only for recipients who live in states and localities offering a full range of programs, with benefits toward the high end of the scale nationwide; and it presumes that recipients have the knowledge, motivation, and opportunity to apply successfully for benefits under many different programs. In reality, this situation is relatively rare.[27]

Welfare Fraud. A preoccupation with welfare fraud and abuse is one of the most enduring aspects of the public debate in the United States. At one extreme the image of the "welfare queen" is deeply ingrained in the American consciousness.[28] On a more mundane level, the public's preoccupation with welfare fraud and abuse expresses itself in a variety of ways, for example: in the findings of public opinion surveys indicating that a majority of Americans agree with the proposition that the "welfare rolls are loaded with chiselers and people who don't want to work"; in pronouncements by public officials that welfare fraud is a serious problem; and in propagation of the idea that government spending could be pared down to size if only all the fraud, waste, and abuse could be wrung out of the welfare system.[29]

Since the early 1970s various studies have attempted to gauge the magnitude of fraud, abuse, and error in AFDC and other public assistance programs (Gardiner and Lyman 1983). While fraught with definitional and methodological problems, these efforts have produced some useful findings. At minimum, they have helped to bring the discussion of welfare fraud out of the realm of fantasy and wild speculation, where it had long been situated.

Official data from 1971 to 1980 reveal that only a tiny fraction of the total AFDC caseload is identified and subsequently prosecuted for fraud. In 1971, the prosecution rate stood at less than 0.2 percent of all AFDC cases, rising to a high of 0.7 percent in 1978.[30] Of course, as for most types of crime, actual prosecution is the end result of a multi-stage filtering process in which many cases are dropped for lack of sufficient evidence or are settled by other means (e.g., payment of restitution). Moreover, it is important to note that cases identified as "possible fraud" and those subsequently prosecuted are typically limited to aggravated (i.e., serious) fraud. Still, data on prosecutions helps to put into realistic perspective the magnitude of serious welfare fraud.[31]

Error rates, which are often confused with incidence of fraud, affect a much larger proportion of cases. Quality control systems established for various public assistance programs in the 1970s have tracked violations of federal and state regulations in awarding benefits to individual cases.[32] These efforts involve regular audits of a sample of the caseload files to determine the accuracy of the grant amount and the recipient's eligibility. Nationally, quality control reports for AFDC in 1980 indicated the following "error rates": 5.0 percent of all cases were ineligible; 10.2 percent were eligible but overpaid; and 4.3 percent were eligible but underpaid (Gardiner and Lyman 1983, 6). The total amount of "overpayment," including ineligibles, was about $290 million out of the total AFDC budget of nearly $12 billion. The source of errors was split about evenly between clients and agency staff.

Of course, official statistics on fraud and error rates are based only on *known* violations of administrative regulations or criminal statutes. What of the cases that go undetected? A partial answer to this question is provided by studies of household composition and income among participants in the Seattle-Denver Income Maintenance Experiment (SIME/DIME) studies. Based on interviews with families receiving income assistance benefits, these studies suggest that the error rates—and, by implication, reports on the incidence of fraud— are underestimated in caseload quality control data. One study found that one-half of the AFDC-matched households in each city had reportable income, of these one-quarter to one-third failed to report this income (Halsey, Nold, and Block cited in Gardiner and Lyman, 1983). The average amount of unreported income was slightly over $320.[33] In addition, some 42 to 47 percent of households failed to report male heads, and around 10 percent overreported the number of children present. Aggregating these effects and projecting the findings on a national basis, Gardiner and Lyman (1983) estimate total overpayments in AFDC to be between a low of $376 million to a high of $3.3 billion per year—or between about 3 and 25 percent of total AFDC spending.

All of these data—indeed, the entire debate over welfare fraud and abuse—need to be placed in the context of prevailing levels of illegal activity of both a serious and petty nature in American society as a whole. While a full discussion of this issue is beyond the scope of this paper, a few examples should suffice: the Internal Revenue Service reports that approximately three-quarters of all individual taxpayer audits result in additional tax payments due; Schwarz (1983) cites U.S. Chamber of Commerce estimates of total losses in the private business sector due to fraud, embezzlement, and other criminal activity to be around 4 percent of all revenues; and estimates of the "underground economy" in the United States in recent years range from 5 to 8 percent of the gross domestic product (The Economist 1987).

In short, welfare fraud is not the huge problem that it is commonly believed to be. It is not inconsequential, but neither does it appear to amount to a major portion of total welfare spending. Cases of aggravated fraud are relatively rare, and even the vast majority of these fall short of the spectacular activities of "welfare queens."

Welfare-Induced Migration. A theme that has surfaced from time to time in the public debate concerns the geographic mobility of welfare recipients.[34] The concern has always been that would-be recipients will migrate to states or localities with higher benefits. Until 1969, when a ruling by the U.S. Supreme Court outlawed residency requirements for welfare applicants, local restrictions on eligibility for public assistance benefits were commonplace.[35]

Specifically addressing the question of welfare's role in attracting migrants to New York City, a 1974 study by the Rand Institute looked at the experience of over 200,000 individuals who had recently moved there. The study found that in the first two years only about 5 percent of the new arrivals went on welfare, although nearly 25 percent could have qualified for benefits. While the group's use of welfare did increase a bit in subsequent years (to about 11 percent before settling down to a rate of 7 percent among those with residence of ten years or longer) the study's authors conclude that the idea that the poor were attracted to New York City by the prospect of generous welfare benefits was "mostly myth."[36]

More recently, discussion of welfare and migration has focused on undocumented aliens, especially those entering the United States from Mexico and Central America. The impact of these immigrants on public expenditures for welfare and related social services has been the focus of intense controversy, especially in the states of the Southwest. Recent studies by Rand (McCarthy and Valdez 1985) and the Lyndon B. Johnson School of Public Affairs (The Undocumented Workers Policy Research Project 1984) help to illuminate the actual impact such immigrants have on social programs.[37]

The Texas study found that there were little use of social services among the sample of undetained immigrants; less than 5 percent reported using AFDC, general assistance, food stamps, or other assistance programs (The Undocumented Workers Policy Research Project 1984, xxix). Nonetheless, over one-quarter of the sample reported using publicly supported health services (mostly children served by public clinics, and adult emergency room admissions for accidents and childbirth) which they commonly paid for in cash. Moreover, almost one-half of the sample made use of legal assistance services, typically related to immigration matters.

The Rand study produced similar findings with respect to Mexican immigrants in California. McCarthy and Valdez (1985) note that "immigrants' service usage varies substantially across services. Their use of education . . . is substantial and probably rising" (48). In contrast, immigrants' use of health care services appears to be about average relative to the age make-up of the population, while their reliance on welfare services is "well below that for comparable low-income populations" (49). Finally, in examining the question of net impact on government program spending, the Rand researchers concluded that, exclusive of educational services, "the average cyclical immigrant pays about $200 to $400 more in taxes than he or she uses in services" (49).

CONSEQUENCES FOR WELFARE REFORM

It is a useful, even an essential, exercise to test common knowledge against the findings of systematic research. But ultimately all such exercises are limited by the fact that most myths and stereotypes are not simply falsehoods that can be confronted and vanquished by empirical evidence. While some misconceptions owe their existence to simple error or absence of knowledge, many of the ideas reviewed in this paper, and many others not addressed here, are rooted in larger belief systems that are not so much counter-factual as they are unfalsifiable—as big questions often are. For example, the answer to the deceptively simple question of whether or not welfare undermines self-reliance presumes that we can first agree on some common definition of what "self-reliance" consists of in a modern society marked by complex webs of economic and social interdependence. It also presupposes that we share at least some value premises about the nature of social and economic inequality. Such broad agreements and common understandings are often simply impossible to achieve. Consequently, even after all the crude misunderstandings are removed from the debate, the wellsprings of ideology that give form and substance to belief systems about social, political, and economic relations will remain, and from them new questions and controversies will inevitably emerge.

Still it is essential to strive to move the debate onto firmer ground, where the play of gross caricature and overwrought polemics—for these are the most common uses to which stereotype and myth are put—is kept to a minimum. To this end, *I submit that a necessary first step toward reforming the welfare system is to reform the welfare debate.* What is yet unknown or not understood about the characteristics of the poor or the nature of dependency is only part of the conundrum of policy reform; a more immediate and less tractable problem is how knowledge, or lack of it, is used or misused. Let me conclude this discussion by offering several illustrations of how the debate has gone astray.

First, gross caricatures of the welfare population reinforce the notion that their situation is so desperate that meaningful progress is all but impossible. This situation breeds a kind of civic pessimism— even cynicism—about the capacity of society to mobilize collective resources to bring about any change for the better. Of course, misconceiving welfare as itself the *cause* of social problems, rather than one of many correlates, only deepens these currents of resignation.

Second, and seemingly paradoxical to the first point, reducing the problems of poverty and welfare dependency to caricature and over-simplification serves to hold out the hope that there is some "magic bullet" that, if correctly aimed, could cure all the ills of the poor. This condition inspires the development of a false optimism that there are easy answers to difficult and complex questions. Indeed, over the years the welfare debate has swung back and forth between poles of despair and hope, pessimism and optimism, a sense that nothing can be done to a feeling that some final solution is within reach. In the end, the net result has been a deadlock.

Third, by their very existence myths and stereotypes tend to undermine the total rationality of the policy-making process. Invoking the welfare mother with ten or more children, the welfare queen, or the unmarried pregnant teenager as conclusive evidence of what is wrong with the welfare system serves no purpose other than to create confusion, inflame emotions, and cloud the picture of who the welfare poor really are and what can be done to help them. What makes good news copy or a flamboyant campaign speech does not necessarily translate into sound public policy. In the case of welfare reform, substance has often been overshadowed by imagery.

Fourth, myths and stereotypes have afflicted the welfare debate with a more subtle kind of disorientation. The attention focused on various sub-themes of welfare reform has often mixed central concerns with peripheral ones, failing to maintain a clear sense of perspective. For example, on their own merits and without myths to impel them, issues such as welfare fraud, welfare induced migration, and welfare inspired fertility would not deserve much attention. The notice paid to these "social problems" reveals more about American society as a whole than it does about the circumstances and behavior of the welfare poor. Of greater intrinsic importance, but still short of what I regard as central to the policy debate, are issues such as intergenerational patterns of welfare use, persistent dependence on welfare, and employment or job training requirements for welfare recipients. These issues are at the forefront of the current welfare reform debate, I would argue, less because they are inherently important than because they each pay homage to a prevailing myth or stereotype. These questions continue to demand a disproportionate amount of the attention of social researchers, politicians, and the public despite the lack of compelling evidence to support the assumptions on which they are based: that the "cycle of dependency" is unbreakable, that long-term welfare use is typical, or that able-bodied adult recipients commonly disdain reasonable offers of employment to remain on welfare.

I do not mean to suggest that none of these questions are worth pursuing, or that the welfare system is not in need of reform. Clearly, current public assistance programs are riddled with problems and profound contradictions that cry out to be corrected. Nor do I dismiss the seriousness of the myriad social problems afflicting the poor: violent crime, drug abuse, broken families, and shattered lives—all are real and all weigh far more heavily on the poor than on other segments of the population. These problems demand our collective attention and action, and while efforts to reform welfare cannot ignore these conditions, we must guard against confusing the symptoms of problems with their causes. My point is that a firmer sense of reality must be brought to bear on the public discussion of welfare and poverty. Myths and stereotypes have been allowed to set a major portion of the agenda for welfare policy reform. Indeed, it is difficult to envision what the debate would look like without them.

The consequence is that fundamental questions have often been ignored or pushed aside in the public debate by a steady stream of non-issues and secondary concerns. The time is long overdue for the discussion of welfare reform to be recast in broad terms of guaranteeing a minimum standard of living to all citizens regardless of employment, marital status, domicile, or other circumstances, rather than as an endless debate over the details of individual social programs. Such a reformulation would draw in many of the deprived segments of the population—the homeless, the working poor, the long-term unemployed—often excluded from the narrow American conception of "welfare" and the myths and stereotypes associated with it.

NOTES

1.   The sources of the headlines and accompanying news stories are, respectively, the *Wall Street Journal* (Salamon 1982), the Los Angeles Times-Washington Post Service (*Albuquerque Journal* 1980), and the Associated Press (*Albuquerque Journal* 1987).

2.   This paper was originally prepared for the symposium "Rethinking Welfare: Beyond Left and Right," sponsored by the Institute of Public Policy, University of New Mexico, April 23–24, 1987. An abbreviated discussion of some of the themes addressed in this paper was published previously in Coughlin (1987). I am grateful to Daniel Firschein for research assistance in preparing this paper. I would also like to thank the New Mexico Department of Human Services for updating some of the data in its public information pamphlet, "Exploding Welfare Myths."

3.   Results of some of these public opinion polls are summarized in Coughlin (1980).

4.   Unless otherwise noted, "welfare" is used in this paper to refer to Aid to Families with Dependent Children (AFDC)—a usage that is itself an example of a prevailing welfare myth. As mentioned in the text, AFDC is neither the only nor the largest public assistance or income transfer program in the United States today.

5.   In the early 1970s the U.S. Department of Health, Education, and Welfare responded by publishing a public information pamphlet designed to dispel some of the prevailing myths about welfare and welfare recipients (U.S. DHEW 1971). At least one state, New Mexico, followed suit, producing its own version of the "Welfare Myths vs. Facts" pamphlet. In the main these efforts were directed at dispelling what can best be described as "conservative myths" about welfare and poverty. In the 1970s and 1980s a number of conservative critics, including Charles Murray, responded by arguing that the lack of progress in the 1960s in combatting poverty was directly attributable to the sway held by "liberal myths" over members of the Washington, D.C., policy establishment. In this paper I have chosen to focus on those misconceptions and misperceptions that have been most widespread throughout the society and most enduring over time. Certainly, at least since the end of the 1960s, public perceptions of welfare in the United States have been shaped by a dominant conservative ideology, which has been especially the case under the Reagan administration. While I by no means rule out the existence of "liberal myths," such ideas have not played a major role in the policy debate in recent years.

6.   Regarding how journalists decide what to report as news, Gans (1979) states "the news depends on and reinforces stereotypes. At times it also invents them, although more often than not the stereotypes journalists create coincide with those invented independently by many other people" (201).

7.   The classic description of the "ecological fallacy" is found in Robinson (1950). Greenstein (1985), among others, has criticized Murray's (1984) highly selective use of state level data in building an indictment of the American welfare system.

8.   See Duncan (1983) for a discussion of this issue in terms of the use of cross-sectional data on poverty to draw inferences about longitudinal trends.

9.   Notable examples here include the question about intergenerational welfare families and concern about welfare fraud. Given the prominence of these themes in the debate, the hard empirical evidence, summarized below, is surprisingly slim. The relationship between welfare and family decisions, such as out-of-wedlock births and breakup of the household, is a similarly controversial and, at least until quite recently, understudied aspect of welfare.

10.   As previously noted, I do not mean to imply here that myths and stereotypes are limited to one end of the ideological spectrum. It is my contention, however, that in American society during the 1970s and 1980s,

and in many respects long before that, the dominant ideology defining the problems of poverty and welfare has been underpinned by the traditional values and beliefs described in the text. In a more general way I am proposing the use of a general analytical framework of the "social construction of reality" developed by sociologists of knowledge (cf. Berger and Luckmann 1966). In this framework, "welfare" and "poverty" are social constructs— essentially social definitions of phenomena that are ordinarily regarded as based in the realm of fact, but which actually represent the development of commonly shared meanings. This process is at the core of how individuals identify and attribute significance to aspects of their social environment.

11.   Lule (1987) sums up the relation between news reports and myth as follows: "[News reports] appear to bear a communal countenance . . . a cultural narrative offering a view of the world's events and suggesting reactions to those events. . . . Myth is a *form*—that is, structure and content—adapted to a *function*, the representation and confirmation of shared belief" (4–5; emphasis in the original).

12.   Sheehan's account is hard to follow on this point. At the time of Sheehan's contact with the family only four of the children were living at home. Mrs. Santana had her first child in Puerto Rico at age fourteen; she married the father and dropped out of school, and within five years gave birth to four more children. Her husband left her shortly thereafter, and she then took up with another man, whom she refers to as her "second husband" even though they never married. She promptly had two more children. Then she moved to New York, where she went to work at a leather goods factory in lower Manhattan. There she met Vicente Santana, whose surname she took even though they too never legally married. With Vicente she had another four children. At the beginning of their relationship, both were employed; but then Vicente was laid off and Carmen Santana, unable to make ends meet, applied for welfare. Soon after, Vicente went back to work at the leather goods factory, but the family continued to receive various forms of public assistance for the next six years. It was not until several years later, after ten years together, that Vicente left for good. At this point the die was cast, and although a succession of "husbands" moved through her life, Mrs. Santana was by then a permanent public charge.

13.   Excerpts of the article were subsequently introduced into the Congressional Record (1981) as an example of, in the words of Representative Richmond, "the failure of current Government [sic] programs to break the cycle of unemployment and poverty." For convenience, page numbers in the text refer to the Congressional Record.

14.   The article gives no surname.

15.   The article is subtitled, "Teen-age pregnancies keep family in Harlem poor; avoiding rats in kitchen." In this way, the writer codes the message that Juanita is black, without saying so explicitly.

16.   Emphasis added in all the quotations.

17.   See Weinberg chapter in this volume for a summary of much of this research.

18.   These data show a steady decline in the incidence of annual poverty through the 1960s, a leveling off during most of the 1970s, and a moderate increase in the 1980s. However, these trends have not been uniform over the entire population, and some groups, such as the aged, have fared better than others.

19.   In 1973, black families made up 45.8 percent of all AFDC households (U.S. Department of Health and Human Services 1982:1). Data for earlier years are found in U.S. Department of Health, Education and Welfare (1977).

20.   As a percent of AFDC families, the figures for Hispanics are as follows: 13.4 percent in 1973, 12.2 percent in 1977, and 13.6 percent in 1979. (U.S. Department of Health and Human Services 1982).

21.   Ronald Reagan is fond of quoting Franklin D. Roosevelt on the deleterious effects of welfare relief on the moral condition of those who receive it.

22.   The data reported in the text are from U.S. Department of Health and Human Services (1982). Similar figures on length of AFDC spells of persons beginning a spell are summarized in U.S. Executive Office of the President (1986).

23.   The figure for New Mexico is higher, standing at 2.8 children in 1986. It reflects overall higher rates of fertility in the state's general population compared to the nation as a whole.

24.   As noted by Lane (1981), a major obstacle to research on this question is that in the real world it is simply not possible to approximate the conditions of a controlled experiment, for example, to determine the fertility choices women would make if AFDC benefits did not exist.

25.   Clearly, decisions about such fundamental matters as marriage and childbearing extend beyond the scope of rational economic calculation. For example, consider the surprising results of studies into the impact of AFDC on family disintegration. A long accepted tenet of the welfare debate is that AFDC causes the break up of families, because in about half of the states AFDC benefits are not available for two parent families. It follows that extending benefits to two parent families would remove the economic incentives that cause families to break up in order to gain program eligibility, and thus more families would remain intact. But actual results of studies of the effect of welfare on marital dissolution have been mixed. On one hand, some studies have found that providing benefits to two-parent families actually increased dissolution rates. On the other, recent analysis of the data from Seattle-Denver Income Maintenance Experiment (SIME/DIME) showed no

significant effect of benefits on rates of family disintegration (cited in U.S. Government Accounting Office 1987:27).

26. Cf. Murray's (1984) discussion of work incentives and welfare, and Greenstein's (1985) critique of Murray.

27. See, for example, U.S. Government Accounting Office (1987), which states: "A study of the New York City welfare system showed that in the early 1970s, the combined benefits from AFDC, Medicaid, Food Stamps, and free school lunches were more than could be earned from any of the city's low-skilled jobs" (25). However, AFDC benefits in New York are among the highest in the nation, and elsewhere in the same report it is noted that, "Because all goals of adequacy are subject to federal and state budgetary constraints, benefits actually provided may be significantly less than the level of adequacy" (15).

28. Popular accounts of "welfare queens" are filled with sensational elements, such as the invention of false identities and ingenious disguises, collection of multiple benefits for fictitious children, purchase of a big house in a ritzy neighborhood and a fleet of expensive automobiles, and so on. Although this kind of outrageous fraud is clearly uncommon—and far beyond what Carmen Santana or Louise Lowman would ever conceive of much less attempt—the theme is significant because it reflects and reinforces a widely shared sentiment that equates welfare with immorality and plays upon the stereotype of the welfare recipient as irresponsible and disreputable.

29. Historically, concern over welfare fraud has gone through several cycles. In 1961 the Ad Hoc Committee on Public Welfare, appointed as part of the Kennedy Administration's welfare reform program, cited eliminating abuse as one of its two main objectives (cited in Axinn and Levin 1982, 250–51). Allegations of fraud and abuse were central to the "war on welfare" in Newburgh, New York (Ritz 1965) and later in California under then-governor Ronald Reagan. In recent years the issue of welfare fraud has subsided somewhat in the public debate. Even recent radical attacks on the welfare system (e.g., Murray 1984) have tended to downplay the fraud question.

30. Data on the disposition of suspected AFDC fraud cases are summarized in Gardiner and Lyman (1983, 29).

31. The difficulty in estimating the actual extent of welfare fraud is part of a general problem that has long vexed criminologists. By its very nature criminal activity tends to be concealed, and thus it is difficult to know how much is actually occurring. This is especially the case in crimes where individuals are not directly victimized and where victimization surveys cannot fill in the gaps in official criminal statistics. Of course, the even larger question of the "real" extent of all forms of deviant behavior in society is unknown and probably unknowable. Nonetheless, the recent studies on

welfare fraud discussed in the text provide a much better basis for estimating the incidence of illegal behavior that anything that was available during the heyday of political campaigns to wipe out welfare fraud in the 1960s and 1970s.

32. Quality control systems were established first in the food stamp program (1971), and subsequently in AFDC (1973), Supplemental Security Income (1974), and Medicaid (1975).

33. The actual figures reported are $322.36 in Seattle, and $354.45 in Denver.

34. As in other areas of welfare, the history of concern about the geographic mobility of the poor dates back to the first Poor Laws in England, first passed during the reign of Henry VIII and later consolidated by Elizabeth I in 1601. Worry about "vagrants" and "sturdy beggars," many of whom had been displaced from rural areas by the enclosure of common land, contributed to the punitive and restrictive character of the early poor laws.

35. Even after the Supreme Court's decision, several states attempted to reinstitute residency requirements (see Waxman 1983, 79). The prospect of descending hoards of would-be welfare recipients—commonly depicted as black—moving from the rural south to cities of the Northeast and Midwest inspired much controversy and a few outbreaks of anti-welfare hostility during the 1960s. This theme was crucial to Newburgh, New York's "war on welfare" in the early 1960s (Ritz 1965).

36. A summary on the Rand study appears in Kihss (1974).

37. Other studies on the impact of immigrants include Community Research Associates (1980a, 1980b) and Villalpando (1977).

BIBLIOGRAPHY

Albuquerque Journal. 1980. "Suspect May Dethrone Current 'Welfare Queen.'" December 20.

———. 1987. "Controversial Mother of 14 Won't Stop." April 18.

Axinn, June, and Herman Levin. 1982. *Social Welfare: A History of the American Response to Need.* New York: Longman.

Bane, Mary Jo, and David T. Ellwood. 1983. "The Dynamics of Dependence: The Routes to Self-Sufficiency." Report prepared for the U.S. Department of Health and Human Services, Office of the Assistant Secretary for Planning and Evaluation. Cambridge: Urban Systems Research and Engineering, Inc.

Berger, Peter L., and Thomas Luckmann. 1966. *The Social Construction of Reality.* Garden City: Doubleday.

Community Research Associates. 1980a. *Undocumented Immigrants: Their Impact on the County of San Diego.* Report prepared for the county of San Diego. San Diego: Community Research Associates.

————. 1980b. *Undocumented Immigrants: Their Impact on the County of Los Angeles.* Report prepared for the county of Los Angeles. San Diego: Community Research Associates.

Congressional Record—House. 1981.:20406–20411.

Coughlin, Richard M. 1987. "Myth and Reality in Welfare Reform." *Quantum* 4 (Fall):4–7.

————. 1980. *Ideology, Public Opinion and Welfare Policy.* Berkeley: Institute of International Studies, University of California.

Duncan, Greg J. 1984. *Years of Poverty, Years of Plenty.* Ann Arbor: Institute for Social Research, University of Michigan.

The Economist. 1987. "The Shadow Economy: Gross Deceptive Product." (September 19):25–28.

Ellwood, David T., and Mary Jo Bane. 1985. "The Impact of AFDC on Family Structure and Living Arrangements." *Research in Labor Economics* 7:137–207.

Gans, Herbert J. 1979. *Deciding What's News.* New York: Pantheon Books.

Gardiner, John A., and Theodore R. Lyman. 1983. *Responses to Fraud and Abuse in AFDC and Medicaid Programs.* Washington, D.C.: U.S. Department of Justice.

Greenstein, Robert. 1985. "Losing Faith in *Losing Ground.*" *The New Republic.* (March 25):12–17.

Holden, Constance. 1987. "Is the Time Ripe for Welfare Reform?" *Science* (October 30):607–09.

Kihss, Peter. 1974. "Study Disputes Welfare 'Myth.'" The *New York Times* (October 6).

Lane, Jonathan P. 1981. "The Findings of the Panel Study of Income Dynamics about the AFDC Program." Mimeographed. Washington, D.C.: Assistant Secretary for Planning and Evaluation, U.S. Department of Health and Human Services.

Lewis, Oscar. 1966. *La Vida.* New York: Random House.

Lule, Jack. 1987. "Myth, Methods and International News." Paper presented to the International Communication Division at the National Convention of the Association for Education in Journalism and Mass Communication, August. San Antonio, Texas.

McCarthy, Kevin F., and R. Burciaga Valdez. 1985. *Current and Future Effects of Mexican Immigration in California.* Santa Monica: Rand.

Murray, Charles. 1984. *Losing Ground.* New York: Basic.

Morgan, James N., Katherine Dickinson, Jonathan Dickinson, Jacob Benus, and Greg Duncan. 1974. *Five Thousand American Families—Patterns of Economic Progress.* Ann Arbor: Survey Research Center, University of Michigan.

Ritz, Joseph. 1965. *The Despised Poor.* Boston: Beacon Press.

Robinson, W. S. 1950. "Ecological Correlations and the Behavior of Individuals." *American Sociological Review* 15:351–57.

Salamon, Julie. 1982. "Welfare Mother Begets 3 Welfare Daughters, Perpetuating Life Style," *The Wall Street Journal* (August 10):1, 24.

Schwarz, John E. 1983. *America's Hidden Success.* New York: Norton.

Sheehan, Susan. 1977. *A Welfare Mother.* New York: New American Library.

Treadwell, David, and Gaylord Shaw. 1981. "Welfare In America—Underclass: How One Family Copes." *Los Angeles Times* (July 5).

The Undocumented Workers Policy Research Project. 1984. *The Use of Public Services by Undocumented Aliens in Texas: A Study of State Costs and Revenues.* Lyndon B. Johnson School of Public Affairs, Policy Research Report No. 60. Austin: The University of Texas.

U.S. Department of Health, Education and Welfare (DHEW), Social and Rehabilitation Service. 1971. *Welfare Myths vs. Facts.* Washington, D.C.: U.S. Government Printing Office.

———. 1977. *AFDC Recipient Characteristic Survey.* Washington, D.C.: U.S. Government Printing Office.

U.S. Executive Office of the President. 1986. *Up From Dependency: A New National Public Assistance Strategy.* Washington, D.C.: Office of Policy Development.

U.S. Department of Health and Human Services (DHHS). 1982. *Aid to Families With Dependent Children, Demographic and Program Statistics, 1979 Recipient Characteristic Study.* Washington, D.C.: U.S. Government Printing Office.

U.S. General Accounting Office. 1987. "Welfare: Issues to Consider in Assessing Proposals to Reform." Draft copy. (February).

Villalpando, M. V. 1977. *A Study of the Impact of Illegal Aliens on the County of San Diego on Specific Socioeconomic Areas.* San Diego: San Diego County Human Resources Agency.

Waxman, Chaim I. 1983. *The Stigma of Poverty.* New York: Pergamon Press.

5

The Economic Effects of Welfare

Daniel H. Weinberg[1]

Twenty years after the War on Poverty was launched, economic dependency remains widespread. The purpose of this chapter is to present a comprehensive review of research on welfare dependency and the impact of welfare programs on the able-bodied nonelderly. Some argue (e.g., Murray 1984) that the poor have become mired in dependency with behavior and attitudes conditioned by the incentives of the social welfare system, which "rewards" those who choose not to work and do not live in two-parent families. In spite of vast increases in social welfare spending and in the numbers receiving means-tested benefits since the mid-1960s, poverty rates have increased since the mid-1970s among families with children and other nonelderly groups. Other social indicators, particularly among blacks, have worsened as well—black youth joblessness and illegitimate births to teenagers increased sharply in the 1970s.

Other analysts challenge the idea that welfare programs create or sustain poverty, partly on grounds that poverty is largely short term. Several researchers, notably Duncan (1984), report that durations of poverty are typically short and that only a small minority are poor for eight or more years in any ten-year period. If poverty and welfare use are predominately transitory, then it is incorrect to argue that most of the poor are caught in a cycle of poverty.

Recent work emphasizes that both views may contain elements of truth. While Duncan is accurate in concluding that most poverty and welfare dependency is short term, it is also true that long-term poverty and dependency is a serious problem for many others. Bane and Ellwood (1983) report that half of all those receiving Aid to Families with Dependent Children (AFDC) benefits will receive those benefits for more than eight years. The situation appears even worse when repeated spells of AFDC receipt are considered. Ellwood (1986a) estimates that 30 percent of those receiving AFDC for the first time will be on the program for at least ten of the next twenty-five years and that 65 percent of AFDC recipients will have eight or more years on AFDC. As Ellwood (1986a) and Murray (1986a) both note, the group that is likely to have the longest welfare durations is young, never-married mothers, a group that has been the focus of much of recent public concern.

The realization that poverty and welfare dependency, especially among single-parent families, often lasts over a decade for certain groups is of serious concern. Children born to unmarried teenage mothers are likely to spend most of their formative years on welfare. Even if public policies have only a modest impact on events associated with or actually leading to welfare dependency, because the majority of AFDC spending is associated with this relatively small group of long-term recipients, new policies might have substantial consequences for reducing the size of the poverty population and spending on it.

Dependency reflects a complex set of individual, social, and economic factors that influence residence, family structure, participation in public assistance programs, and work decisions simultaneously and interactively. Isolating the effect of one factor (say welfare benefits) on one aspect of behavior (say teenage pregnancy) may lead to an inadequate understanding of what is taking place. Three insights are key. First, a full understanding of behavior requires that we consider the full set of choices. Second, both perceived choices and actual opportunities guide behavior. Third, attitudes and values are a critical determinant of behavior and will cause different people facing identical choices to behave differently.

DYNAMICS OF DEPENDENCY

To understand the effects of welfare, one must first understand the dynamics of dependency. Typical government reports provide only a cross-section snapshot of welfare use. They do not provide information on turnover (entry and exit), nor do they examine the duration of welfare receipt. To understand the causes of dependency, we must distinguish between short- and long-term welfare recipients: who they are and why they enter and leave the programs.

The Time Pattern of AFDC Receipt.[2] The most systematic research on the patterns of dependency has relied on analyses of longitudinal data (data that follow a sample of persons over a period of time) and case record data for AFDC recipients.[3] Despite technical imperfections in these data sets (e.g., small sample sizes, excluded years of data, annual measurements only, limited program coverage), the data have allowed researchers to identify with a reasonable degree of confidence many of the demographic factors closely associated with differing spells of AFDC receipt. Researchers have approached these data in a number of different ways. Several studies (e.g., Harrison 1977, Rein and Rainwater, 1978, Coe 1981, Duncan 1984) were based on point-in-time observations of welfare duration. They were essentially a "snapshot" of the AFDC caseload at one moment. Subsequently, a number of researchers, most prominently Plotnick (1983), Bane and Ellwood (1983), O'Neill et al. (1984), and Ellwood (1986a), have analyzed the AFDC duration using "spells," or continuous periods, of AFDC use. Ellwood (1986a) has also examined total time on welfare.

Until recently there were some puzzling contradictions. Early research, such as Boskin and Nold (1975) and Rydell et al. (1974), summarized by Lyon (1977) and Hutchens (1982), gave the impression of a highly dynamic welfare population. Average stays were judged to be short, and the fraction of people who spent a considerable period on AFDC was found to be small. Nevertheless, it was commonly believed that lengthy welfare dependence was chronic and pervasive.

In recent years, the contradiction appears to have been clarified. Bane and Ellwood (1983) and Plotnick (1983) point out that the methods used in the earlier analyses can give a misleading impression of welfare dynamics for two reasons. First, the earlier analyses failed to distinguish between those persons entering the AFDC rolls at a given point in time (a cohort) and the make-up of the rolls at a point in time. Looking only at those beginning their time on welfare indicates that caseload turnover is high, because it does not capture the build-up over time of long duration recipients. Some in the entering cohort will remain on AFDC for a short period, while others will stay much longer. Long spells account for a disproportionate part of the caseload. Second, analysts often failed to consider that the relative impact of long spells would be underrepresented in any snapshot of the data. In any data set, there will inevitably be some whose welfare episodes started or ended in the period outside the sampled period. The observed durations for these truncated spells will be far shorter than the actual durations.

Most recent literature recognizes these problems. Three recent studies are in general agreement about the duration of AFDC spells— Bane and Ellwood (1983), who analyzed the PSID; O'Neill et al. (1984), who analyzed the NLS, the PSID, and AFDC case records; and Ellwood (1986a), who reanalyzed the PSID. As shown in Table 5.1,

- A majority of AFDC spells are short-term, lasting two years or less, while fewer than one-sixth can be thought of as long-term, lasting eight or more continuous years.

Table 5.1   Distribution of Length of AFDC Spells and Total Time on Welfare

Duration	Persons beginning a spell				Persons on AFDC at a point in time	Persons beginning first AFDC spell	Persons on AFDC at a point in time
	(1)	(2)	(3)	(4)	(5)	(6)	(7)
1–2 years	48%	61%	59%	69%	15%	30%	7%
3–7 years	35	27	25	24	36	40	28
8 or more years	17	12	16	7	49	30	65
Data Source:	PSID	NLS	AFDC Case Records (1965 Cohort)	(1975 Cohort)	PSID	PSID	PSID

Length of Individual Spell (columns 1–4); *Total Time on Welfare (includes multiple spells)* (columns 5–7)

Sources: PSID: Ellwood (1986a)
NLS, AFDC Case Records: O'Neill et al. (1984)
(Table adapted from Duncan and Hoffman, 1986.)
Notes: PSID = Panel Study of Income Dynamics
NLS = National Longitudinal Survey

- At any moment, one-half of all AFDC recipients are in the midst of long-term spells.

The short-term nature of most welfare spells is reflected in the figures in the first four columns of Table 5.1. They are based on individuals who *began* AFDC spells *at any time* between the mid-1960s and the late 1970s. They show that between one-half and two-thirds of AFDC spells lasted one or two years, and fewer than one-sixth of the spells lasted eight or more years.[4]

Viewed in this way, it seems clear that long-term welfare receipt is relatively uncommon; it certainly does not accurately reflect the welfare experience of the majority of recipients. In contrast, the distribution of completed AFDC spell lengths for recipients observed at a given point in time is quite different. The estimates of completed spell lengths in the fifth column show that when using this measure, short spells characterize only one-sixth of current recipients, while one-half are in the midst of long spells, lasting eight or more years.

The large difference between the two ways of examining time on welfare may seem paradoxical but occurs because longer-term recipients have a higher probability of being on welfare at a given time than those who have shorter welfare spells. An example from Bane and Ellwood (1983) using hospitalization spells illustrates the point. Consider a thirteen-bed hospital in which twelve beds are occupied for an entire year by twelve chronically ill patients, while the other bed is used by 52 patients, each of whom stays exactly one week. Viewed over the course of a year, out of the sixty-four patients using hospital services, about 80 percent (52/64) spent only one week in the hospital. However, on any given day, about 85 percent of patients (12/13) were in the midst of long spells of hospitalization.

One of the most important lessons from the longitudinal evidence is that while the welfare population at any point is composed predominantly of long-term users, the typical recipient is a short-term user. If one assumes that long- and short-term recipients have the same average benefit (actually an underestimate of the benefit of the long-term recipient relative to the short-term one), it is clear that the majority of AFDC program resources go to support the long-term recipients. However, the analyses which focus on completed spells understate the total time on welfare. For example, an individual could spend a high proportion of her adulthood receiving welfare and yet have short welfare spells via high turnover.

The research of Bane and Ellwood (1983) and Ellwood (1986a)

confirms that multiple spells of AFDC receipt are indeed fairly common. Ellwood (1986a) constructs an estimate of the *total* expected time on AFDC for individuals first beginning an AFDC spell and for individuals on AFDC at any given point. His estimates, shown in the final two columns of Table 5.1, indicate that about 30 percent of new AFDC recipients can expect to experience only one or two years of total receipt, while a similar proportion will have eight or more total years of receipt.

One difficulty in this type of analysis is determining the impact of changes in welfare policy on welfare duration. For example, existing data are not extensive enough to indicate the impact of the changes in AFDC law incorporated in the Omnibus Budget Reconciliation Act (OBRA) of 1981 on welfare duration. This issue can only be resolved with many more years of observations.

Entry and Exit from AFDC.[5] Besides examining spell length, it is also useful to examine the determinants of entry to and exit from the program. Hutchens (1981) finds asymmetries in the determinants of AFDC entry and exit for female-headed households that do not change marital status. He identifies the level of AFDC benefits as the dominant determinant of entry and exit and that changes in wage rates and nonwage income are more important in explaining entry than exit.

However, Bane and Ellwood report that *most AFDC turnover is a result of major changes in family structure* (see Table 5.2), mitigating the relevance of Hutchens' work. Specifically, family structure changes account for three-quarters of all entries onto AFDC: 45 percent are due to divorce or separation and 30 percent are due to birth of a child to an unmarried childless woman. Only 12 percent of entries occur because a single female head's earnings decline. Ellwood (1986a) finds that 35 percent of all women exit from AFDC due to marriage, 11 percent due to loss of eligibility because the child leaves home or becomes too old to retain eligibility and 21 percent due to an increase in the female head's earnings. However, these results are based on a classification hierarchy that counts simultaneous earnings and family structure changes as the latter. Consequently, this approach will understate the importance of earnings changes in AFDC turnover.

Exits from AFDC because of marriage occur uniformly throughout a spell of welfare receipt, but exits because of earnings typically occur early on (O'Neill et al. 1984), with two-thirds of all earnings exits occurring within the first three years of receipt (Bane and Ellwood). Nonetheless, some 40 percent of those who exit due to earnings continue to earn incomes less than the poverty level in the year after their exit, although by the second year those who left by marriage are somewhat more likely to be poor than those who left via an earnings increase (Bane and Ellwood). Yet, earnings are an important route off of AFDC for some. Ellwood (1986b) reports that 42 percent of former recipients (including both those who earn and those who marry their way off) earn more than six thousand dollars in their first year off the program. For former recipients who both marry and increase their earnings, it is difficult to know just how crucial the earnings are to leaving AFDC. Of those who don't marry but move off AFDC within a year or two of first receiving benefits with substantial earnings in that first year off, many have worked in the year prior to welfare receipt and are better educated (high school or more). Further, the level of AFDC benefits influences whether earnings

Table 5.2   Events Associated With the Beginnings and Endings of AFDC Spells

Beginnings		Endings	
Divorce/Separation	45%	Marriage	35%
Childless, unmarried woman becomes a female head with children	30	Children leave parental home	11
Earnings of female head fell	12	Earnings of female head increased	21
Earnings of others in family fell	3	Earnings of others in family increased	5
Other income fell	1	Transfer income increased	14
Other (including unidentified)	9	Other (including unidentified)	14
All	100%	All	100%

Sources: "Beginnings": Bane and Ellwood (1983).
"Endings": Ellwood (1986a).
(Table adapted from Duncan and Hoffman, 1986.)

cause an exit from welfare. In low benefit states, work is more likely to result in an exit, precisely because the benefit is low.

Both Bane and Ellwood and O'Neill et al. find that blacks were no less likely than whites to earn their way off AFDC, but were considerably less likely to marry their way off.[6] In fact, according to O'Neill et al., "the entire effect of race on the probability of exit seems to be generated by a difference in the probability of exit via marriage across races."

Do women who ultimately escape dependency through earnings do so by a sudden leap to a job, or is the process gradual, involving increasing work hours and improving wage rates? Ellwood found that for those that leave AFDC through work, the process is gradual. Women who eventually leave with earnings of six thousand dollars or more worked a great deal even two years prior to the time that they left AFDC completely. This suggests the gradual accumulation of job skills. In their next-to-last year of AFDC receipt, some two-thirds of women who later left AFDC with high earnings worked, and most of them worked more than five hundred hours. By contrast, of those who left via other routes, only one-third worked at all in the next-to-last year and only one-fifth worked more than five hundred hours. It is important to emphasize that these findings are based on data collected before the 1981 changes in the AFDC law which reduced the proportion of recipients with earnings; the pattern may now be somewhat different.

CORRELATES OF LONG-TERM DEPENDENCY

Studies of the correlates of long-term dependency reveal that the probability of receipt, AFDC spell length, and recidivism vary markedly according to a number of recipient characteristics.[7] Bane and Ellwood, O'Neill et al., and Ellwood (1986a) have conducted the most extensive multivariate analyses of these factors to determine marginal effects.[8]

- *Age of Female Head.* The age of the female head of household significantly affects how long AFDC is received, with younger heads more likely to remain on the program longer.
- *Teenage Motherhood.* While women starting AFDC spells are more likely to have had a child as a teenager than the general population, early childbearing does not appear to be associated

with longer AFDC *spells*. However, teen mothers are more likely to spend longer *total* time on AFDC.

- *Number of Children.* Ellwood finds that more children increased both AFDC spell length and recidivism. O'Neill et al. find that only the number of children under age six mattered, and also that women who give birth while on AFDC tend to remain on the rolls longer.

- *Age of Children.* As noted, O'Neill et al. report that women with children under age six are likely to have longer AFDC spells. Bane and Ellwood find no such correlation, although Ellwood has found that of women who leave the rolls, those whose youngest child was over age six were less likely to return to AFDC.

- *Race.* Bane and Ellwood find that non-whites have longer AFDC spells, but Ellwood, in reanalyzing the PSID data, found no significant correlation. However, he reports that blacks are significantly more likely to return to AFDC after an earlier spell. O'Neill et al. find a significant association between race and duration, noting that some 68 percent of blacks, but only 42 percent of whites, remained on AFDC for longer than one year, while 31 percent of blacks and 13 percent of whites remained on for five or more years.

- *Schooling.* Education is highly correlated with spell length, with high school dropouts much more likely to experience long AFDC spells than those who completed high school.

- *Work Experience.* Work experience is strongly associated with AFDC spell length, with little or no prior work experience leading to longer stays.

- *Wage Rate.* The lower the female head's wage rate prior to her receiving welfare, the longer her expected stay.

- *Income.* Almost half of recipients had incomes below the poverty line in the year prior to welfare receipt.

- *Health.* Being disabled leads to longer AFDC stays.

- *Social-Psychological Factors.* Researchers do not find that social-psychological factors (e.g., motivation, efficacy) affect spell length.

- *AFDC Experience.* The elapsed duration of an AFDC spell is not a good predictor of future time on the rolls because of the prevalence of recidivism. Nor does AFDC participation itself affect the probability of leaving the program (Blank 1986).

- *AFDC Benefit Levels.* Higher AFDC benefit levels are associated with longer stays.
- *State Administrative Practices.* In analyzing case records, O'Neill et al. find some evidence that state administrative practices, as measured by error rates, can affect spell length, with tighter administration reducing duration.
- *State Economic Conditions.* State economic conditions, as measured by the state manufacturing wage and unemployment rate, appear generally to affect duration on AFDC, with higher wages and lower unemployment associated with shorter stays.

Taking all these factors into consideration, including the correlation among characteristics, *the group that is most likely to spend a long time on AFDC is young, black, never-married women with young children who had their first child as a teenager and dropped out of school and have little or no prior work experience.* The group most likely to spend a short time on AFDC is older, divorced or separated, whites with older children, a high school education, and some prior work experience.

These findings were confirmed by Murray's (1986a) detailed examination of PSID cases. Murray emphasizes, in particular, the much longer AFDC dependency experiences of younger, never-married female heads of household who have not completed high school.

> Age is a primary discriminator [of subsequent AFDC experience]. Prior marital status is probably worth much more attention than the research literature has given it. Educational attainment is important. . . . Most [new, unmarried, uneducated AFDC mothers under 39] remain on AFDC for long periods of time. Of the unmarried women who had less than a high school degree, 64 percent were on AFDC for [at least] ten consecutive years. . . . The typical person stayed on AFDC for several years, didn't remarry successfully, didn't get into the labor market while on AFDC, and remained poor at the end of the [ten-year] followup [period] except for the grace of welfare income. (Murray 1986a, 61–63)

WELFARE AND WORK

The major alternatives to welfare dependency are work, remaining dependent on parental support, and marriage. This section examines how the structure of a welfare program affects the choices made by recipients between dependency and work.

AFDC Work Programs. Welfare programs have used two approaches to encourage recipients to work: financial incentives and work requirements. The Work Incentive (WIN) program, established in 1967, requires able-bodied recipients (with children six years of age or older) to register for the program and participate in required activities or face the loss of the caretaker's benefits. (In the AFDC-Unemployed Parents program, the entire family loses eligibility.) Under the 1981 OBRA, allowable work activities were expanded to include WIN demonstration programs, Community Work Experience Programs (CWEP), and work supplementation (e.g., grant diversion, using the benefit payment to subsidize private sector jobs). Job Search, as a specific work-oriented activity that could be required of recipients, was added as an option in 1982. These work programs are aimed at enhancing the future employability of AFDC recipients either by leading directly to a job or by providing potentially valuable work experience.

Mead (1986) argues that in order to avoid creating long-term dependency on welfare, the government must insist on reciprocity—a *quid-pro-quo* for providing a welfare benefit. A work, training, or job search requirement, in his view, should not be viewed as a sanction, but as a necessary part of the social contract implicit in providing transfer payments to those in need. Child care (at home) alone is not a sufficient social benefit or a sufficient obligation to justify the transfer payment. Acceptance of the concept of reciprocity, he argues, is essential if work or efforts to find work are to be integral parts of a welfare program.

Evaluations of the pre-1982 WIN program have generally been negative. The program has been found to be inefficient in providing employment, though the failure of these evaluations to use control groups (a methodological problem discussed below) raises questions as to their reliability. Due to severe funding constraints WIN focused resources on recipients who were more "job-ready" in an attempt to maximize placement rates. This made the program look better, but the net impact was actually larger for those participants who were *less* job-ready (Schiller 1976, Gordon 1978), as most of those "placed" actually found their own jobs. Further, Rein (1982) states, "legislative priorities, federal guidelines, state limitations, and caseworker discretion had severely limited compulsory participation in WIN for AFDC mothers". (6)

Since 1982 the Manpower Demonstration Research Corporation

(MDRC) has conducted a large-scale, multi-year study with random assignment to experimental and control to measure the effectiveness of innovative state AFDC work programs, with emphasis on programs permitted on a demonstration basis by the 1981 legislation.[9] Among mandatory WIN demonstration programs, job search is a more prominent activity than work experience. West Virginia operates an open-ended mandatory work program targeted primarily to the mostly male AFDC-Unemployed Parent population rather than the mainly female AFDC-Basic caseload. Other states (e.g., Arkansas, California, and Illinois) have established a two-stage program: job search, followed by a limited work obligation for those who have not found unsubsidized jobs in the first component. Virginia also requires job search of everyone, with CWEP an option in an array of succeeding mandatory services. Maryland's program provides a mix of education and training services (including job search and unpaid work experience) that are matched to enrollee's needs or preferences in much the same way as are the offerings of the Massachusetts' Employment and Training (E.T.) Choices program. Some states (including New Jersey and Maine) have avoided mandatory approaches altogether and have implemented voluntary on-the-job training programs with private employers, using grant diversion as a funding source. Findings from six of the projects—in San Diego, California; Arkansas; Virginia; West Virginia; Chicago, Illinois; and Baltimore, Maryland—have been reported (see Table 5.3).

In four of the six sites (San Diego, Arkansas, Baltimore, and Virginia), results indicate that the work programs tested produced significant employment gains for AFDC women of between 3.3 and 5.6 percentage points. In three of these sites, earnings increases ranged from $676 to $1043; in the fourth, Virginia, earnings increased only $81. There were no significant increases in employment or earnings in Chicago or West Virginia. Only Arkansas showed a significant decline in the fraction ever receiving AFDC while in four of the six (San Diego, Arkansas, Chicago, and Virginia), average AFDC payments declined for the experimentals relative to the controls.

In addition to measuring the net impact of the work programs, the evaluations estimated their net benefit or cost, for participants in the program, taxpayers, government, and society as a whole. Increased earnings for participants in San Diego, Baltimore, and Virginia outweighed the loss of AFDC benefits and increase in taxes. This was not true in Arkansas, where the reduction in benefits was not matched by increases in earnings, or in Chicago and West Virginia, where there were no gains in earnings. Nevertheless, the majority of participants in all sites were positive about their work assignments—they felt the work requirements were fair and believed they were making a useful contribution. All programs are estimated to be of net benefit from the taxpayers' perspective (which counts the value of output produced) and the San Diego, Virginia, Chicago, and Arkansas programs are estimated to have saved the government money. All six programs show net benefits to society as a whole.

In sum, these results suggest that

- most work programs have only a modest effect on earnings, employment, and AFDC receipt, and
- for most work programs, savings can offset costs in a relatively short period of time.

Work Incentives. The alternative to imposing work requirements in the AFDC program is the approach of attempting to induce people to work, rather than requiring them to. This was tried from 1967 to 1981 in the form of an earnings disregard. Recipients were allowed to keep part (the first thirty dollars plus one-third) of all earnings (plus an allowance for work expenses). By creating this financial incentive to work it was believed that more recipients would work, gain the confidence and experience necessary for self-support, and eventually become independent.

One potential problem with this approach is that more people remain eligible for some benefit. To illustrate, with a 100 percent tax rate and an AFDC benefit of $300 per month for those with no income, only those with less than $300 per month of income would remain eligible. With "30-and-a-third" and work expenses of $60, all those with earnings under $570 per month would remain eligible for a benefit. Adding the 30-and-a-third provision creates at least a theoretical incentive for all those with earnings between $360 and $570 (and possibly higher incomes) to reduce their work hours and become eligible for a benefit. Of course, not all jobs offer flexible hours.

Strong evidence that generous transfer payments can reduce work effort came from the income maintenance experiments operated between 1968 and 1978 in various parts of the country, with the Seattle and Denver Income Maintenance Experiments (SIME/DIME) being the largest. SIME/DIME involved about five thousand families, equally divided between experimentals and controls. The cash

Table 5.3   Summary of Impacts of AFDC Work Programs

Outcome	Experimental-Control Difference	Percentage Decrease/ Increase
SAN DIEGO—Applicants. Job search workshop followed by work experience.		
Ever employed during 15 months	+ 5.6%***	+ 10%
Ever received AFDC payments during 18 months	− 0.4%	0%
Avg. total earnings during 15 months	+$ 700 ***	+ 23%
Avg. total AFDC payments received during 18 months	−$ 288 **	− 8%
ARKANSAS—Applicants and Recipients. Job search workshop followed by individual job search and work experience.		
Ever employed during 33 months	+ 4.5%*	+ 12%
Ever received AFDC payments during 36 months	− 3.7%*	− 5%
Avg. total earnings during 33 months	+$ 676 **	+ 27%
Avg. total AFDC payments received during 36 months	−$ 430 ***	− 14%
CHICAGO—Applicants and Recipients. Individual job search followed by activities including work experience.		
Ever employed during 15 months	+ 1.0%	+ 3%
Ever received AFDC payments during 18 months	− 0.1%	0%
Avg. total earnings during 15 months	+$ 57	+ 3%
Avg. total AFDC payments received during 18 months	−$ 70 *	− 2%
BALTIMORE—Applicants and Recipients. Multicomponent, including job search, education, training, and work experience.		
Ever employed during 33 months	+ 4.8%***	+ 7%
Ever received AFDC payments during 36 months	− 0.1%	0%
Avg. total earnings during 33 months	+$1043 ***	+ 16%
Avg. total AFDC payments received during 36 months	−$ 63	− 1%

Continued next page

Table 5.3   *Continued*

VIRGINIA—Applicants and Recipients. Job
search followed by work experience, education,
or training.

Ever employed during 9 months	+ 3.3%*	+ 12%
Ever received AFDC payments during 12 months	− 0.1%	0%
Avg. total earnings during 9 months	+$ 81	+ 8%
Avg. total AFDC payments received during 12 months	−$ 84 **	− 4%

WEST VIRGINIA—Applicants and Recipients.
Work experience.

Ever employed during 15 months	− 0.4%	− 2%
Ever received AFDC payments during 21 months	+ 0.8%	+ 1%
Avg. total earnings during 15 months	$ 0	0%
Avg. total AFDC payments received during 21 months	−$ 40	− 1%

Notes: These estimates are regression-adjusted to control for pre-random assignment characteristics of sample members. The definitions of applicants and recipients in Chicago and West Virginia are not strictly comparable to the other sites.
***Experimental effect statistically significant at the 0.01 level.
**Experimental effect statistically significant at the 0.05 level.
*Experimental effect statistically significant at the 0.10 level.
Sources: Gueron (1988).

transfer offered to experimental families in SIME/DIME, as in the previous income maintenance experiments, consisted of a series of negative income tax plans.

A negative income tax is simply a cash transfer program in which there is: a) a maximum benefit (called the guarantee) for which a family is eligible if it has no other income, and b) a rate (called the benefit reduction or tax rate) by which the maximum benefit is reduced as other income rises. The combination of a guarantee and a tax rate defines an income level (called the break-even level) at which the benefit falls to zero. Families whose incomes rise above this break-even level no longer receive benefits, although they retain program eligibility and regain benefit entitlement should their income fall below the break-even level at some later date. In contrast to AFDC, a negative income tax typically lacks categorical eligibility tests (e.g., absence of a spouse) or work requirements. In all the experiments, more than one version of the negative income tax treatment was tested. This was to provide information on how behavioral responses might differ as program structure varied—making the results useful for predicting response to a wide range of cash transfer plans. Control families remained eligible for normal AFDC, Food Stamp, and other benefits.

In SIME/DIME the provision of a guaranteed income more generous than AFDC along with lower than 100 percent marginal tax rates on earnings reduced hours of work by 9 percent among husbands, 20 percent among wives, 25 percent for single female heads of household (Robins and West 1980), 43 percent for males who remained non-heads of household, 33 percent for male non-heads of household who became husbands, and 42 percent for female non-heads who do not marry (West 1980). West finds no response for males and females who become unrelated individuals and females who become wives. (See U.S. Department of Health and Human Services, 1983, for the complete findings.) As with any short-term experiment, these findings may understate the labor supply reduction if a negative income tax is fully implemented because the behavioral response to a permanent program is likely to be larger.

Robins (1985) has summarized the average labor supply response from all four income maintenance experiments (SIME/DIME, Gary, Rural, and New Jersey). He finds the following effects on annual hours of work of a program with a guarantee about the poverty level and a marginal tax rate of about 50 percent: a 5 percent reduction for husbands, 21 percent for wives, 13 percent for single female heads, and 22 percent for youths. He also estimates the effect on the employment rate: a 4 percent reduction for husbands, 22 percent for wives, 16 percent for single female heads, and 20 percent for youths.

The work disincentive effects of the AFDC program have been the focus of substantial research though few studies examine different demographic groups separately. Masters and Garfinkel (1977) find no consistent effect of program parameters on hours of work. Coe and Duncan (1985) point to the relatively rapid movement off welfare and the receipt of income from both work and AFDC as evidence that disincentives, if they exist, cannot be too powerful. Plant (1984) finds that the failure to exit via earnings has been the result of low wages rather than work disincentives.

Other studies reach different conclusions. Levy (1979) concludes that higher guarantees (the maximum benefit payable to a family with no other income) reduce work effort, but that higher program tax rates (the rate at which benefits are reduced as earnings increase) increase work effort overall. (As described above, while higher tax rates may reduce the work effort of recipients, they also reduce the number of people who are eligible to receive benefits. The additional work from those people no longer eligible more than offsets any reduced work effort of those who remain on the rolls.) Barr and Hall (1981) report similar results. Blau and Robins (1986) utilized individual labor market histories to examine movement on and off the welfare rolls and find a significant work disincentive effect of welfare programs, particularly on the transition into employment. They also find that welfare programs lengthened the time spent unemployed or out of the labor force.

Hausman (1981) finds that raising the annual guarantee by one thousand dollars on the margin would reduce the annual work by an average of 120 hours for all female family heads. Moffitt's (1983) estimates imply a similar but smaller response of ninety hours. There is less agreement between Hausman and Moffitt on the effects of a tax rate change. While Hausman also shows that lowering the tax rate would induce a large increase in the work effort of current recipients, his econometric methods are controversial. Indeed, in contrast, Moffitt estimates a statistically and economically insignificant impact. In effect averaging the Hausman and Moffitt results, Danziger et al. (1981), in a summary of the literature on the full labor supply effects of the AFDC program, estimate that the program as a whole led to an average annual reduction of 180 work hours of female household heads in 1977. They guess that food stamps and housing assistance would account for an additional reduction of roughly ninety hours.

Additional information on the impact of the AFDC work incentives is available from studies of the impact of the 1981 OBRA changes. The general findings are that working recipients did not stop working and nonworking recipients did not change their rate of entrance into the labor force, despite arguments that increases in the tax rate (the 1981 OBRA returned the tax rate on earnings to 100 percent by eliminating the "30-and-a-third" earnings disregard after four months) would induce reduced work effort (Research Triangle Institute 1983, Hutchens 1984). Analysts have speculated that the small proportion of AFDC recipients who have jobs also have a strong work ethic and are willing to work even in the face of a 100 percent tax rate on earnings.

Studies of the work disincentive effects of the 1981 OBRA, however, are hampered by other changes in the AFDC program (e.g., changes in the gross income limit) and in the economy (onset of a recession). Moffitt (1986) speculates that OBRA may well have had disincentive effects that were disguised by the state of the economy, though his analysis inappropriately uses the overall unemployment rate rather than the rate specific to female heads of household (which shows a different pattern).

In sum, the research evidence supports the conclusion that high AFDC benefit levels discourage work, but does not support the conclusion that high AFDC tax rates also discourage work by recipients.

One major shortcoming of the studies cited above is their limited focus on AFDC. Fraker and Moffitt (1985) have extended the studies of the labor supply effects of AFDC by modeling jointly the effects of AFDC and Food Stamps on female household heads. They estimate that elimination of the Food Stamp program would increase the mean hours of work of female household heads from 20.9 to 21.4 hours per week (roughly twenty-six hours per year). The AFDC program was estimated to have only a slightly larger effect on female heads (increasing the mean to 21.5 hours per week) despite its larger benefit amounts because offsetting increases in food stamp benefits would occur if the AFDC program were eliminated. The effect of eliminating both programs would be to increase mean hours worked by female household heads by 73 hours per year (from 20.9 to 22.3 hours per week), more than either program taken individually. Small changes in program parameters (such as the benefit reduction rate) were estimated to have only small effects on hours of work.

Employment and Training Programs.[10] Evaluations of work related training programs that have been used to enhance the employability of disadvantaged populations, including welfare recipients, generally find that earnings gains are positive for women and nonexistent for men. The effectiveness of these programs has been reviewed by Bassi and Ashenfelter (1986). Employment and training programs have increased earnings for women chiefly by raising their hours of work rather than their hourly wage. Because women generally worked fewer hours prior to the programs than did men, it is easier for them to improve their earnings.

Evaluations of subsidized training programs typically rely on information about samples of enrolled individuals. For example, the data set used by most evaluators of the Comprehensive Employment and Training Act (CETA), the Continuous Longitudinal Manpower Survey (CLMS), presents information on economic outcomes for a sample of individuals who enrolled in the different subsidized training, employment and job placement programs offered under CETA. As Stromsdorfer et al. (1985) point out, the results must be interpreted with caution. It appears that the most reliable studies are those that use experimental random assignment, rather than evaluation studies that use only comparison groups in a quasi-experimental design.

Supported Work was designed to test a program of intensive employment and support services for individuals facing the most severe problems in finding and maintaining employment—ex-offenders, former drug addicts, long-term AFDC recipients, and unemployed drop-out youth. The evaluation of the National Supported Work Demonstration (Hollister et al. 1984), using random assignment, finds that such an intensive intervention has a significant and sustained effect on both the hours of work and the earnings of the AFDC target group (long-term recipients), but not for the other groups. They estimate that their results are applicable to the 17 percent of the AFDC population whose situations are similar to the demonstration participants.

The Job Corps provides economically disadvantaged youths between sixteen and twenty-one years with basic education, vocational training, and related services in a residential setting. Rees (1986) has summarized the studies of Job Corps:

> The results of studies of the Job Corps are at best mixed. Kiefer (1979) finds negative effects on earnings for whites of both sexes in the Job Corps but positive effects for blacks of both sexes . . . Mallar et al. (1982) find significant positive effects, except for women with children. Gay and Borus (1980) find negative effects for all whites and for black females. (625)

Rees also points out that "similarly mixed results were obtained in studies of the Neighborhood Youth Corps," citing the same works by Kiefer and Gay and Borus (see also Barocci 1982).

Mallar et al.'s (1982) evaluation of Job Corps is probably the most careful. They examined the economic impact of the program by comparing a four-year follow-up of a sample of participants with a comparable group of unenrolled youths. They find that Job Corps had a positive and sizeable impact on its participants and that the program's economic benefits for society exceeded its costs, with the social investment paid back in about three years. (Economic benefits to society as a whole are typically measured in terms of goods and services produced by participants, and reduced crime prevention costs. Specifically, Job Corps members averaged six hundred dollars per year (15 percent) more earnings, worked more than three weeks more on average per year, obtained 27 percent more high school diplomas, had fewer serious health problems, were less dependent on welfare and unemployment insurance, and appeared to be involved in fewer serious crimes.

There have been numerous evaluation surveys of the pre-Comprehensive Employment and Training Act (CETA) manpower programs carried out under the Manpower Development and Training Act (MDTA), including an extensive survey by Perry et al. (1975) and another by Barocci (1982). Many of the evaluations of the pre-CETA period examined a specific local program, while others focused on some of the major program interventions (examples are Ashenfelter 1978 and Kiefer 1979). Nothing was done in an experimental context, however, so few definitive conclusions about the effectiveness of MDTA programs can be drawn.

Most of the national studies of CETA have been conducted by Westat (e.g., Westat 1982), although several other investigators have recently completed work using the CLMS files. In addition, there are recently published surveys of CETA programs and their outcomes by Taggart (1981), Barocci (1982), and the U.S. General Accounting Office (1982).

With the exception of the analysis by Dickinson et al. (1985), these analyses of CETA are roughly consistent in their estimation of the net labor market impact of CETA. They generally agree that *the returns in annual earnings increases to adult women who participated in CETA were positive, large, and nominally statistically significant* (Stromsdorfer et al. 1985).[11] For all women, the estimate of the *net* program impact of CETA ranges from three hundred dollars to twelve hundred dollars per year depending on whether one examines the impact of work experience or the classroom training treatments. The impacts of on-the-job training and public service employment fall within this range. The evidence is consistent with a finding that white women fare better than nonwhite women for any program treatment, but the reasons for this are not known other than possible race discrimination. Finally, if these are the true net impacts and if they do not decay over four or five years, the CETA program appears to be cost-effective.

The general pattern of findings for CETA is consistent with patterns found for its predecessor, the Manpower Development and Training Act—at least for adult women (see Ashenfelter 1978). However, the range of results within and across studies is disturbingly large and no particular point estimate can be said to be the correct one. Given the methodological problems with the CLMS and Current Population Survey (CPS) data sets used for the analyses, the results by themselves cannot serve as a reliable guide to education and training investment decisions for CETA or its successor, JTPA. In particular, if, as is likely to be the case, selection bias exists, the returns to women may be overstated since many of the women who were CETA participants may have entered the labor market in the absence of CETA. (Additionally, they may also have acquired training and educational services on their own.) In fact, an expert panel (Stromsdorfer et al. 1985) recently concluded that "the estimates of net impact on CETA are not reliable and that the true net impacts of CETA are still open to question," (2) though CETA may be "a reasonable social investment for disadvantaged adult women." (12)

Effects of employment and training programs targeted specifically to welfare recipients have recently been reanalyzed by Grossman et al. (1985), exploiting some additional follow-up data that had not previously been analyzed. They reanalyzed five data sets: 1) the Louisville WIN Individual Employment Service sample, 2) the Louisville Group Job Search sample, 3) the Supported Work AFDC sample, 4) the Employment Opportunity Pilot Projects (EOPP) sample, and 5) KETRON's Longitudinal WIN sample. The results of the reanalysis by Grossman et al. reveal no major new findings, though they strengthen the conclusions that can be drawn from the evaluations. The analyses of the longer-term follow-up data for Supported Work and the Louisville WIN projects confirmed that the impacts of both job-search assistance and employment and training interventions will tend to stabilize within the first two years following program enrollment, with the stabilization of welfare impacts lagging slightly behind that of earnings impacts.

The reanalyzed findings indicate that job-search assistance programs, which tend to be short-term and low-cost, can be expected to have small and persistent impacts on employment and earnings, but lead to only very small (and relatively short-lived) reductions in welfare receipt. In contrast, the longer and more costly employment and training services seem to have sizeable, lasting impacts on earnings ($600 to $1000 per year), while the estimated impacts on welfare dependency are more ambiguous, ranging from sizeable reductions for two of the three programs (EOPP and Supported Work) to no long-term effects for the third (Louisville WIN). It is as yet unknown how the elimination of the earnings disregard (after four months) by OBRA might affect these effects.

Grossman et al. (1985) point out that although there is little consistent evidence of targeting strategies that would have improved the earnings gains associated with employment and training interventions, the results suggest a number of potential targeting strategies that may result in larger welfare savings from these more extensive services. These include targeting high school dropouts who do not have recent work experience, those who have young children (especially those with more than one child), and those who have been on welfare for a relatively long time.

Bassi and Ashenfelter (1986) conclude that "employment and training programs have been neither an overwhelming success nor a complete failure in terms of their ability to increase the long-term employment and earnings of disadvantaged workers." Employment and training programs have never covered a very large proportion of the potential target group, but even if they had, there is little evidence they could have significantly reduced pre-transfer poverty.

WELFARE AND FAMILY STRUCTURE

The third choice available to a poor woman with children is marriage. Marriage rates have fallen among the general population in recent years. The annual marriage rate per one thousand women ages fifteen to forty-four has dropped from 148.0 in 1960 to 103.1 in 1981 (a 30 percent decline) while the number of divorces per one thousand married women age fifteen and over has more than doubled in the same period, from 9.2 to 22.6. It is difficult to untangle the effects of welfare from more pervasive social influences and the effects of other policies, such as no-fault divorce, that have occurred during this period.

After remaining more or less constant from 1940 to 1960, the proportion of mother-only families grew 37 percent for both whites and blacks during the 1960s and 40 percent for whites and 35 percent for blacks during the 1970s (McLanahan et al. 1986). In 1983 there were over 7.2 million families headed by a single mother in the United States, or about 23 percent of all families (14 percent of all white families and 48 percent of all black families). Demographers estimate that about 42 percent of white children and about 84 percent of black children born in the late 1970s will live for some time with a single mother before they reach the age of eighteen (Bumpass 1984, Hofferth 1985).

Mother-only families face a higher risk of poverty than other demographic groups. The poverty rate of those in mother-only families actually declined until the late 1970s, only to rise (along with that of other groups) after 1978. The "feminization of poverty" refers to the period between 1967 and 1978 when the proportion of the poor living in female-headed families was increasing. In 1967, 21 percent of the nonelderly poor lived in female-headed families and 41 percent lived in two-parent families. By 1978, 35 percent of the poor lived in female-headed families and only 30 percent in two-parent families. This change was in large part due to the growth in the number of female-headed families and to the relative improvement in economic well being of other demographic groups (Garfinkel and McLanahan 1985). The argument has been made that making welfare more attractive by increasing its benefits makes marriage less attractive an alternative and reduces a woman's likelihood of creating and maintaining a two-parent family.

As noted above, another element of the conceptual choice model of behavior is whether to have children. Teen pregnancy and childbearing out of wedlock often have long-term negative consequences on both the mothers and the children. The illegitimacy rates of adolescents are the highest ever observed in this country. Over half of all births to women under twenty are out-of-wedlock and 39 percent of all out-of-wedlock births were to teenagers in 1982 (U.S. Department of Health and Human Services 1984a). Unwed teenage mothers are more likely to be poor and on welfare: nationally, roughly 50 percent of AFDC mothers had their first child as a teenager. Teen pregnancies complicated by poverty are also risky; because of insufficient prenatal care, the infant death rate is 200 percent greater among infants born to teens, and these infants are three times more likely to suffer birth defects. Further, several indicators of social pathology such as child abuse and drug addiction are also associated with this population. A major reason teenage girls drop out of school is teenage pregnancy. In addition, children of adolescent mothers experience significant social and economic disadvantages. The children of adolescent mothers are more likely to live in low-income families and to be raised by poorly educated parents (Moore 1986).

Some researchers, such as Janowitz (1976), Vining (1983), and Gilder (1983), assert that AFDC increases illegitimacy, especially among teenagers, by providing them with a means of escape from unpleasant home environments that they otherwise could have little hope of leaving. By allowing women to support themselves without a marriage, the existence of welfare is also said to create more opportunity to bear children.

Marriage, Divorce, and Welfare. A common claim is that AFDC actually encourages the formation of one-parent families because eligibility for two-parent families is only available when one of the parents is incapacitated. Otherwise, the second parent must be absent from the home except in those states that operate the AFDC-Unemployed Parent (UP) program that provides benefits to families where the main breadwinner works less than one hundred hours in a month. Through AFDC-UP, eligibility can be established through the unemployment of the principal earner. It is alleged that the lack of the AFDC-UP program in half the states encourages marital break-up and the failure of families to form. There is no evidence, however, that either of these problems is more severe in states without the UP program.

A further allegation is that because AFDC-UP rules require a recent attachment to the labor force, a requirement not satisfied by many young fathers, the mothers of the children cannot form a home with the fathers because that would make the children ineligible for AFDC. However, many states have general assistance programs that provide substantial cash benefits similar to AFDC for such families (e.g., California, Illinois, Massachusetts, Michigan, New York—see Urban Systems Research and Engineering, 1983). Despite this assistance, the major urban areas in all of these states have severe problems with out-of-wedlock births to teenagers.

There is some evidence to support the view that welfare increases family break-up. Honig (1974), based on data from the 1960s, estimates that a 10 percent increase in AFDC benefits would increase the number of beneficiaries due to marital break-up among whites by some 15 percent and among blacks by some 7 percent. Bahr (1979) also finds that those who received AFDC, food stamps, or other public assistance were more likely to have dissolved their marriages than those not receiving welfare (this finding held among low-income whites but not low-income blacks), and that the remarriage rate of divorced families was three times greater among non-AFDC than AFDC recipients.

Others have found contradictory or unconvincing results. Using data similar to Honig's, Minarik and Goldfarb (1976) report that AFDC encouraged stability, though the effects were not significant. Ross and Sawhill (1975) find significant dissolution effects for nonwhites but not for whites. Cutright and Madras (1976) conclude that AFDC benefits do not affect marital disruption but do increase the likelihood that separated or divorced mothers would head their own households instead of living in subfamilies.

The most detailed study of these issues was carried out by Ellwood and Bane (1985), who examine the impact of welfare on family structure and living arrangements using CPS data to compare marital dissolution and living arrangements for: 1) mothers likely and unlikely to be AFDC recipients ("likely vs. unlikely recipients"); 2) women who are or are not mothers in high- and low-benefit states ("eligibles vs. non-eligibles"); and 3) changes over time in family structure and benefit levels. They find that in 1975, had the average state increased its AFDC benefits by one hundred dollars per month (quite a substantial change in most states), there would have been a 10 percent increase in the number of divorced or separated mothers, with a more substantial effect for young women (perhaps as high as 50 percent more for very young mothers), and an estimated 25–30 percent increase in the formation of independent households (reduction in subfamilies), again with a more substantial effect for young mothers. *In other words, higher AFDC benefits are associated with more young mothers (e.g., teenagers) leaving either their husbands or their parents to live independently.* (See Table 5.4 for their detailed estimates.)

131

Table 5.4   Estimated Impact of a $100 Per Month Increase in AFDC Maximum Benefits in 1975

	Research Methodology		
Impact Variable	Likely vs. Unlikely Recipient Comparisons	Eligibles vs. Non-Eligibles Comparisons	Over Time Comparisons
LIVING ARRANGEMENTS OF SINGLE MOTHERS			
Overall	30% decrease in sub-families (living with the woman's parents)	N/A	25–30% decrease in sub-families (living with the woman's parents)
Sub-groups	50–100% increase in % of young single mothers living independently	N/A	N/A
DIVORCE/SEPARATION			
Overall	10% increase in divorced/separated mothers	5–10% increase in divorced/sep-arated mothers	10% increase in divorced/separated mothers
Sub-groups	50% increase in very young di-vorced/separated mothers	N/A	N/A
SINGLE PARENTHOOD (includes childbearing and failure to marry or stay married)			
Overall	5% increase in single mothers	N/A	N/A
Sub-groups	Largest effect for white women over 24; small effect for women under 24	N/A	N/A
FEMALE HEADSHIP (includes childbearing, failure to marry or stay married, and living independently)			
Overall	15% increase in female heads	N/A	No significant impact
Sub-groups	50–100% increase in female heads under 24	N/A	N/A

N/A = not available
Source: Ellwood and Bane (1985), Table 1.

Duncan and Hoffman (1986), among others, point out a number of methodological problems with the Ellwood and Bane (1985) study. They argue that the model was poorly specified and failed to account adequately for nonwelfare choices available to the individual. Further, changes in AFDC as a result of the 1981 OBRA or consideration of the full package of benefits (AFDC plus food stamps plus Medicaid) may change the impacts.

This latter result, that higher AFDC benefits are associated with fewer multigenerational households, is confirmed by Scheirer (1983). She finds that states with higher levels of AFDC benefits have a much lower proportion of families living with the youngest child's grandparents. Her hypothesis was that, given an adequate economic basis, AFDC mothers prefer to establish their own independent households rather than relying on relatives for economic support. She found that living in a three-generation household had no effect on the AFDC mother's current work or schooling. Hutchens et al. (1986) report that for those subfamilies receiving assistance, AFDC is likely to reduce the recipients' current employment but increase somewhat the likelihood of school attendance, especially for young mothers.

Studies using longitudinal data yield mixed results. Hoffman and Holmes (1976) report that families living in states with high AFDC benefits are 6 percent more likely than the average to dissolve their marriages while similar families in low-benefit states are 6 percent less likely to do so. On the other hand, Ross and Sawhill (1975) in a similar analysis of the same data, find no significant welfare effects. Hutchens (1979) estimates that an increase in the level of AFDC benefits reduces the probability of remarriage. Sawhill et al. (1975) find that persons living in states with higher AFDC payment levels do not have higher separation rates. There is, however, some evidence that receiving AFDC inhibits the marriage and remarriage of women who head families (only 5 percent of those receiving welfare remarry within four years compared to 15 percent of those not receiving it). On the other hand, the level of welfare benefits does not seem to affect remarriage. Danziger et al. (1982) conclude that reducing welfare benefits would result in only a slight decrease in the number of female household heads.

McLanahan et al. (1986) use some of these findings to draw out some implications for low-income women.

> Using [the Ellwood and Bane and the Danziger et al.] studies, we estimate that the increase in [AFDC] benefits led to a 9 to 14 percent increase in the prevalence of single motherhood between 1960 and 1975, . . . no more than one-seventh of the overall growth. . . . It seems reasonable to assume that welfare benefits played little or no role in the marital decisions of those in the top half of the income distribution. . . . Thus, if the growth in benefits accounted for 15 percent of the total growth in single motherhood, it could possibly account for 30 percent of the growth within the bottom part of the income distribution. (7)

McLanahan et al. conclude that other factors also affect marital decisions. For example, increases in economic opportunities for women can account for a substantial part of the increase in single motherhood for whites (and a smaller portion of that for blacks).

Studies of intact families receiving income transfers under the income maintenance experiments show that providing benefits to two-parent families did not uniformly reduce marital instability. Even though it was thought that the AFDC program, by providing income support only to families without both parents present, encouraged family break-up, it was found that when income support was provided to intact families, the split rates for these families were *higher*, not lower, than those of comparable low-income families, although the results were not consistent across income support levels, races, or even experiments (Bishop 1980). Apparently, guaranteed incomes for both men and women create an "independence effect," facilitating marital dissolution theretofore inhibited by financial difficulties. Income maintenance payments increased the proportion of families headed by single females. For blacks and whites the increase was due to the increase in marital dissolution; for Hispanics the increase was due to a decrease in marital formation (Groeneveld et al. 1980).[12]

Other demographic factors may affect the marriage decisions of black women. One alternate hypothesis concerns the role of employment prospects and potential earnings of young men in influencing marriage decisions of young persons generally. Wilson and Neckerman (1986) point to male joblessness as the major determinant of changes in the structure of black families. Because of the poor labor market prospects of black men, black women are more likely to delay marriage and are less likely to remarry. Wilson and Neckerman construct a "male marriageable pool index"—the ratio of employed, civilian men to women of the same race and age group—and find that black women, especially young black women, face a shrinking pool of marriageable black men. The pool has not shrunk for white women; rather, the increase in white women living alone is due chiefly to increased economic independence. Thus, low rates of black employment may be in large part responsible for the declines in marriage and increases in divorce and separation in the black community and the increased reliance of black women on welfare for support. On the other hand, men may not work because they perceive that welfare supports their families.

In order to study the problems of black male youth unemployment, researchers from the National Bureau of Economic Research developed a Survey of Inner-City Black Youth ages sixteen to twenty-four in Boston, Chicago, and Philadelphia. The results of several analyses of the survey are presented in Freeman and Holzer (1986). The topics covered the youth's standard work activities, his desire to work, his use of drugs, his participation in illegal activities, his perceptions of the labor market, his attitudes and family background, and his typical daily activities. The study "found no single factor to be *the* cause of the black youth employment problem."

> A variety of social and economic factors have contributed to the crisis. On the demand side of the market, we find evidence of several determinants, including local labor market conditions and demographics, discriminatory employer behavior, and the unattractive characteristics of the job held. On the supply side of the market, we find aspirations and churchgoing, opportunities for crime, the family's employment and welfare status, education, and the willingness to accept low-wage jobs all to be important factors. Overall, we see a picture in which many black youths face unappealing labor market choices and therefore find other ways to obtain income and spend their time. (17)

Unfortunately, they are fairly pessimistic about the future: "The labor market problems of inner-city black youths are not likely to diminish greatly as they grow older . . . [because] . . . the typical out-of-school, nonemployed youth spends his time on activities that do little to raise his employability" (9).

Welfare and Illegitimacy. Another key issue is whether welfare has increased illegitimacy. AFDC benefits might lead to illegitimacy because such benefits are generally limited to poor, female-headed families. AFDC reduces the cost of maintaining a single-parent family and of having additional children out of wedlock. Although the rise in illegitimacy over the last twenty years, particularly among young black women, coupled with the tremendous increase in cash and noncash transfers to households, lends support to this theory, the magnitude of the impact on welfare is not so clear.

Early studies by Cutright (1970, 1971, 1972), Fechter and Greenfield (1973), Winegarden (1974), Moore and Caldwell (1977) and Moore and Burt (1982) find no relationship between the level of welfare benefits and illegitimacy. Moore (1980) finds no effects of welfare on teenage childbearing, but Janowitz (1976) reports a positive relationship between welfare benefits and illegitimacy among nonwhites, although not among whites.

In contrast, McLanahan (1985) points out that the illegitimacy rate was declining during most of the time welfare benefits were increasing. This apparent difference results from different definitions. The illegitimacy ratio (the ratio of nonmarital births to all live births) rose throughout the 1970s. The illegitimacy rate (the ratio of nonmarital births to the total number of single women ages fifteen to forty-four, those at risk for such a birth) tell a different story. As McLanahan (1985) notes, "For black women, the illegitimacy rate rose sharply between 1945 and 1960, leveled off between 1960 and 1965, and began to decline after 1965. For whites, it increased during the late sixties, declined during the early seventies, and rose again during the late seventies" (3). McLanahan argues that the *rate* is a more appropriate statistic than the *ratio:*

> If one is interested in describing the experience of a particular group, e.g., children, the ratio is the appropriate statistic. It tells us what proportion of children are born to nonmarried women and presumably what proportion are at high risk of poverty. If, however, one wants to talk about behaviors and propensities, the *rate,* not the *ratio,* is the appropriate statistic. The illegitimacy rate tells us what proportion of nonmarried women are having children out of wedlock. If the propensity of nonmarried women to have children is increasing, it should be reflected by an increase in the illegitimacy rate. (3)

In the most sophisticated study of the issue, Ellwood and Bane (1985) find "no evidence that welfare influences childbearing decisions of unmarried women" (198) (See Table 5.3). Wilson and Neckerman (1986), in summarizing the literature on the relationship between welfare and family structure, state:

> To sum up, this research indicates that welfare receipt or benefit levels have no effect on the incidence of out-of-wedlock births. AFDC payments seem to have a substantial effect on living arrangements of single mothers, but only a modest impact on separation and divorce. The extent to which welfare deters marriage or remarriage among single mothers is addressed only indirectly . . . and here the evidence is inconclusive. (251)

Murray (1985) postulates that the effect of welfare on illegitimacy may be explained by a *threshold effect*—welfare makes it economically viable to keep a baby born out of wedlock:

> At some very low level, welfare benefits have no causal effect on poor single women having and keeping babies. At some higher level (higher than any existing package), welfare benefits would make having a baby so economically beneficial for a poor person that it would in itself be a "cause" of such behavior. Between these extremes, a break point exists. . . . Once this break point is passed, welfare benefits become an enabling factor: they do not cause single women to decide to have a baby, but they enable women who are pregnant to make the decision to keep the baby. If in all states the package of benefits is already large enough to have passed the break point for a large proportion of the potential single mothers, then the effects [of] increases in the welfare package as measured by Ellwood and Bane will be very small. (441)

These threads of explanation are woven together by Murray (1986b) who suggests that "welfare does not *bribe* poor women to have babies, it *enables* them to do so." Further, it is not just the AFDC benefit that matters, it is the total package of benefits, both cash and in-kind. This package does not vary in value among states by nearly as much as do AFDC benefits alone. Murray then broadens his model of behavior to include aspects of the "marriageable male" hypothesis presented above: "At the same time that women were becoming enabled to support a child without having to rely on a man, men in poor communities were becoming less reliable. . . . The existence of an extensive welfare system permits the woman to put less pressure on the man to behave responsibly" (6–7). He then adds another element:

> The changes in welfare *and* changes in the risks attached to crime *and* changes in the educational environment reinforced each other. Together, they changed the incentive structure facing young people and they changed status rewards associated with behaviors [in ways] that make escape from poverty [more difficult]. . . . Beginning in the mid-1960s, a concentrated effort was made by the reformers to keep schools from acting in . . . punitive ways toward pregnant girls, and these efforts were largely successful. . . . A community that subsists on illegal sources of income and that is victimized by widespread violent crime is socially disorganized in crucial ways. To put it roughly, good folks no longer set the standards. (8–9)

He then suggests that both the failure of schools to act in punitive and stigmatizing ways toward pregnant girls and increases in crime negate attempts to maintain the social stigma against illegitimate births. This leads him to a final argument that only by improving the *character* of poor young people can any progress be made in reducing illegitimacy. Murray's model provides one unifying perspective, but its hypotheses are largely untestable because it seems politically impossible to totally eliminate cash transfers, even on an experimental basis.

In sum, there is weak evidence that AFDC affects family structure. The debate regarding these effects is far from resolved, however. Not until studies are done using a more complete specification of the welfare package (including non-AFDC benefits), the choices available to poor women (including accounting for "marriageable males"—see Wilson and Neckerman 1986), the environment (e.g., abortion availability), and attitudes, preferences, and expectations, will some of the uncertainties be resolved.

Welfare and Child Support. The shift in AFDC caseloads from widow-headed families to families headed by divorced, separated, or never-married women meant that welfare benefits increasingly represented a payment that was required because of the lack of voluntary financial support from the absent parent. Establishment and enforcement of child support obligations is a state responsibility. The first federal legislation was in 1950, which required state welfare agencies to notify law enforcement officials when a child receiving AFDC benefits had been abandoned. Congress enacted measures to increase the collection of child support payments from absent parents. The most important was the establishment in 1975 of the Child Support Enforcement Program (Title IV-D of the Social Security Act). The statute authorized federal matching funds to be used for locating absent parents, establishing paternity, obtaining child and spousal support, and enforcing the support obligations owed by absent parents to their children and the spouse (or former spouse) with whom the children are living. The program required the provision of child support enforcement services for both welfare and nonwelfare families. In 1984 Congress passed legislation that required all states to begin withholding child support payments from the wages of non-compliant absent parents after a one-month delinquency.

Temple et al. (1986) have estimated that cost avoidance—the *indirect* savings when a family leaves or stays off the AFDC, food stamps, or Medicaid programs—because of child support collections was between $269 million and $1 billion in the May 1983–April 1984 period. About half of the saving was in the AFDC program, one-third in the food stamp program, and the remaining one-sixth in the Medicaid program. These figures represent savings comparable to child support collections on behalf of AFDC families reported by the Office of Child Support Enforcement of $1 billion in FY 1984 (U.S. Department of Health and Human Services, 1984b).

Although the literature on the relationship between child support payments and dependency has been small relative to the fact that nonpayment of child support is a major factor keeping families dependent on welfare, there are a number of recent studies. Much of the work to date deals with three main questions. What is the size of the underpayments by absent parents? What determines the amounts of payments made by absent fathers and the amounts received by custodial parents? To what extent are these underpayments responsible for the low-income status of custodial parents and their children? Unfortunately, much of the literature has been produced with highly imperfect data because of small samples, the use of characteristics of custodial women to proxy for the former husband's characteristics, the highly limited data on informal payments by never-married fathers, and the inability to obtain information from a large, paired sample of both parents.

Survey data show that the amount of child support underpayments is quite large, though there is anecdotal evidence that there is some informal (unreported) support, both cash and in kind. CPS data from 1983 show that, based on reports from custodial mothers, a large proportion (42 percent) of women raising children without a father present had not been awarded child support payments. Of those with a child support award, 76 percent received payments that averaged about 80 percent of the full award. Of those with an award, 24 percent received no payment, 26 percent received only a partial payment, and 50 percent received the full amount owed. Poor mothers were less likely than other mothers to have obtained an award and less likely to receive a payment (given a receipt of child support award). The average annual amount paid to poor mothers was $1,425 in 1983, or about one thousand dollars less than amounts received by nonpoor mothers, probably due in part to the likelihood that their former spouses are poor as well.

Robins and Dickinson (1983) found that "marital status is a strong predictor of receipt of welfare and of child support." According to results from their analysis of the CPS, half of unwed mothers end up on welfare and less than one in ten receive child support. Divorced mothers, on the other hand, have only a 30 percent chance of receiving welfare and more than half receive child support. When they examined the welfare/child-support linkage from another perspective, Robins and Dickinson found that single mothers receiving child support are significantly less likely to receive welfare than single mothers who receive no child support. However, many of the characteristics that determine welfare recipiency also influence (in the opposite direction) whether a family receives child support. They conclude that "child support alone has a fairly limited impact on welfare recipiency." Part of the reason for such a relatively small impact of child support may be low award amounts. Since their data indicate that the average monthly child support award amount is only about two-thirds the average monthly AFDC benefit, child support alone is not sufficient to cause the average mother to become ineligible for welfare.

Several studies, including Cassetty (1978), Jones et al. (1976), and Chambers (1980), document that earnings of absent parents affect the size of their child support payments. In addition, Chambers and Jones et al. found evidence that enforcement policies caused increased payments by absent parents. Sorenson and MacDonald (1981) used

1977 AFDC survey data on mothers heading families to show that the presence and size of the child support award had the most significance in explaining ultimate receipts by welfare recipients. Economic and demographic characteristics of the mothers, considered as indicators of the absent father's ability to make payments, influenced the size of the award, but had little impact on payments, given the size of the awards. In contrast, Beller and Graham (1985) found, using data on a national sample of custodial mothers from a 1979 CPS supplement, that predicted father's income (again based on custodial mother characteristics) influenced both the size and presence of an award and actual payments.

A draft study by Lerman (1986) is one of the first to examine the characteristics of absent fathers in any detail. While few young men became fathers before their early twenties, those who did often lived away from their children. Fatherhood patterns shift significantly between the late teenage years and the mid-twenties. About one-half of twenty to twenty-one-year-old fathers are absent fathers, but only about one-third of twenty-four to twenty-five-year-old fathers are absent. The interplay between marriage and fatherhood varied by race. Hispanic young men showed high marriage and fatherhood rates. Whites married at relatively high rates but delayed having children. Blacks fathered children at the highest rates, but had the lowest marriage rates. Since black young men experience sharply higher unemployment rates than whites, the black-white differences in family status are consistent with the explanation that male joblessness keeps families from forming and/or destabilizes existing families. However, the evidence about Hispanic young men runs in the opposite direction. The high unemployment rates faced by Hispanic young men apparently have not prevented them from starting and maintaining families with children.

Lerman carried out a multivariate analysis to determine the independent effects of various factors on whether young men were childless, absent fathers, or resident fathers in 1983 and on whether a childless man became an absent father in the 1979–1983 period. He finds that young absent fathers are more likely to come from a low-income family, have lived in a family that received welfare (for whites and Hispanics, but not blacks), have low aptitude (as measured on Armed Forces Qualification Tests of reading and math comprehension), and have higher early sexual activity. However, even after taking account of both differences in personal characteristics (e.g., employment, sexual activity) and family background (e.g., prior welfare status), the probability of being an absent or resident father *continued* to differ by race. Thus, attitudes and cultural factors captured by the race variable may exert a direct influence.

A key issue concerning dependency is whether the absence of child support payments limits the capacity of women to escape poverty and welfare. This issue is addressed by Robins (1986): ". . . child support enforcement may represent an effective means for reducing AFDC program costs. However, because the current legal system establishes such low child support award amounts, it does not appear to be an effective anti-poverty device" (786). The state of Wisconsin is about to begin an experiment to test whether their Child Support Assurance Program will increase child support payments (by fathers or through the program's direct minimum payment) and lesson welfare dependence. By providing an income floor not tied directly to welfare, the program would raise the income threshold at which mothers qualify for AFDC and encourage more self-support as an alternative to welfare (Corbett et al. 1986). Child support payments might also contribute to reduced welfare dependency by increasing remarriage rates. Unfortunately, Beller and Graham's findings cast doubt on the positive impact of child support payments on both the remarriage mechanism and the earnings route out of dependency. However, Garfinkel (1985) points out that Beller and Graham only examine the effects of child support awards, not payments, and this limitation reduces one's confidence in their conclusions.

MIGRATION AND WELFARE

Differences in state welfare benefit levels may have an important influence on migration patterns. The massive movement of blacks from the south to the north and from rural to urban areas may have exerted a major influence on the nature and character of both rural and urban poverty. Finally, the apparent retreat of black middle- and upper-class families from the worst central city neighborhoods may have altered the institutions and role models which served to hold neighborhoods together. This latter possibility has been emphasized recently by Wilson (1985) and by Lemann (1986).

There are a few studies of the influence of welfare benefit levels on migration; but *most evidence suggests that people, with the possible exception of some subgroups, are not motivated by welfare benefit levels to leave low-benefit states and migrate to high-benefit ones.* (For a summary of some of this literature, see Cebula 1979.) Gallaway (1967), Gallaway et al. (1967), and Sommers and Suits (1973) fail to find a significant relationship between migration and welfare benefit levels. Fields (1979) finds no consistent aggregate effect of welfare on migration.

On the other hand, some have found different results, particularly when migration patterns are disaggregated by race. Kaun (1970), Cebula and Shaffer (1975), Glantz (1973), and DaVanzo (1972) find higher migration rates into areas with higher welfare payments for some groups, but numerically, the effects were not large. Cebula et al. (1973) finds that welfare may be an important determinant of black migration; this is confirmed by Ziegler (1976) and Kau and Sirmans (1976). Pack (1973) finds that higher AFDC levels inhibit white in-migration.

A recent study by Gramlich and Laren (1984) finds a relationship between AFDC benefit levels and migration. When AFDC recipients move, they are more likely to move to a high-benefit state than a low-benefit one. Since very few AFDC households make an interstate move in any one year, this tendency manifests itself only over the long run.

Nevertheless, it seems clear that the level of welfare payments has not played a major role in determining migration flows. One possible explanation for the contradictory effects is offered by Fields (1979):

[My results provide] only meager support for the view that higher welfare benefits attract migrants. A more persistent effect is the finding that a higher percentage of welfare recipients leads to greater out-migration. Taken together, [these] results suggest that welfare benefits influence migration in two somewhat offsetting ways. On the one hand, low income workers may be moving to locations where benefits are higher and easier to obtain. On the other hand, there also seems to be significant "flight from blight" on the part of the non-poor. (30)

This is a difficult problem to disentangle. The overlapping and possibly opposite effects of welfare benefit levels on in- and out-migration for different racial and income groups have so far made determining the definitive impacts of welfare on migration impossible.

ATTITUDES, INTERGENERATIONAL TRANSMISSION
OF WELFARE DEPENDENCY, AND THE UNDERCLASS

As pointed out by Hopkins (1986), the effects of welfare, to the extent they exist, come about in one of two ways. The interaction of welfare program characteristics (such as a work disincentive or the benefit level) with a recipient's existing attitudes could cause the recipient to *choose* to rely on welfare as the main source of support. Or, welfare could alter the recipient's underlying attitudes toward welfare receipt as dependency lengthens.

There is no statistical evidence that welfare itself changes attitudes. Duncan and Hoffman (1986) note that events such as wage or employment changes generally lead to changes in one's perception of control over her environment (e.g., Andrisani 1978, Hill et al. 1985). O'Neill et al. (1984) and Hill et al. (1985) find no effect of welfare receipt on recipients' perceptions of efficacy and feeling of control. Similarly, Goodwin (1972) finds no effect of welfare receipt on attitudes toward work. Unfortunately, most measures of attitudes are poor predictors of behavior. This casts doubt on all studies of these issues, particularly those that rely on generalized attitudes (e.g., efficacy) rather than on specific attitudes (e.g., toward welfare).

Hopkins (1986) suggests that attitudes play a major role in the intergenerational transmission of dependency.

> Regardless of whether dependent attitudes are pre-existing or are produced by welfare receipt, such receipt could catalyze the formation of dependent attitudes among children. Such hypothesized intergenerational transmission of dependency is, in fact, a recurrent theme in the literature on the causes of poverty. (14)

The best-known proponents of the "culture of poverty" thesis— that the poor (or some identifiable subgroup of the poor) have a distinct, separate culture and that this culture keeps them mired in poverty—are Clark (1965), Banfield (1970), Harrington (1962), Lewis (1968), and Miller (1968). They all argue that poverty is more than low income, but one feature of a lifestyle whose characteristics (dependency, illegitimacy, instability) are problems as well. For those writers, the poor (or some subgroup) are characterized by psychological inadequacies that lead to behavioral dependence. However, their conclusions are often based on impressionistic evidence, though

Moynihan (1965) used decennial census statistics of changing family structure by race to buttress similar arguments.

If true, the existence and persistence of a culture of poverty has major implications for poverty policy. If poverty and dependency are culturally and psychologically based, poverty cannot be eliminated solely by providing either additional resources (transfer payments) or opportunities (jobs). The first step would require a change of attitude by those in this culture of poverty to resemble mainstream attitudes and values more closely. If the deviant attitudes and values of this subset of the poor could not be changed, there would be little hope that poverty policy would be fully effective. Yet abandoning efforts to help those thus trapped in poverty opens the government to charges that it is "blaming the victim."

The existence of a culture of poverty was strongly contested in the 1960s and later (see Patterson 1981), but lack of explicit models linking motivation to achievement has prevented serious testing. These arguments have resurfaced as descriptions of an underclass containing, among others, long-term welfare-dependent mothers (see Auletta 1982, Bernstein 1982). Recently, Wilson (1985) and Lemann (1986) have argued that the flight of middle-class blacks from ghettos resulting from the relaxation of overt racial discrimination in housing has left an isolated black underclass behind, one without role models to demonstrate the ways out of poverty and dependency. As Wilson describes:

> Accompanying the black middle-class exodus has been a growing movement of stable working-class blacks from ghetto neighborhoods to higher-income neighborhoods in other parts of the city and to the suburbs. . . . Today's ghetto neighborhoods are populated almost exclusively by the most disadvantaged segments of the black urban community, [those] who are outside the mainstream of the American occupational system. Included in this group are individuals who lack training and skills and either experience long-term unemployment or are not part of the labor force, individuals who are engaged in street criminal activity and other forms of aberrant behavior, and families who experience long-term spells of poverty and/or welfare dependency. (546)

Corcoran et al. (1985) examine longitudinal data on individuals and families and conclude that the culture of poverty and underclass arguments are inappropriate models for viewing all the poor. They find that only a small subset of individuals who come into contact with poverty remain poor for an extended period and that most long-term poor are old, disabled, or live outside of large urban areas. Further, they find no consistent evidence that the motivational and psychological characteristics of individuals affect subsequent achievement, either within or across generations:

> A series of systematic tests by Hill (1981), Hill et al. (1985) and Hill and Ponza (1983, 1985), [examined] 14 years of PSID data on young adults and their parents. [Hill and her colleagues] found that only a small proportion of women growing up in heavily welfare-dependent homes themselves became heavily dependent on welfare as adults and, indeed, that there was no significant link at all for blacks between the welfare dependency of parent and child. (Hopkins 1986, 14)

This was confirmed by Antel (1986) who analyzed the effects of parental welfare participation on the subsequent fertility and schooling decisions of young women from welfare families. Estimation of a statistical model that explicitly corrected for the effects of unobserved characteristics using the 1979–1983 National Longitudinal Survey of Youth led him to the conclusion that parental participation in welfare had no effect on young girls' fertility or high school completion. Unfortunately, when he adds two more years of data, Antel (1987) reaches a different conclusion:

> Family welfare participation encourages the fertility and discourages the high school completion of daughters. According to these two indicators of future welfare dependency, children exposed to welfare at home, after controlling for observed and unobserved factors, are more likely to become dependent on welfare. (21)

If welfare affects attitudes toward work, that effect could reduce the recipient's ability and/or inclination to become self-sufficient and thus prolong her period of dependence. O'Neill et al. (1984) find such a "duration dependence," meaning that the longer one's welfare spell at a particular point in time the longer her total spell could be expected to be, but they were unable to determine if it was a statistical artifact. Ellwood (1986a) derived a similar result. However, Goodwin (1981) argues that there is no evidence that time on welfare dependency is caused by preference for welfare.

The finding that only a small group of welfare recipients account for the majority of total time on welfare is consistent with the existence of an underclass. More research needs to be done to characterize this long-term dependent population and determine whether its characterization is consistent with theories of the underclass. As Wilson (1985) has argued,

> Thoughtful explanations of the rise of inner-city social dislocations . . . should emphasize the dynamic interplay between ghetto-specific cultural characteristics and social and economic opportunities. This would necessitate taking into account the effects not only of changes in American economic organization but also of demographic changes and changes in the laws and policies of the government as well. In this connection, the relationships between joblessness and family structure, joblessness and other social dislocations (crime, teenage pregnancy, welfare dependency, etc.) and joblessness and social orientation among different age groups would receive special attention . . . [augmented] with empirical data on the ghetto underclass experience and on conditions in the broader society that have shaped and continue to shape that experience. This calls for a number of different research strategies ranging from survey to ethnographic to historical. (556)

UNANSWERED QUESTIONS

The previous sections highlighted some of the research regarding welfare. This section focuses on what remains to be studied.

Dynamics of Dependency. More needs to be learned about the characteristics of the long-term dependent. Are long-term dependents generally homogeneous in behavior and attitudes or are there many subgroups? If there are subgroups, what distinguishes among them? How many can be characterized as part of an underclass? Are they concentrated in inner cities or rural areas? Is there any trend over time in the number or demographic characteristics of long-term dependents? Has or can any government program affect their length of stay on welfare? What do we know about the causes of such dependency?

While the majority of AFDC spells are short-term, not much is known about those spells, particularly those lasting less than a year. What causes them and how do they end? Are they a reflection of real long-term need, of a temporary reduction in circumstances, or a reflection of administrative "churning" (erroneous apparent changes in eligibility)? Do those suffering short spells of dependency suffer many or only a few spells before returning to self-support? These kinds of questions could possibly be addressed when longitudinal data from the Survey of Income and Program Participation (SIPP) become available, covering thirty consecutive months, though the sample of AFDC recipients is small.

Not enough is known about the total lengths of stay on the Food Stamp program. Indeed, multiple benefit receipt and long-term dependency on more than one program has been little studied. For example, Weinberg (1985, 1987) has characterized multiple transfer program participation in one month using SIPP and its precursor, but until the longitudinal file is available little can be done to analyze multiple benefit receipt over time. Other longitudinal data sets have only limited information on multiple transfer program receipt.

Correlates of Dependency. Quite a lot is known about the correlates of AFDC dependency. It would be useful to know more about what leads to long-term Food Stamp recipiency and how it relates to long-term AFDC recipiency. It would also be valuable to understand more about the role of neighborhood on the use of welfare. For example, is there any evidence that living in an area where there is a substantial concentration of welfare recipients leads children in these areas to become welfare recipients as adults?

Welfare and Work. The individual program and total joint effects of work incentives built into welfare programs have yet to be definitively established. Indeed, little is known about the effects of work incentives in the Supplemental Security Income program. Further, the long-term effects of work incentives may differ from the short-term effects, for example, Moffitt (1986) has argued that we have yet to see the full effects of the 1981 changes in AFDC. More research is needed on the effects of the Medicaid "notch": Do families use welfare as a way to get Medicaid because of poor health? Do families stay on AFDC because they don't want to lose their Medicaid status? Does the transition coverage recently enacted (providing extensions of Medicaid coverage for those earning their way off of AFDC) encourage more recipients to become self-supporting?

Along with the analysis of work incentives, more analysis of work programs is needed. With regard to work programs directly tied to welfare programs, further analysis of the WIN demonstrations now underway (focusing on longer-term follow-up and analysis of more states) would allow more generalizable conclusions. Mandatory participation in employment and training programs by those with young children is important to investigate as well. As part of this analysis, can we determine whether the availability or cost of supportive services (e.g., day care, transportation) changes the effectiveness of work programs for welfare recipients. Can the skills necessary to be qualified for entry level jobs that prepare individuals for jobs that pay enough to support a family be taught effectively? Also, does displacement occur, that is, do the graduates from work programs take the jobs of others, resulting in no net gain in employment?

Welfare and Family Structure. Most important of the unanswered questions in this topic area is the total effect of the full package of welfare benefits on separation, divorce, and remarriage. To date, the major studies of this issue have focused on the effects of differences between states in the level of AFDC benefits, a difference mitigated by the provision of other transfers such as Medicaid and Food Stamps. In particular, a thorough examination of Murray's (1986) threshold effect (AFDC as enabling rather than inducing) and the interrelationships between welfare, youth unemployment, and teenage pregnancy and out-of-wedlock births are vital to a better understanding of the effects of welfare on family structure.

Migration and Welfare. Though it seems clear that welfare benefit levels are not a major determinant of migration flows, the definitive impacts of welfare on migration are not known. As with other unanswered questions, one way to resolve the inconsistencies may be to study the effects of multiple transfer benefits.

Welfare and Child Support. Not enough is known about absent parents (primarily fathers)—their incomes, family circumstances, geographic proximity to their children, ability to pay child support. A nationally representative survey of these individuals, preferably matched to the custodial parents, would help design public strategies to encourage more child support by absent parents. Additional information is also needed on the effectiveness of certain child support enforcement activities, such as paternity establishment and wage withholding for delinquent payments authorized by the 1984 amendments. It is also important to evaluate carefully more positive approaches such as more visitation and more joint custody. There will be additional insights into the role of child support from the Wisconsin Child Support Assurance Project (Corbett et al. 1986) as well.

Attitudes, Intergenerational Transmission of Welfare Dependency, and the Underclass. More needs to be done on understanding the values and attitudes of the poor—how they are formed and how they change. Is there an underclass? Though defining an underclass is not intrinsically very informative, its identification might prove enlightening. Is there intergenerational transmission of dependency, that is, is chronic welfare dependency a culture (set of values) that is transmitted from parent to child? The evidence suggests that there is not a lot, but the image of a three-generation welfare family is too persistent to ignore. Has middle- and upper-class black migration out of central cities contributed to underclass culture? If so, is there any way of reversing the trend?

Further, substantial additional research is needed on the causes of dependency and the process by which women choose the welfare alternative. What role do attitudes play in dependent behavior and how might public policy affect them?[13]

NOTES

1.   The views expressed in this paper are those of the author and should not be construed as necessarily representing the official position or policy of U.S. Department of Health and Human Services or any office therein. An earlier and more lengthy version of this chapter was originally prepared for the White House Office of Policy Development in July 1986. The author wishes to thank the following individuals for their comments and suggestions without in any way associating them with the statements contained herein: Steven Cole, Deirdre Duzor, David Ellwood, Walton Francis, Peter Germanis, Kevin Hopkins, Gabrielle Lupo, Carol McHale, John Pencavel, William Prosser, Christine Schmidt, Reuben Snipper, and Ernst Stromsdorfer.

2.   This section draws in part from Duncan and Hoffman (1986).

3.   The principal sources of longitudinal data are the Panel Study of Income Dynamics (PSID), which provides information on representative samples of recipients and nonrecipients from 1968 through the present; the now-concluded Ohio State National Longitudinal Surveys (NLS), which provide such information beginning in 1969; and a new NLS data set on youth, begun in 1979. A fourth set of data is derived from AFDC case records, beginning with cases opened in 1965.

4.   Rank (1985), using life-table analysis (cross-classification of initial states by outcomes), confirmed that most families remain on welfare (measured broadly in his study as AFDC, food stamps, or Medicaid) for a relatively short time.

5.   This section is based in part on Hopkins (1986) 9–10.

6.   Using NLS data, O'Neill et al. also find blacks less likely to exit by either means.

7.   This summary is based on Hopkins (1986).

8.   O'Neill et al. rely primarily on NLS data (though analyzing PSID and case-load statistics as well) and the others use only PSID data.

9.   This description is drawn from Gueron (1988).

10.   This section is based on Stromsdorfer et al. (1985).

11.   This discussion of the effects of CETA is based on Stromsdorfer et al. (1985) 8–10. They examined the studies by Ashenfelter and Card (1984), Bassi (1983), Bloom and McLaughlin (1984), Dickinson et al. (1984), Finifter (1983), Geraci (1984), and Westat (1984).

12.   Cain (1986) has recently called these findings into question.

13.   Readers interested in different perspectives on the literature on long-term welfare dependency are urged to consult two studies sponsored by the U.S. Department of Health and Human Services, Office of the Assistant Secretary for Planning and Evaluation—Ellwood (1987) and Hopkins (1987)—completed after this summary was written. Also useful is U.S. Office of Policy Development (1988).

BIBLIOGRAPHY

Andrisani, Paul J. 1978. *Work Attitudes and Labor Market Experience.* New York: Praeger.

Antel, John J. 1986. "The Inter-Generational Transfer of Welfare Dependency: Program Effects on Future Welfare Dependency." Prepared for the U.S. Department of Health and Human Services, Office of the Assistant Secretary for Planning and Evaluation under Grant No. 84–ASPE–096A. Houston: University of Houston.

Antel, John J. 1987. "The Intergenerational Transfer of Welfare Dependency." Prepared for the U.S. Department of Health and Human Services, Office of the Assistant Secretary for Planning and Evaluation. Houston: University of Houston.

Ashenfelter, Orley. 1978. "Estimating the Effects of Training Programs on Earnings." *Review of Economics and Statistics* 60.

Ashenfelter, Orley, and David Card. 1984. "Using the Longitudinal Structure of Earnings to Estimate the Effect of Training Programs." Working Paper No. 1489. Cambridge: National Bureau of Economic Research.

Auletta, Kenneth. 1982. *The Underclass.* New York: Random House.

Bahr, Stephen J. 1979. "The Effects of Welfare on Marital Stability and Remarriage." *Journal of Marriage and the Family* 41:553–60.

Bane, Mary Jo, and David T. Ellwood. 1983. "The Dynamics of Dependence: The Routes to Self-Sufficiency." Prepared for the U.S. Department of Health and Human Services, Office of the Assistant Secretary for Planning and Evaluation. Cambridge: Urban Systems Research and Engineering, Inc.

Banfield, Edward C. 1970. *The Unheavenly City.* Boston: Little, Brown.

Barocci, Thomas A. 1982. "Employment and Training Programs in the 1970s: Research Results and Methods." In *Industrial Relations Research in the 1970s: Review and Appraisal,* edited by T. A. Kochan et al., 95–148. Madison: Industrial Relations Research Association.

Barr, Nicholas, and Robert Hall. 1981. "The Probability of Dependence on Public Assistance." *Economica* 48:109–24.

Bassi, Laurie J. 1983. "The Effect of CETA on the Postprogram Earnings of Participants." *Journal of Human Resources* 18:539–56.

Bassi, Laurie J., and Orley Ashenfelter. 1986. "The Effects of Direct Job Creation and Training Programs on Low-Skilled Workers." In *Fighting Poverty,* edited by S. Danziger and D. Weinberg, 133–151. Cambridge: Harvard University Press.

Beller, Andrea H., and John W. Graham. 1985. "Variations in the Economic Well-Being of Divorced Women and Their Children: The Role of Child Support Income." In *Horizontal Equity, Uncertainty, and Economic Well-Being,* edited by M. David and T. Smeeding. NBER Studies in Income and Wealth. Vol. 50. Chicago: University of Chicago Press.

Bernstein, Blanche. 1982. *The Politics of Welfare: The New York City Experience.* Cambridge: Abt Books.

Blank, Rebecca M. 1986. "How Important is Welfare Dependence?" Discussion Paper No. 821–86. Madison: Institute for Research on Poverty.

Bishop, John H. 1980. "Jobs, Cash Transfers and Marital Instability: A Review and Synthesis of the Evidence." *Journal of Human Resources* 15:301–34.

Blau, David M., and Philip K. Robins. 1986. "Labor Supply Response to Welfare Programs: A Dynamic Analysis." *Journal of Labor Economics* 4:82–104.

Bloom, Howard S., and Maureen A. McLaughlin. 1982. *CETA Training Programs—Do They Work for Adults?* A Joint Congressional Budget Office-National Commission for Employment Policy paper. Washington, D.C.: U.S. Government Printing Office.

Boskin, Michael J., and Frederick C. Nold. 1981. "A Markov Model of Turnover in Aid to Families with Dependent Children." *Journal of Human Resources* 10(4):467–81.

Bumpass, Larry L. 1984. "Children and Marital Disruption: A Replication and Update." *Demography* 21:71–82.

Cain, Glen. 1985. "Comments on Murray's Analysis of the Impact of the War on Poverty on the Labor Market Behavior of the Poor." In *Losing Ground: A Critique.* Institute for Research on Poverty Special Report No. 38. Madison: Institute for Research on Poverty.

Cain, Glen G. 1986. "The Income Maintenance Experiments and the Issues of Marital Stability and Family Composition." In Alicia H. Munnell (ed.) *Lessons from the Income Maintenance Experiments.* Proceedings of a conference sponsored by the Federal Reserve Bank of Boston and the Brookings Institution.

Cassetty, Judith. 1978. *Child Support and Public Policy.* Lexington: Lexington.

Cebula, Richard J. 1979. *The Determinants of Human Migration.* Lexington: Lexington.

Cebula, Richard J., Robert M. Kohn, and Lowell E. Gallaway. 1973. "Determinants of Net Migration to SMSAs, 1960–1970." *Mississippi Valley Journal* 9:59–64.

Cebula, Richard J., and B. K. Schaffer. 1975. "Analysis of Net Interstate Migration: Comment." *Southern Economic Journal* 41:690–93.

Chambers, David. 1980. *Making Fathers Pay.* Chicago: University of Chicago Press.

Clark, Kenneth B. 1965. *Dark Ghetto: Dilemmas of Social Power.* New York: Harper and Row.

Coe, Richard D. 1981. "A Preliminary Empirical Examination of the Dynamics of Welfare Use." In *Five Thousand American Families—Patterns of Economic Progress Volume IX,* edited by M. Hill, D. Hill, and J. Morgan. Ann Arbor: Institute for Social Research.

Coe, Richard D., and Greg J. Duncan. 1985. "Welfare: Promoting Poverty or Progress?" *Wall Street Journal* (May 15).

Corbett, Thomas, Irwin Garfinkel, Ada Skyles, and Elizabeth Uhr. 1986. "Assuring Child Support in Wisconsin." *Public Welfare* 44:33–39.

Corcoran, Mary, Greg J. Duncan, Gerald Gurin, and Patricia Gurin. 1985. "Myth and Reality: The Causes and Persistence of Poverty." *Journal of Policy Analysis and Management* 4:516–36.

Cutright, Phillips. 1970. "AFDC, Family Allowances and Illegitimacy." *Family Planning Perspectives* 2:4–9.

———. 1971. "Illegitimacy: Myths, Causes and Cures." *Family Planning Perspectives* 3:26–48.

———. 1972. "Illegitimacy in the United States: 1920–1968." In *Demographic and Social Aspects of Population Growth,* edited by C. Westoff and R. Parke. Washington, D.C.: U.S. Government Printing Office.

Cutright, Phillips, and Patrick Madras. 1976. "AFDC and the Marital and Family Status of Never Married Women Age 15–44: United States 1950–1970." *Sociology and Social Research* 60:314–27.

Danziger, Sheldon, Robert Haveman, and Robert Plotnick. 1981. "How Income Transfers Affect Work, Savings, and Income Distribution." *Journal of Economic Literature* 19:975–1028.

Danziger, Sheldon, George Jakubson, Saul Schwartz, and Eugene Smolensky. 1982. "Work and Welfare as Determinants of Female Poverty and Household Headship." *The Quarterly Journal of Economics* 98:519–34.

DaVanzo, Julie. 1972. *An Analytic Framework for Studying the Potential Effects of an Income Maintenance Program on U.S. Interregional Migration.* Report R-1081-EDA. Santa Monica: Rand Corporation.

Dickinson, Katherine P., Terry R. Johnson, and Richard W. West. 1984. "An Analysis of the Impact of CETA Programs on Participants' Earnings." Menlo Park: SRI International.

———. 1985. "Summary of an Analysis of the Impact of CETA Programs on Participants' Earnings and Implications for Evaluating JTPA." Menlo Park: SRI International.

Duncan, Greg J. 1984. *Years of Poverty, Years of Plenty.* Ann Arbor: Institute for Social Research.

Duncan, Greg J., and Saul D. Hoffman. 1986. "Longitudinal Evidence on the Use and Effects of Welfare." Paper presented at the Association for Public Policy Analysis and Management meetings (December 1985), and the conference "The Political Economy of the Transfer Society" (February 1986).

Ellwood, David T. 1986[a]. *Targeting the Would-be Long Term Recipient of AFDC: Who Should be Served?* Princeton: Mathematica Policy Research.

———. 1986[b]. "Working Off Welfare: Prospects and Policies for Self-Sufficiency of Female Family Heads." Discussion Paper #803–86. Madison: Institute for Research on Poverty.

Ellwood, David T., and Mary Jo Bane. 1985. "The Impact of AFDC on Family Structure and Living Arrangements." *Research in Labor Economics* 7:137–207.

Ellwood, David T. 1987. *Understanding Dependency: Choices, Confidence, or Culture?* Waltham: Brandeis University, Center for Human Resources.

Fechter, A., and S. Greenfield. 1973. "Welfare and Illegitimacy: An Economic Model and Some Preliminary Results." Urban Institute Working Paper No. 963–37. Washington, D.C.: The Urban Institute.

Fields, Gary S. 1979. "Place-to-Place Migration: Some New Evidence." *Review of Economics and Statistics* 61:21–32.

Finifter, David H. 1985. "Estimating Net Earnings Impact of Federally Subsidized Employment and Training Programs: What Have We Learned and Where Do We Go From Here?" Department of Economics Working Paper. Williamsburg: College of William and Mary.

Fraker, Thomas, and Robert Moffitt. 1985. "The Effect of Food Stamps on Labor Supply: A Bivariate Selection Model." Prepared for the U.S. Department of Agriculture Food and Nutrition Service under Contract No. FNS–53–3198–3–120. Princeton: Mathematica Policy Research.

Freeman, Richard B., and Harry J. Holzer (eds.). 1986. *The Black Youth Employment Crisis.* Chicago: University of Chicago Press.

Gallaway, Lowell E. 1967. *Interindustry Labor Mobility in the U.S.* U.S. Department of Health, Education, and Welfare, Social Security Administration. Research Report No. 18. Washington, D.C.: U.S. Government Printing Office.

Gallaway, Lowell E., R. F. Gilbert, and P. E. Smith. 1967. "The Economics of Labor Mobility: An Empirical Analysis." *Western Economic Journal* 5:211–23.

Garfinkel, Irwin. 1985. "Comment [on Beller and Graham]." In *Horizontal Equity, Uncertainty, and Economic Well-Being,* edited by M. David and T. Smeeding. NBER Studies in Income and Wealth. Vol. 50, Chicago: University of Chicago Press.

Garfinkel, Irwin, and Sara McLanahan. 1985. "The Feminization of Poverty: Nature, Causes, and a Partial Cure." Discussion Paper No. 776–85. Madison: Institute for Research on Poverty.

Gay, Robert S., and Michael E. Borus. 1980. "Validating Performance Indicators for Employment and Training Programs." *Journal of Human Resources* 15:29–48.

Geraci, Vincent J. 1984. *Short-Term Indicators of Job Training Program Effects on Long-Term Participant Earnings.* Project Working Paper No. 2 under Contract No. 20–48–82–16 to the U.S. Department of Labor, Employment and Training Administration.

Gilder, George. 1983. "Child Allowances: Out of the Welfare Trap." *Wall Street Journal* (September 22).

Glantz, Frederic B. 1973. *The Determinants of the Interregional Migration of the Economically Disadvantaged.* Report 52. Boston: Federal Reserve Bank of Boston.

Goodwin, Leonard. 1972. *Do the Poor Want to Work?* New York: Vintage Books.

Goodwin, Leonard. 1981. *The Impact of Federal Income Security Programs on Work Incentives and Marital Stability.* Prepared for the U.S. Department of Labor, Employment and Training Administration, Office of Research and Development under Grant No. 5I–25–77–05.

Goodwin, Leonard. 1983. *Causes and Cures of Welfare.* Lexington: Lexington.

Gordon, Jesse E. 1978. "WIN Research: A Review of the Findings." In *The Work Incentive Experience,* edited by C. D. Garvin, A. D. Smith, and W. J. Reid. Montclair: Allanheld, Osmun.

Gramlich, Edward M., and Deborah S. Laren. 1984. "Migration and Income Redistribution Responsibilities." *Journal of Human Resources* 19:489–511.

Groeneveld, Lyle P., Michael T. Hannan, and Nancy Brandon Tuma. 1980. "The Effects of Negative Income Tax Programs on Marital Dissolution." *Journal of Human Resources* 15:654–74.

Grossman, Jean B., Rebecca Maynard, and Judith Roberts. 1985. *Reanalysis of the Effects of Selected Employment and Training Programs for Welfare Recipients.* Princeton: Mathematica Policy Research.

Gueron, Judith M. 1986. *Work Initiatives for Welfare Recipients: Lessons from a Multi-State Experiment.* New York: Manpower Demonstration Research Corporation.

Gueron, Judith M. 1988. "State Welfare Employment Initiatives: Lessons from the 1980s." *Focus* 11:17–24.

Harrington, Michael. 1962. *The Other America.* New York: MacMillan.

Harrison, Bennett. 1977. "Labor Market Structure and the Relationship Between Work and Welfare." (mimeo). Cambridge: Department of Urban Studies and Planning, Massachusetts Institute of Technology.

Hausman, Jerry. 1981. "Labor Supply." In *How Taxes Affect Economic Behavior,* edited by H. J. Aaron and J. A. Pechman. Washington, D.C.: Brookings Institution.

Hill, Martha S. 1981. "Some Dynamic Aspects of Poverty." In *Five Thousand American Families—Patterns of Economic Progress, Volume IX* edited by M. Hill et al. Ann Arbor: Institute for Social Research.

Hill, Martha S., Sue Augustyniak, Greg Duncan, G. Gurin, J. K. Liker, J. Morgan, and M. Ponza. 1985. *Motivation and Economic Mobility of the Poor.* ISR Research Report. Ann Arbor: Institute for Social Research.

Hill, Martha S., and Michael Ponza. 1983. "Intergenerational Transmission of Dependence: Does Welfare Dependency Beget Dependency?" Paper presented at Southern Economic Association meetings in Washington, D.C.

———. 1985. "Poverty Across Generations: Is Welfare Dependency A Pathology Passed on From One Generation to the Next?" Ann Arbor: Institute for Social Research.

Hofferth, Sandra L. 1985. "Updating Children's Life Course" *Journal of Marriage and the Family* 47:93–116.

Hoffman, Saul D., and J. Holmes. 1976. "Husbands, Wives and Divorce." In *Five Thousand American Families—Patterns of Economic Progress, Volume IV* edited by G. Duncan and J. Morgan. Ann Arbor: Institute for Social Research.

Hollister, Robinson G., Jr., Peter Kemper, and Rebecca Maynard. 1984. *The National Supported Work Demonstration.* Madison: University of Wisconsin Press.

Honig, Marjorie. 1974. "AFDC Income, Recipient Rates, and Family Dissolution." *Journal of Human Resources* 9:303–22.

Hopkins, Kevin R. 1986. "A Choice-Based Approach to Studying Welfare Dependency." Discussion Paper HI–3787P. Alexandria, Va.: Hudson Institute.

———. 1987. *Welfare Dependency: Behavior, Culture, and Public Policy.* Alexandria, Va.: Hudson Institute.

Hutchens, Robert M. 1979. "Welfare, Remarriage, and Marital Search." *American Economic Review* 69:369–79.

———. 1981. "Entry and Exit Transitions in a Government Transfer Program: The Case of Aid to Families with Dependent Children." *Journal of Human Resources* 16:217–37.

———. 1982. "Recipient Movement from Welfare Toward Economic Independence: A Literature Review." Paper prepared for the Council of State Planning Agencies and the U.S. Department of Health and Human Services.

———. 1984. "The Effects of OBRA on AFDC Recipients: A Review." Discussion Paper #764–84. Madison: Institute for Research on Poverty.

Hutchens, Robert M., George Jakubson, and Saul Schwartz. 1986. "Living Arrangements, Employment, Schooling, and Welfare Recipiency of Young Women." Prepared for the U.S. Department of Health and Human Services, Office of the Assistant Secretary for Planning and Evaluation under Grant No. 84–ASPE–095A.

Janowitz, Barbara S. 1976. "The Impact of AFDC on Illegitimate Birth Rates." *Journal of Marriage and the Family* 38:485–94.

Jones, Carol, Nancy Gordon, and Isabel Sawhill. 1976. *Child Support Payments in the United States.* Washington, D.C.: Urban Institute.

Kau, J. B., and C. F. Sirmans. 1976. "New, Repeat, and Return Migration: A Study of Migrant Types." *Southern Economic Journal* 43:1144–48.

Kaun, David E. 1970. "Negro Migration and Unemployment." *Journal of Human Resources* 5:191–207.

Kiefer, Nicholas M. 1979. "The Economic Benefits from Four Government

Training Programs." In *Research in Labor Economics: Evaluating Manpower Training Programs,* edited by F. E. Bloch, 159–86. Greenwich: JAI Press.

Lemann, Nicholas. 1986. "The Origins of the Underclass." *The Atlantic Monthly* (June–July).

Lerman, Robert I. 1986. "What Influences Young Men to Become Absent and Resident Fathers?" Prepared for the U.S. Department of Health and Human Services, Office of the Assistant Secretary for Planning and Evaluation under Grant No. 84–ASPE–097A.

Levy, Frank. 1979. "The Labor Supply of Female Household Heads, or AFDC Work Incentives Don't Work Too Well." *Journal of Human Resources* 14:76–97.

Lewis, Oscar. 1968. "The Culture of Poverty." In *Poverty in America,* edited by L. Ferman, J. Kornbluh, and A. Haber, rev. ed. Ann Arbor: University of Michigan Press.

Lyon, David W. 1977. "The Dynamics of Welfare Dependency: A Survey." Prepared for the Ford Foundation by the Welfare Policy Project, Institute of Policy Sciences and Public Affairs, Duke University.

Mallar, Charles, Stuart Kerachsky, Craig Thornton, and David Long. 1982. *Evaluation of the Economic Impact of the Jobs Corps Program: Third Follow-up Report.* Prepared for the U.S. Department of Labor, Employment and Training Administration, Office of Policy, Evaluation, and Research under Contract No. 23–34–76–06. Princeton: Mathematica Policy Research.

Masters, Stanley H., and Irwin Garfinkel. 1977. *Estimating the Labor Supply Effects of Income Maintenance Alternatives.* New York: Academic Press.

McLanahan, Sara. 1985. "Charles Murray and the Family." In *Losing Ground: A Critique.* Madison: Institute for Research on Poverty.

McLanahan, Sara, Irwin Garfinkel, and Dorothy Watson. 1986. "Family Structure, Poverty and the Underclass." Paper prepared for the Workshop on Contemporary Urban Conditions sponsored by the Committee on National Urban Policy of the National Research Council.

Mead, Lawrence M. 1986. *Beyond Entitlement: The Social Obligations of Citizenship.* New York: Free Press.

Miller, Walter B. 1968. "Focal Concerns of Lower Class Culture." In *Poverty in America,* edited by L. Ferman, J. Kornbluh, and A. Haber, rev. ed. Ann Arbor: University of Michigan Press.

Minarik, Joseph J., and Robert S. Goldfarb. 1976. "AFDC Income, Recipient Rates, and Family Dissolution: A Comment." *Journal of Human Resources* 11:243–50.

Moffitt, Robert. 1983. "An Economic Model of Welfare Stigma." *American Economic Review* 73:1023–35.

――――. 1986. "Work Incentives in the AFDC System: An Analysis of the 1981 Reforms." *American Economic Review* 79:219–23.

Moore, Kristin A. 1986. *Children of Teen Parents: Heterogeneity of Outcomes*. Final Report to the Center for Population Research, National Institute for Child Health and Human Development, U.S. Department of Health and Human Services under Grant No. HD–18427–02. Washington, D.C.: Child Trends, Inc.

――――. 1980. *Policy Determinants of Teenage Childbearing, Final Report*. Washington, D.C.: The Urban Institute.

Moore, Kristin A., and Martha Burt. 1982. *Private Crisis, Public Cost*. Washington, D.C.: Urban Institute Press.

Moore, Kristin A., and Steven B. Caldwell. 1977. "The Effect of Government Policies on Out-of-Wedlock Sex and Pregnancies." *Family Planning Perspectives* 9:164–69.

Moynihan, Daniel P. 1965. *The Negro Family: The Case for National Action*. Washington, D.C.: U.S. Department of Labor, Office of Policy Planning and Research.

Murray, Charles. 1984. *Losing Ground: American Social Policy, 1959–1980*. New York: Basic.

――――. 1985. "Have the Poor Been 'Losing Ground?'" *Political Science Quarterly* 100:427–445.

Murray, Charles, with Deborah Laren. 1986[a]. "According to Age: Longitudinal Profiles of AFDC Recipients and the Poor by Age Group." Prepared for the Working Seminar on the Family and American Welfare Policy.

Murray, Charles. 1986[b]. "No, Welfare Isn't Really the Problem." *The Public Interest* 84:3–11.

O'Neill, June A., Douglas A. Wolf, Laurie J. Bassi, and Michael T. Hannan. 1984. *An Analysis of Time on Welfare*. Final report to the U.S. Department of Health and Human Services. Washington, D.C.: The Urban Institute.

Pack, J. R. 1973. "Determinants of Migration to Central Cities." *Journal of Regional Science* 13:249–60.

Patterson, James T. 1981. *America's Struggle Against Poverty 1900–1980*. Cambridge: Harvard University Press.

Perry, Charles R., Bernard E. Anderson, Richard L. Rowan, Herbert R. Northrup, Peter P. Amons, Stephen A. Schneider, Michael E. Sparrough, Harriet Goldberg, Larry R. Matlack, and Cornelius A. McGuinness. 1975. *The Impact of Government Manpower Programs in General and on Minorities and Women*. Philadelphia: University of Pennsylvania Press.

Plant, Mark W. 1984. "An Empirical Analysis of Welfare Dependence." *American Economic Review* 74:673–84.

Plotnick, Robert. 1983. "Turnover in the AFDC Population: An Event History Analysis." *Journal of Human Resources* 18:65–81.

Rank, Mark R. 1985. "Exiting from Welfare: A Life-Table Analysis." *Social Service Review* 59:358–76.

Rees, Albert. 1986. "An Essay on Youth Joblessness." *Journal of Economic Literature* 24:613–28.

Rein, Martin, and Lee Rainwater. 1978. "Patterns of Welfare Use." *Social Service Review:* 511–34.

Rein, Mildred. 1982. *Dilemmas of Welfare Policy: Why Work Strategies Haven't Worked.* New York: Praeger.

Research Triangle Institute. 1983. *Final Report: Evaluation of the 1981 AFDC Amendments.* Prepared for the U.S. Department of Health and Human Services.

Robins, Philip K. 1986. "Child Support, Welfare Dependency, and Poverty." *American Economic Review* 76:768–88.

———. 1985. "A Comparison of Labor Supply Findings from the Four Negative Income Tax Experiments." *Journal of Human Resources* 20:567–82.

Robins, Philip K., and Katherine P. Dickinson. 1983. *Child Support and Welfare: An Analysis of the Issues.* Prepared for the U.S. Department of Health and Human Services, Social Security Administration. Grant No. 18–P00174. Menlo Park: SRI International.

Robins, Philip K., and Richard W. West. 1980. "Labor Supply Response Over Time." *Journal of Human Resources* 15:524–44.

Ross, Heather L., and Isabel V. Sawhill. 1975. *Time of Transition: The Growth of Families Headed by Women.* Washington, D.C.: The Urban Institute.

Rydell, C. Peter, Thelma Palmerio, Gerard Blais, and Dan Brown. 1974. *Welfare Caseload Dynamics in New York City.* Report R–1441–NYC. New York: Rand Institute.

Sawhill, Isabel V., Gerald E. Peabody, Carol A. Jones, and Steven B. Caldwell. 1975. "Income Transfers and Family Structure." Working Paper 979–03. Washington, D.C.: The Urban Institute.

Scheirer, Mary Ann. 1983. "Household Structure Among Welfare Families: Correlates and Consequences." *Journal of Marriage and the Family* 45:761–71.

Schiller, Bradley, with David Miller, William Cameron, Michael Temple, and Doris Hull. 1976. *The Impact of WIN II: A Longitudinal Evaluation of the Work Incentive Program (WIN).* Prepared by Pacific Consultants with Camil Associates and Ketron, Inc. for the U.S. Department of Labor, Employment and Training Administration, Office of Policy, Evaluation and Research under Contract No. 53–3–013–06.

Sommers, P. M., and D. B. Suits. 1973. "Analysis of Net Interstate Migration." *Souther Economic Journal* 40:193–201.

Sorenson, Annette, and Maurice McDonald. 1981. "Child Support: Who Pays

What to Whom?" Paper presented at the Wisconsin Workshop on Child Support, at the Institute for Research on Poverty, April 22–23.

Stromsdorfer, Ernst, Howard Bloom, Robert Boruch, Michael Borus, Judith Gueron, Alan Gustman, Peter Rossi, Fritz Scheuren, Marshall Smith, Frank Stafford. 1985. *Recommendations of the Job Training Longitudinal Survey Research Advisory Panel* [to Office of Strategic Planning and Policy Development, Employment and Training Administration, U.S. Department of Labor].

Taggart, Robert. 1981. *A Fisherman's Guide: An Assessment of Training and Remediation Strategies.* Kalamazoo: W. E. Upjohn Institute for Employment Research.

Temple, Michael G., Virginia K. Graham, and William L. Dreifke. 1986. *Final Report on the Design and Implementation of a Methodology for Estimating Cost Avoidance in the Child Support Enforcement Program.* Prepared for the U.S. Department of Health and Human Services, Office of Child Support Enforcement under Contract No. 600–83–0170. Wayne, Pa.: KETRON, Inc.

U.S. Department of Health and Human Services, National Center for Health Statistics. 1984a. "Advance Report of Final Natality Statistics." *Monthly Vital Statistics Report* 33 (September 28):6, Supplement.

———, Office of Child Support Enforcement. 1984b. *9th Annual Report to Congress for the Period Ending September 30, 1984.*

———, Office of the Assistant Secretary for Planning and Evaluation. 1983. *Final Report of the Seattle-Denver Income Maintenance Experiment.* Washington, D.C.: U.S. Government Printing.

U.S. General Accounting Office. 1982. *CETA Programs for Disadvantaged Adults—What Do We Know About Their Enrollees, Services, and Effectiveness?* Washington, D.C.: U.S. Government Printing Office.

U.S. Office of Policy Development, Interagency Low Income Opportunity Advisory Board. 1988. *Up From Dependency: A New National Public Assistance Strategy. Supplement 4: Research Studies and Bibliography.*

Vining, Daniel R., Jr. 1983. "Illegitimacy and Public Policy." *Population Development Review* 9:105–10.

Weinberg, Daniel H. 1985. "Filling the 'Poverty Gap': Multiple Transfer Program Participation." *Journal of Human Resources* 20:64–89.

———. 1987. "Filling the 'Poverty Gap,' 1979–1984." *Journal of Human Resources.* 22:563–73.

West, Richard W. 1980. "The Effects on the Labor Supply of Young Nonheads." *Journal of Human Resources* 15:574–90.

Westat, Inc. 1982. *Net Impact Report No. 1 (Supplement No. 1): The Impact of CETA on 1978 Earnings: Participants in Selected Program Activities Who Entered CETA During FY 1976.* Prepared for U.S. Department of

Labor, Employment and Training Administration under Contract No. 23–24–75–07. Rockville: Westat, Inc.

―――. 1984. *Summary of Net Impact Results.* Prepared for U.S. Department of Labor, Employment and Training Administration under Contract No. 23–24–75–07. Rockville: Westat, Inc.

Wilson, William. 1985. "Cycles of Deprivation and the Underclass Debate." *Social Service Review* 59:541–59.

Wilson, William, and Katherine Neckerman. 1986. "Poverty and Family Structure: The Widening Gap Between Evidence and Public Policy Issues." In *Fighting Poverty: What Works and What Doesn't,* edited by S. Danziger and D. Weinberg, 232–59. Cambridge: Harvard University Press.

Winegarden, C. R. 1974. "The Fertility of AFDC Women: An Econometric Analysis" *Journal of Economics and Business* 26:159–66.

Ziegler, J. A. 1976. "Interstate Black Migration: Comment and Further Evidence" *Economic Inquiry* 14:449–53.

6

Work Programs in Welfare and the Difference They Make

Gary Burtless

Work requirements for welfare recipients are appropriate under certain circumstances. . . . Receipt of full benefits should be conditioned on the fulfillment of family responsibilities and work requirements. (Meyer 1986, x)

. . . the poor in turn have obligations to their families and to society. Work requirements, child support, family planning, meeting educational commitments—all are advanced as obligations which society can ask of the poor if it is providing meaningful benefits. (Center for National Policy 1987, 15)

Adults, excluding the elderly and disabled, have the obligation to work or prepare themselves for work. Single parents also have an obligation to work or prepare for work at least part time if they are able, reflecting society's changed expectations. (Task Force on Poverty and Welfare 1986, 9)

Recipients of welfare should be required to take part in work (or time limited training programs) as a condition of obtaining benefits. (American Enterprise Institute 1987, 111)

The preceding quotes are all taken from recent reports on American welfare reform. Each quotation reflects the view of a recent commission or study group investigating public assistance. These commissions have included specialists and nonspecialists from across the political spectrum. Remarkably, each commission concluded that

163

able-bodied assistance recipients should be compelled to work or to participate in education and training programs in exchange for public assistance benefits.

This consensus on the desirability of work and training require-ments in welfare is new. If the same kind of work or training obliga-tion had been suggested as recently as five years ago, many advocates of public assistance programs would have been outraged.

People have changed their views on work and training obligations for a variety of reasons. Some have been impressed by new evidence about the effectiveness of these obligations. Others have been per-suaded by the argument that, in exchange for guaranteed minimum income benefits, able-bodied assistance recipients have a moral re-sponsibility to do something in their own behalf. Middle-class work-ing mothers (and the spouses and relatives of these mothers) are less impressed than they once were with the argument that single moth-ers must be excused from work in order to care for their children. Finally, some advocates of greater aid for the poor now realize that the public may be unwilling to finance higher benefits without some concrete demonstration that assistance recipients are actively seek-ing to improve their own condition.

One basic question will be addressed here: "What can we expect of work and training obligations imposed on public assistance recip-ients?" The basic expectation that most of us harbor for work/wel-fare programs is contained in the old adage, "Give a man a fish and you feed him for a day; teach a man to fish and you feed him for a lifetime." (In discussing public assistance, it would be more accurate to substitute "woman" for "man" and "her" for "him.") We can hope, but hardly expect, that teaching a welfare recipient to fish will feed her for a lifetime. Many assistance recipients have acute problems or shortcomings in addition to their need for training and work experi-ence.

Education, training, and work experience as basic strategies for reducing poverty are inherently risky. We can spend one hundred dollars, one thousand dollars, or even ten thousand dollars to provide education and work experience to an assistance recipient, but the investment does not *guarantee* that a well-paid job will materialize, nor does it assure us that the trainee will be able to perform a job if a good one is found. In contrast to investment in training or unpaid work experience, the same sum of money spent on cash benefits, food stamps, subsidized housing, or medical assistance will almost certainly help poor children and their parents. These kinds of "investments" do not represent a gamble. They will definitely improve the well-being of the intended beneficiary. The effect of education and unpaid work experience is inherently less certain.

In the remainder of this paper, I will briefly consider four points:

- The training and work experience programs we have developed for welfare recipients have often turned out to be reasonably effective in raising participants' earnings.
- These work and training programs are gradually assuming a new role in welfare. They are being used to screen out current and prospective beneficiaries rather than to develop new employment skills among participants.
- Whatever the basic goal of these programs, state and federal officials have been seeking program models that are cheap and reasonably effective, and they have recently found one—structured job search assistance.
- The hope of eliminating (or even significantly reducing) public assistance through education and work programs alone is an illusory one. Unless other costly steps are taken, these programs will have only a modest overall impact. While this does not imply that we should abandon current efforts to improve the work and training opportunities available to welfare recipients, it does suggest that these programs by themselves will not put a major dent in poverty.

The Earnings Impact. Training and certain work experience programs appear to work moderately well in raising earnings and reducing welfare dependency, especially among single mothers. Statisticians and economists have completed dozens of studies of the effectiveness of work training programs. Evaluations of the old CETA program consistently showed that occupational training and work experience programs were more effective in raising the employment and earnings of welfare mothers than in helping any other group (Barnow 1987, Taggart 1981). The experimental Supported Work program, conducted by the Manpower Demonstration Research Corporation (MDRC), showed the same result for an ambitious (and expensive) work experience program (MDRC 1980). MDRC's recent evaluations of various state work/welfare initiatives have yielded a similar set of findings. Not only are these programs more helpful for single mothers than for men on welfare, they also seem to be most effective for women who have not had recent work experience and who have been on the welfare rolls for one or more years (Friedlander and Long 1987).

The work/welfare experiments provide evidence that is most directly relevant to recent reform efforts. These experiments were instituted under federal legislation passed in 1981 that encouraged states to enforce a work related obligation on a higher percentage of AFDC recipients than had previously participated in the Work Incentive (WIN) program. The response of individual state governments to this legislation has been described in recent reports by the General Accounting Office (1987) and Congressional Budget Office (1987). MDRC, in cooperation with eleven states instituting new work/welfare programs, conducted thorough assessments of several of the more innovative plans. In eight of the states, MDRC persuaded program administrators to measure the effectiveness of their programs using random assignment of eligible AFDC recipients to treatment and control groups. This analytical method yields estimates of short-run program impact that are highly reliable.

Six of the best evaluations were conducted in Arkansas, Illinois, Maryland, Virginia, West Virginia, and San Diego, California.[1] All six experiments involved enrollees from the AFDC program, and three also included enrollees from the AFDC-Unemployment Parent program, which provides cash assistance to two-parent families. Five of the six experiments tested a program of unpaid community work experience, commonly known as "workfare." In four of these five programs assignment to an unpaid workfare job only occurred after the AFDC recipient had participated in several weeks of supervised or unsupervised job search effort. If employment was found during this period of job search, the welfare client was not assigned to a workfare position.

In theory, participants in workfare were required to work a specified number of hours each month, usually computed as the monthly welfare grant divided by the state or federal minimum wage rate. The work assignment could last up to thirteen weeks or, in one of the experiments, indefinitely. However, workfare participation was not as common as these rules imply. Among AFDC recipients enrolled in the Arkansas program, only 3 percent participated in a workfare job. Approximately 7 percent participated in Illinois; 10 percent in Virginia; and 20 percent in San Diego.

In some experiments a moderately high percentage of recipients who failed to comply with the program rules were penalized. For example, in the Illinois job-search experiment about 15 percent of treatment-group members were sanctioned for noncompliance with the rules. A sanctioned family could lose the portion of the monthly welfare grant due to the adult member. Outside of Illinois a much smaller percentage of participants was sanctioned. There was also a wide range across the six states in the cost of the tested programs. The mandatory job-search program in Illinois was relatively cheap, costing $125 to $140 per enrollee, while the work and training program in Baltimore was relatively costly, with about $1,000 spent on an average person served.

The largest short-run impact on AFDC recipients' earnings was found in the San Diego program that combined job-search assistance with a workfare obligation for those who could not find employment during job search. Over the second through the sixth calendar quarters following participants' enrollment in the program, the San Diego treatment raised enrollees' earnings by about one-quarter (or $560 per year) above the level observed in the control group, which did not participate in the innovative plan. In the Arkansas, Maryland, and Virginia experiments earnings gains were less than half as large, while there was little or no earnings impact in the Illinois and West Virginia programs.

MDRC also measured the welfare savings that resulted from the tested programs. The largest savings were found in San Diego, where AFDC benefits fell by about 8 percent, or two hundred dollars a year. Moderate savings were detected in Arkansas and Virginia, while only slight savings—3 percent or less—were found in Illinois, Maryland, and West Virginia. The programs were generally cost effective, in the sense that modest outlays on job search assistance or workfare resulted in either moderate earnings gains or slight-to-moderate welfare savings.

The recent experiments suggest that work and training programs can be successful in raising the employability of the able-bodied poor and can even raise participants' earnings by enough to offset the direct and indirect costs of the programs. This is good news for advocates of welfare reform who believe that a work or training obligation in public assistance will improve the self-sufficiency of the able-bodied poor. The bad news is that the good news is not good enough. While work and training programs for welfare recipients can be cost effective, they are not effective enough by themselves to substantially reduce dependency among the poor. The longer-term impact of the programs on participants is modest.

MDRC has found that about one year after women enrolled in the work/welfare demonstrations the earnings of participants averaged only about $30 per month more than the earnings in a randomly selected group of nonparticipants. The earnings gain resulted in a 2 to 4 percent reduction in welfare dependency rates on average and a somewhat larger percentage reduction in welfare outlays (Friedlander and Long 1987, v-viii). This impact is obviously quite modest. Some participants were probably helped a great deal by the programs, but most were helped only a little or not at all.

This evidence is intensely disappointing to social reformers who hope to change the lives of the poor through work and training programs. Some lives are changed; most are not. From a cold accounting perspective, the programs are nonetheless worthwhile. Their benefits are substantial compared to their modest costs. The programs work, but they do not work miracles.

A Discipline Device. If participation in work or training programs is mandatory for adults who receive welfare, the programs can serve a different kind of function. Mandatory participation provides a powerful signal that work and self-sufficiency are *expected* of welfare recipients. If the work and training requirement is effectively enforced, the programs provide a way to remove from the rolls welfare recipients who do not actively attempt to improve their own lives.

Many people unfamiliar with welfare think that this goal can be attained at low cost and with little effort. However, it can be expensive and administratively burdensome to provide a public employment or training opportunity for *every* adult recipient who is physically able to work. The provision of child care and transportation services to single mothers is far from cheap. Creating paid or unpaid public jobs requires real resources. The jobs must be found and then supervised. Welfare caseworkers must closely track recipients who are expected to work and then enforce the work and training requirement. I am not aware of any work/welfare program that has successfully imposed a work obligation on a high percentage of welfare mothers who are physically capable of working. The participation rates mentioned above in the recent workfare experiments are suggestive. The cost of imposing a work or training obligation on every single mother is just too high.

When work and training programs are used as a disciplinary mechanism in public assistance they must be judged by somewhat different criteria than the ones discussed earlier. Even if the programs do not raise the unsubsidized employment and earnings of participants, they may still be judged successful if they deter people from applying for public assistance or if they remove noncomplying participants from the rolls. A "successful" program may actually *raise* the incidence of poverty by reducing outlays on public assistance while failing to increase the wage earnings of the poor.

Three of the six work/welfare experiments mentioned above—those in Arkansas, Illinois, and West Virginia—were not very expensive. They each cost less than three hundred dollars per AFDC recipient served. But even these inexpensive programs were moderately successful in imposing a work-related obligation on more clients than had faced such obligations in the past. Even though two of these inexpensive programs—the ones in Illinois and West Virginia—failed to raise participants' earnings, all three programs achieved at least small reductions in welfare benefits. These welfare savings probably occurred because the perceived cost of receiving benefits had been raised.

Critics of workfare contend that this type of "success" is inadmissible in a program whose main function must be to improve the well-being of poor children and their families. But that kind of criticism is receding. As noted above, there is growing evidence that many of the programs may actually raise the earnings of single mothers. MDRC has even obtained evidence that the programs are acceptable (and perhaps desired) among welfare recipients themselves (e.g., see Friedlander et al. 1986). Taken as a whole, the MDRC studies of work/welfare programs suggest that mandatory work and training requirements may raise the incomes of single-parent welfare families, but reduce the incomes of two-parent families receiving AFDC-UP.

A Cheap Work/Welfare Program. Whether they wish to raise the earnings of the poor or simply reduce dependency on public assistance, state and local officials are seeking cheap and administratively feasible work/training programs. Comprehensive occupational training and workfare programs are expensive. The welfare department must first seek out training and work opportunities, then it must ensure that all eligible recipients are placed in these positions. Over the last seven or eight years, departments around the country have discovered a feasible and apparently effective new approach to training—"job-search assistance."

Job-search programs combine instruction in job-finding techniques with a formal, intensive, and systematic program of job seeking. These programs typically require that participants spend several hours per day engaged in search related activities (preparation of resumes, telephoning prospective employers, and pounding the pavement to find job leads). The idea is not to teach someone how to fish, but to teach him or her to find an existing job in the fishing industry. By assumption, the job seeker is already capable of performing some jobs, though the jobs may be menial ones (for example, lugging dead fish from the dock to the back of a truck). In any event, no new *occupational* training is offered. The virtue of job-search programs, from an administrative point of view, is that the obligation to look for work can be enforced quite easily and inexpensively. Welfare recipients may not be required to participate in these programs full time, of course. But they would be required to participate periodically, say, twice each year for a period of six to eight weeks.

The work/welfare experiments show just how inexpensive job-search programs can be. The most elaborate and costly job-search program was the one conducted in San Diego, which required outlays of about $540 to $610 per person enrolled in the experimental treatment. Job seekers in San Diego were given extensive help in looking for jobs and were closely monitored in their search for employment. By contrast, the program in Illinois was only one-quarter the cost of the one in San Diego, and it provided almost no actual assistance to job seekers. Most of the outlays in the Illinois program were devoted to ensuring that job seekers contacted a minimum number of potential employers each month and were sanctioned if they failed to bring in periodic proof of these employer contacts.

The experience in these demonstrations suggests that a work related obligation can be imposed at little cost or at high cost, depending on the level of training or support services offered. A program need not require much resources if it only obligates AFDC recipients to attend job-search orientation meetings and then to prove they have in fact engaged in some search efforts. But it can be far more expensive to provide the training and support services to ensure that these search efforts pay off in terms of better job finding.

As noted above, many job-search programs also turn out to be reasonably successful in getting participants into jobs. Arguably, the programs are almost as effective in raising participant earnings as more ambitious (and expensive) training or work experience programs. (In fact, several of the work/welfare demonstrations examined by MDRC relied primarily on providing job-search assistance to welfare recipients. The job-search assistance programs seemed to be about as effective as other approaches tested.) The job-search approach can raise participant earnings in one of two ways. It is conceivable that some participants are genuinely ignorant about the best method to search for a job, and the program helps them by providing decent instruction. Alternatively, the program might simply force participants to devote more time to searching for work. By spending more time and effort, participants find a job earlier than they otherwise would.

This limited degree of success would probably not satisfy most advocates of work and training programs for the poor. Many of the jobs that welfare recipients find are low-wage, dead-end jobs that provide no way out of poverty, even if the jobs end up providing full-time, year-round employment. Before rejecting job-search assistance programs out of hand, however, we should remember that nearly *all* successful work and training programs, including those that are far more expensive, succeed for the same reason. They increase the time that participants spend in jobs, but they have little effect on the types of jobs that participants find. The gain in employment is worthwhile and should not be lightly dismissed. But the gain is not large enough to remove most dependent families permanently from poverty.

Modest Expectations. The current enthusiasm for work/training programs in welfare is based partly on an illusion. Many voters and politicians believe that by providing training or unpaid work experience to poor breadwinners while changing no other aspect of our labor market, we can eventually eliminate the jobs that are associated with poverty incomes. The facts do not support this pleasant illusion. Not only does our labor market contain low productivity *people* (whose productivity we can plausibly expect to raise), it also contains millions of low productivity, poorly paid *jobs*. As long as those jobs are available some people will hold them. If these people happen to have dependent children, their families will probably be

171

poor. The wages from a full-time, year-round poorly paid job are often too low to bring larger families above the poverty threshold.

In deciding what kind of work or training program should be offered to welfare recipients, we should also bear in mind the unavoidable clash of interest between taxpayers on one hand, and AFDC beneficiaries on the other. Elaborate work and training programs, such as Supported Work or CETA public service jobs programs, can substantially raise the earnings of the welfare recipients who participate in them. But these programs can cost ten thousand dollars or more per participant served, and they may not represent bargains to taxpayers who are primarily interested in reducing net government outlays on the poor. Even if the programs eventually raise the earnings of participants by much more than ten thousand dollars, there is little assurance that the associated reduction in welfare benefits will offset the direct cost of the work or training program.[2] Though the well-being of the poor may be improved by the program, taxpayers are left holding the bill for costly work or training that has not achieved equivalent savings in welfare outlays.

In addition, if receipt of welfare is required in order to participate in a successful program, many people who would otherwise avoid public assistance may apply for welfare in order to receive the training. A successful work or training program may thus make welfare more attractive and lead to higher case rolls, at least in the short run. The training program could raise public dependency (or fail to reduce dependency) even as it increased participants' earnings.

As noted above, recent work/welfare experiments have demonstrated that certain types of programs can be attractive to taxpayers since added outlays on work or training result in welfare savings that are even larger. Often, however, these programs are cost effective from the taxpayer's standpoint because they make welfare recipients worse off; that is they reduce welfare benefits without simultaneously raising wage earnings. Since the obligations associated with work or training programs frequently make participation in public assistance more burdensome, families leave the rolls faster than they would in the absence of the program. The job-search program in Illinois, for example, costs little to administer and failed to raise participant earnings. But it did achieve welfare savings by encouraging recipients to cut short their stay on public assistance.

Clearly, if policy makers attempt to retain all the benefits of a work or training program for taxpayers rather than for welfare recipients, they must coerce program participation among the recipient population; for example, they must make public assistance payments contingent upon participation in the work program. While this type of participation requirement can make the program relatively cheap to administer if zealously enforced, it will place an extra burden on recipients and could reduce their participation in public assistance and depress their net incomes. Dependency would decline and taxpayers would be better off, but the well-being of the poor could be harmed.

If we sincerely wish to reduce poverty among families with children we will have to do much more than impose work and training obligations on poor breadwinners who receive welfare. Work and training requirements can apparently yield small but meaningful benefits to the poor, but such obligations will not yield enough benefits to reduce child poverty significantly or to satisfy the high expectations of most taxpayers. To eliminate or substantially reduce poverty among able-bodied adults we must either create a new mechanism for sorting people into jobs or break the present link between family income and productivity in a job. One way to achieve the former is to assure that adults with dependents are favored in hiring for well-paid jobs. A way to achieve the latter is to raise public assistance payments for the working poor or to subsidize the wages of poor breadwinners who have child dependents. Training and work experience programs, by themselves, will do little to improve the income prospects of poor children or their parents.

I will close by noting a subtle and gradual shift in policymakers' attitudes toward work and training programs in welfare. The programs were formerly seen as a ladder out of poverty and dependency. Research and evaluation efforts were focused on designing ladders to be as effective as possible in raising people from different target groups.

But the analogy of a ladder no longer applies. The ladder has turned into a cudgel. Even if work and training programs do not offer a way out of poverty, mandatory participation in such programs can be used as a club to move assistance recipients off the welfare rolls. The idea is to impose obligations on recipients either to emphasize society's expectation that welfare recipients have an obligation to become self-sufficient or to make welfare receipt as unpleasant as possible. The goal of these programs has shifted from reducing poverty to reducing dependency. I see a subtle, but very important, distinction between those two goals.

NOTES

1. Good summaries of these experiments can be found in CBO (1987) and in the individual evaluation reports prepared by MDRC. I have largely relied on these two sources for basic information about the experiments.

2. This is because some of the earnings gains resulting from the program are enjoyed by welfare recipients who would have escaped the rolls even without any special government help. It is also because a ten thousand dollar gain in gross earnings on the part of a typical welfare recipient almost never causes welfare grants to fall by the full ten thousand dollars. Recipients themselves get to keep some of the gain.

BIBLIOGRAPHY

American Enterprise Institute. 1987. *A Community of Self-Reliance: The New Consensus on Family and Welfare.* Milwaukee: Marquette University Press.

Barnow, Burt S. 1987. "The Impact of CETA Programs on Earnings: A Review of the Literature." *Journal of Human Resources* 22:157–93.

Center for National Policy. 1987. *Work and Welfare: The Case for New Directions in National Policy.* Washington, D.C.: Center for National Policy.

Congressional Budget Office. 1987. *Work-Related Programs for Welfare Recipients.* Washington, D.C.: U.S. Congressional Budget Office.

Friedlander, Daniel, Marjorie Erickson, Gayle Hamilton, and Virginia Knox. 1986. *Final Report on the [West Virginia] Community Work Experience Demonstrations.* New York: Manpower Demonstration Research Corporation.

Friedlander, Daniel, and David Long. 1987. *A Study of Performance and Measures and Subgroup Impacts in Three Welfare Employment Programs.* New York: Manpower Demonstration Research Corporation.

General Accounting Office. 1987. *Work and Welfare: Current AFDC Work Programs and Implications for Federal Policy.* Washington, D.C.: U.S. Government Printing Office.

Manpower Demonstration Research Corporation (MDRC). 1980. *Summary and Findings of the National Supported Work Demonstration.* Cambridge: Ballinger.

Meyer, Jack A., ed. 1986. *Ladders out of Poverty: A Report of the Project on the Welfare of Families*. Washington, D.C.: American Horizons Foundation.

Taggart, Robert S. 1981. *A Fisherman's Guide: An Assessment of Training and Remediation Strategies*. Kalamazoo: W. E. Upjohn Institute.

Task Force on Poverty and Welfare (New York State). 1986. *A New Social Contract: Rethinking the Nature and Purpose of Public Welfare*. Albany: State of New York Executive Chamber.

III
Policy Positions

7

Up From Dependency: The President's National Welfare Strategy

John A. Daeley

In his 1986 State of the Union Address, President Reagan called for an evaluation of all programs that meet the financial, educational, social, and safety concerns of poor families and a new strategy to promote "real and lasting emancipation" from welfare. In response to the president's charge, the White House Domestic Policy Council's Low-Income Opportunity Working Group made an exhaustive study of welfare and poverty. This report, *Up From Dependency* (U.S. Executive Office of the President 1986), was based on discussions with Americans from all walks of life, including current and former welfare recipients, those who deliver public assistance, the nation's governors, government officials, scholars, and many others. The report assesses the welfare system and its successes and failures, describes the frustrations felt by America's poor, and proposes a basic change in public assistance policy, which has now been incorporated into legislation that has been submitted to the Congress.

OVERVIEW

America's public assistance system is composed of fifty-nine major federal welfare programs on which federal and state governments spent more than $132 billion in fiscal year 1985. These fifty-nine programs comprise a centralized welfare system that requires over six thousand pages of federal law and regulation. It is overseen by a score of congressional committees and managed by eight major federal departments through numerous agencies in the fifty states and territories, through hundreds of thousands of welfare workers. The Census Bureau estimates that more than fifty-two million Americans benefit from some welfare program during the course of a year (U.S. Executive Office of the President 1986, 10).

One of the most obvious problems with the welfare system is that this multitude of programs with its excessively complex regulations, diverse eligibility requirements, and varying benefit levels often leads to confusion and demoralization for poor families seeking assistance. The system is so complex that it can be impossible to figure out how to get the help that is needed. Families may have to go from office to office to apply for assistance from several programs. Even when programs are administered in one location, a family will often need to see different eligibility workers for different programs. Recipients also say that the rules and reporting demands often strip them of dignity and stigmatize them as lazy and dishonest.

Not only is the complexity of the system frustrating for recipients, but the trend toward noncash benefits has diminished their personal choice and self-responsibility. Welfare recipients can spend cash to meet their needs as they see them, but with noncash benefits they become more dependent on the decisions of others.

One justification for the many and complex rules of the welfare system is that they ensure that welfare goes only to the most needy. Upon inspection, however, the complexity of the system often undermines this goal. In fact, current welfare spending is more than double the "poverty gap," or the amount it would take to lift all Americans above the official poverty level. This can happen when the rules do not specifically target those in need and when noncash benefits and the income of other family or household members are ignored in determining eligibility and benefits. Because individual needs and capabilities differ, public assistance benefits and opportunities should not be tied to a federally determined standard. Whenever possible precision must be applied to determine individual needs, and benefits must be tailored accordingly.

The welfare system also creates incentives that undermine the attractiveness of work to welfare recipients. Many welfare recipients can receive more on welfare than they can earn by working. There is no clear evidence on how welfare benefits should be structured to produce greater work effort. For example, altering the benefit reduction rate when earnings increase may promote work effort for some welfare recipients, but others may reduce their work effort to get more welfare and leisure time (SRI International 1983).

Welfare's impact on poverty cannot be separated from its impact on families. Among the welfare poor today, families as we usually think of them often are not being formed. Since 1960 the percentage of babies born to unmarried mothers has more than tripled, and too often these babies are being born to mothers and fathers who are themselves only children (U.S. Bureau of the Census 1984, 70).

Lastly, the traditional responsibility of the local community to aid those of its members who are in need of assistance has become undermined by the tendency to impose solutions constructed in Washington. In bypassing the community, federal welfare ignores local resources that could help support individuals and families as they attempt to escape dependency. The welfare system cares mainly that benefits and services are delivered and rules obeyed. The modern welfare state does not involve citizens actively in their community's efforts to resolve its local problems or promote the integration of state, local, and voluntary resources.

TIME FOR CHANGE

There is now general and, apparently, bipartisan agreement that the welfare system needs overhaul. While there is much consensus on the direction of reform, there is disagreement on many issues. Attempting to work them out on the national level could doom any meaningful welfare reform, as it has several times in the past. While we have some research on work requirements, when it comes to sweeping changes to restructure the whole welfare system, we have to admit that current research and demonstration results do not provide a basis for knowing what will work and what won't on a system-wide basis. On this point, it is useful to remember past experiences with major "welfare reforms." Over a period of years both Republican and Democratic Administrations introduced varieties of welfare reform proposals based upon the negative income tax. Income Maintenance Experiments (the largest in Seattle and Denver) led to results that were contrary to initial expectations. As a result, even some of the strong supporters of those welfare proposals now agree that it was best that they were not adopted into national law.

We need further experimentation supported by sound evaluation before we embark on national system-wide welfare reform.

As we examine the potential for reform, we must be cautious in designing changes and firm in our commitment to make them. Millions of people depend on welfare for sustenance; untested changes in national rules and benefits can easily make matters worse. Our changes must be real improvements; they must encourage real self-reliance among individuals and families, and they must enable communities to strengthen themselves. There will be many proposals for sweeping restructuring of our complex public assistance system. Rebuilding the welfare system requires new conceptualization, bold innovation, and responsiveness to local conditions. Before we make changes to the system from the top down, we should seek evidence from the bottom up about what works in real communities and states.

There are several reasons for conducting many different demonstrations simultaneously. It is not obvious that what works in one part of the country would be as effective elsewhere. Similarly, because the welfare population is heterogeneous the needs of population subgroups will differ. The proposed demonstrations would free states to tailor assistance to the specific needs of these groups and the localities in which they live, while at the same time meeting broad, national goals for welfare. Also, because there is little agreement on the best approach, operating several demonstrations permits many competing innovative ideas, and allows us to discover how best to promote self-sufficiency and economic independence. Federal legislation enacted since 1981 has given states new tools and increased latitude; this allows them to undertake employment and training programs designed to increase the self-sufficiency of welfare recipients. Numerous state governments have taken advantage of these laws to implement reforms that put a premium on reducing dependency and instilling a sense of pride and accomplishment among welfare recipients. Several rigorous evaluations have been done of the innovative reforms in AFDC, and we have learned valuable lessons from them: AFDC recipients want to work, and employment and training programs can give them the skills and experience they need to work. Given the heartening results of the states' innovations in AFDC, there is every reason to believe that our proposal will lead to significant reforms in a broad range of programs.

Despite the negative impact of the federal welfare system, there are hundreds of community self-help initiatives around the country. Any successful welfare reform effort must acknowledge the importance of creating solutions that can be adapted to the unique character of fifty states and thousands of diverse communities.

NEW GOALS

The president's proposal offers a chance to strengthen the existing system by creating an opportunity for testing new and better ways of helping the poor. *Up From Dependency* outlines ten specific goals to guide states, local governments, community organizations, and individuals in building a better welfare system through innovative experimentation. These goals are:

1. Insure that public assistance is an adequate supplement to other resources in meeting essential needs.
2. Focus public assistance resources on reducing future dependency on public assistance.
3. Individualize determinations of need for public assistance, and make such determinations, to the extent possible, through local decisions.
4. Provide public assistance only to those in need and only to the extent of that need.
5. Make work more rewarding than welfare.
6. Require that those who are able to work do so for their public assistance benefits.
7. Encourage the formation of economically self-reliant families.
8. Require public assistance recipients to take greater responsibility for managing their resources, and encourage community based administration of public assistance.
9. Create opportunities for self-reliance through education and enterprise.
10. Reduce the future cost of public assistance by reducing the need for it.

PROPOSED LEGISLATION

The Low-Income Opportunity Improvement Act of 1987, which the president transmitted to Congress on February 26, 1987 and which has been introduced as S. 610, creates a process by which we can reach these policy goals. The report to the president emphasizes that welfare is a *system* of programs. The president's legislative proposal of my department (Health and Human Services) treats public assistance as a system, too. The bill provides broad waiver authority, which makes state sponsored, community based demonstrations of alternative welfare programs possible. Currently, a few programs have limited waiver authority to test alternative ways to meet their objectives. Nevertheless, waiver authority that cuts across program lines to allow for system-wide demonstration efforts does not exist. The administration is proposing to allow states to incorporate into a demonstration the funding they otherwise would receive from any program that alleviates poverty. In addition, the program must currently have a means-test, in law or practice (that is, income and resources must be under a certain level); or the funds must be distributed to grantees by a method which includes the size of the low-income population. This covers a wide range of programs.

There has been considerable alarm expressed about which programs might be included. The administration thinks that putting the *criteria* in the statute, instead of a list of programs, will clarify that we are talking about programs intended to help low-income people. The administration does not expect that any state will want to include in its demonstration all the programs currently fitting these criteria. In fact, there probably are some means-tested programs that no state would want to include. All the same, it is important to recognize the systematic nature of welfare. Under the bill, the administration will look closely at a state demonstration that proposes to include any program fitting the general criteria.

The filing for demonstration waiver authority must make clear exactly what the state intends to do: *specifically, programs to be included, who participates, principles for eligibility and benefit determination, form and amount of benefits, and innovative ways in which the demonstration is expected to meet the needs of the low-income population and also reduce dependency.* Involvement of communities in supporting the efforts of individuals and families to become self-sufficient must be described. With other specifics of the scope of the demonstration, the filing *must* describe the evaluation efforts the state plans to undertake so that at the end of the demonstration we will have generally acceptable evidence as to whether the demonstration succeeded in its objectives.

One thing heard often in discussions with the governors is that the states need a single place from which to get federal approval for their welfare reform ideas. To accommodate these wishes, the administration proposes that state filings be submitted to an Interagency Low-Income Opportunity Board. The board will be made up of representatives of the departments with responsibility for the major public assistance programs. The board's chairman will be appointed by the president. The Interagency Low-Income Opportunity Board is intended to speak with one voice to the states, while reflecting the various voices of the executive agencies responsible for public assistance programs. If the board's chairman determines that a filing meets programmatic and budgetary requirements; that the civil rights of individuals and families, under all applicable laws, will be protected; and that the proposed demonstration is structured to permit a sound evaluation of its results; the filing will be certified.

The agencies with responsibility for programs included in the demonstration will estimate the amount of funds the demonstration site would have received during its first year under the laws then in effect. That amount will be payable to the state for expenditures under the demonstration. Since many of these demonstrations will not be state wide, the federal agencies will have to review and use information supplied by the states to determine just what the funding for the included programs would have been in the communities included in the demonstrations. Each year's funding will be calculated based upon the laws in effect for the programs included. This means that if the allocations or funding levels for national programs change, the demonstrations will be affected in the same manner. Drafters of the bill think that this method of funding will show the continued support of the administration for the demonstrations.

The administration thinks that commitment to the demonstrations is also evident in the provision that permits states to keep any funds they save by making gains in reducing dependency. The bill would permit a state to put these savings to any use that primarily benefits the low-income people of the demonstration area.

The administration has confidence that both federal and state welfare program resources could be used with considerably *more* effectiveness if the law gave governors the flexibility to design demonstration programs according to the needs and realities of their states and communities. Governor Sununu of New Hampshire made clear in his remarks before the Committee on Ways and Means that, if the choice were more dollars with federal strings or more flexibility to use the dollars he was getting now, he would want the flexibility. This administration believes that many governors share that view. As documented in *Up From Dependency,* there is sufficient federal and state funding now, in dozens of programs, to both reduce dependency and meet the needs of those who cannot provide for themselves. All program managers at all levels need to make the best possible use of the available resources.

The bill also provides for sound evaluation of the demonstrations. This is a hard lesson we learned with the CETA and WIN programs. Like the negative income tax proponents, every advocate of a program is sure that it will succeed. Work and training programs, however, have not always had the kind of evaluations which stand up to scientific scrutiny. Evaluation can provide the means to contemplate policy changes. For example, today it is hard to find someone who disagrees with the idea that AFDC recipients should participate in work activities. One important reason for the consensus is that there have been a series of well-designed evaluations of the impact and cost effectiveness of these work activities. They work and we can show it. Consequently this bill provides for evaluations of the demonstration programs, so that the results will be carefully measured.

The governor in the state undertaking a demonstration must submit a final report to the board assessing the demonstration's achievements and shortcomings, including recommendations regarding the demonstration's national significance. The board's chairman must submit an annual report to Congress regarding the progress of the demonstrations.

SUMMARY

The Low-Income Opportunity Improvement Act of 1987 provides a reasonable course for reform of the *system* of welfare programs. Waiver authority will be broad enough to allow a community to improve the way the system works, not just this program or that program. Care will be taken that low-income people's rights are protected and that their needs are met. We will learn considerably more about what works to reduce dependency because we will have sound evaluations of demonstrations, drawing from the bottom up, on the experience and innovations of communities and states.

Most important, state and community efforts to better target welfare resources, eliminate or reduce work disincentives, increase individual choice, and strengthen families will result in new and exciting opportunities for low-income individuals and families to increase their social and economic self-sufficiency.

In January 1987, President Reagan put it this way in his remarks on the state of the union, "We will never abandon those who, through no fault of their own, must have help. But let us work to see how many can be freed from the dependency of welfare and made self-supporting."

NOTES

Since the presentation of this paper, a number of different plans have been introduced into the congressional debate surrounding welfare reform. As is sometimes the case, the proposal now supported by the administration has had the benefit of congressional interest and evaluation and contains some variation from proposals described in this presentation.

A number of features are common to both this proposition and the "Republican Welfare Reform Bill" introduced by the Honorable Hank Brown (R-CO). Among these are a comprehensive employment and training program, and more flexibility for states in program design and administration; states may now operate demonstration programs involving up to twenty-two separate welfare programs.

BIBLIOGRAPHY

U.S. Bureau of the Census. 1984. *Statistical Abstract of the United States.* 104th ed. Washington, D.C.: U.S. Government Printing Office.

U.S. Executive Office of the President (EOP). 1986. *Up From Dependency: A New National Public Assistance Strategy.* Washington, D.C.: Office of Policy Development

SRI International. 1983. *Seattle/Denver Income Maintenance Experiment.* Washington, D.C.: U.S. Government Printing Office.

8

Welfare Reform: Prospects and Challenges

A. Sidney Johnson, III

With the establishment of a greatly expanded job development program to reach everyone who wants to and can work, we should also move to revamp our archaic and unworkable welfare system. We should do away with the various qualifying categories and make need the only requirement for assistance. Building in incentives against idleness, we should establish minimum national assistance standards, with appropriate adjustments in particular states and areas on the basis of the local cost of living; and the federal government should take over the principal responsibility for the cost.

Expanded jobs program, revamping the welfare system, need as the only requirement for assistance; incentives to work; minimum assistance standards; a major federal role. The above paragraph could well be a summary of H.R. 1720, the welfare reform legislation under consideration in the United States Congress in the summer of 1988. It could be but it is not. The paragraph was written in 1967. Twenty-one years ago. It appears near the end of a book called *Alarms and Hopes* (Harris 1967), a book assessing the problems of poverty and racism in the 1960s, written by then-senator Fred Harris (D-Okla.).

Clearly some have been addressing poverty and the need for welfare reform far longer than others. And those, including the author, who work with Congress in 1988 appreciate the groundwork laid by Senator Harris and others in past years, past decades.

In 1988 there is a historic opportunity in the making on the issue of welfare reform. No one attempting to address the issue a year or so ago would have dreamt that major, comprehensive welfare reform might actually happen in 1988. The issue has moved farther, more quickly, than could have been imagined.

Serious legislation is pending before Congress as this volume goes to press. The House Ways and Means Committee reported a bill, the Family Welfare Reform Act, H.R. 1720, and it gained House approval in December 1987. In June 1988, by an overwhelming margin, the Senate passed a more limited bill, the Family Security Act, S. 1511, introduced by Senator Daniel Patrick Moynihan (D-N.Y.).

THE EMERGING CONSENSUS

The historic opportunity exists in part because of a convergence of views. A consensus has developed gradually over recent years, among liberals and conservatives, Republicans and Democrats. That consensus has to do not only with agreement on the *need* for welfare reform, but also on some of the specific policies that must be put in place to make such reform a reality.

A starting point in describing that consensus is the work done by the American Public Welfare Association. Three years ago the state human service commissioners concluded that they had a responsibility, as individuals and as a group, to respond to the worsening situation of children living in poverty. They initiated a policy development project entitled, "Investing in Poor Families and Their Children: A Matter of Commitment." The project's first report dealt with income security, education and employment, and teenage pregnancy; it was issued in November 1986. That report, *One Child in Four,* (APWA 1986), contains their recommendations for comprehensive welfare reform.

Shortly after the APWA steering committee held its first meeting in January 1986, President Reagan called for a White House study of low-income assistance programs. That announcement, contained in his February 4, 1986 State of the Union message, helped focus public attention on the issue of poverty and the need for welfare reform.

Former Arizona Governor Bruce Babbitt and former HEW Secretary Arthur Flemming convened a panel of political moderates, academics, and former government officials under the title, "The Project on the Welfare of Families." Governor Babbitt said at the time that it would be a major alternative voice to the White House welfare reform. The Babbitt group's report, *Ladders Out of Poverty,* (Babbitt and Flemming 1986), was published in December 1986.

New York Governor Mario Cuomo convened his Task Force on Poverty and Welfare. The American Enterprise Institute, a conservative Washington, D.C., think-tank, called a group of scholars and former government officials together to draft recommendations for welfare reform. In February 1986 the National Governors' Association adopted a welfare reform policy (NGA 1987) closely resembling the APWA report and strongly emphasizing education, training, and jobs for welfare recipients.

While these reports have not been carbon copies of each other, there are some major threads running through nearly all of them.

The Contract. One thread of the emerging consensus has to do with the idea of reciprocal obligations between individuals and society. The APWA report, for example, calls for "contracts" between a poor family and the human service agency, setting out what is expected of each—the work or training that the client will undertake, for example, and the services such as child care and transportation that will be provided by the agency. The report to Governor Cuomo was actually titled "Toward a New Social Contract," embodying the notion that poor families and the government have obligations to each other.

Work in Place of Welfare. The second thread in this consensus follows directly from the idea of reciprocal obligations. It has to do with the area of work and training for work. There is a consensus that sees work as the alternative to welfare, and for the most part sees government as the entity responsible for instituting training and education programs that can make employability a reality for poor parents.

Historically, there has been a strong sense in the United States that anyone who *could* be self-sufficient *should* be self-sufficient—individuals should earn their own way and be responsible for the maintenance of their family. We *value* self-sufficiency. We value the ability of individuals to take care of themselves and their families. What has changed, somewhat, in recent years has been the notion of just who should work, and how and why the government should be part of ensuring that those who can work, do work.

Obviously, when aid to families with dependent children (AFDC) was begun in the 1930s, it was to benefit widows and orphans. It was designed as a maintenance system for women and children, with no thought given to mothers actually entering the work force. As the pattern of women working outside the home has changed so, too, has our notion of what can be reasonably expected of a poor mother with children.

There is not yet unanimity on this, but a growing proportion of American policy makers believe that it is legitimate to expect women who are single parents to enter the work force. This assumes that they have the training and ability, that jobs are available, and that support services including child care, transportation, and medical care are available, so that seeking employment is a rational choice for a single mother to make.

The APWA welfare reform proposal, the National Governors' Association policy, and major legislation before Congress would require parents with children over age three to participate in a welfare-to-work program. Many agree that major emphasis must be given to services for those individuals who are difficult to employ, including those with a greater "employability deficit," and those who may be dependent on welfare over a long period of time. The Cuomo report goes farther than most of the other studies in the jobs area; it recommends guaranteeing jobs in public or private nonprofit agencies or organizations for those who have successfully completed training in the welfare-to-work program. This would ensure that these "graduates" receive wages rather than benefit checks.

Child Support Enforcement. A third major thread found in nearly all of the recommendations for welfare reform is stronger child support enforcement to hold absent fathers accountable for the maintenance of their children. Senator Moynihan made this the centerpiece of his legislation, titled the Family Security Act of 1987, S. 1511. He argues that policy should begin with parental support for children, and that "child support supplements" or cash benefits are the last recourse when support from parents is not adequate to meet children's needs.

Stringent enforcement of child support orders, including paternity determinations, is a policy recommendation that cuts across all ideological lines. No one quarrels with parental responsibility for children. In testimony and other public statements, the Reagan Administration finds this the most promising feature of many welfare plans, notwithstanding the fact that the administration's budget office has recommended reductions in federal support for state enforcement efforts.

Benefit Improvements. There are other elements critical to comprehensive welfare reform on which the consensus has yet to be fully developed. First and foremost has to do with the current benefit structure in the AFDC program. The APWA report; the governors' recommendation; the Federalism Act, S. 2926, introduced in 1986 by Senator Daniel Evans (R-Wash.); and the studies by the Babbitt and Cuomo groups recognize the need for some improvement in welfare benefits if self-sufficiency is ever to be a reality for poor families. Nevertheless, the Reagan Administration and many Republicans in Congress oppose benefit increases at the federal level, arguing however wrongly that bringing benefits in line with living costs might make welfare more attractive than self-sufficiency. The administration has proposed, instead, further experimentation at the state and local level, with federal assistance capped at current levels.

The human service commissioners in their report (APWA 1986, 22) recommended something they call a family living standard—a nationally mandated, but state-specific standard—that would be based on actual need and real living costs in each state. A family living standard would accomplish a goal mentioned in the paragraph cited earlier, an assistance system based on need, not on deprivation, family structure, or an artificial construct like the current "poverty index."

Under this proposal, federal legislation and regulations would establish what it takes to sustain a family, from housing, to food, to clothing and so on. Each state would then cost out that "market-basket" in order to produce a realistic standard for assistance. Benefits would be based on the difference between that standard and a family's income.

There have been efforts over time to introduce a national minimum benefit standard in the AFDC program. One argument has to do with equity; other federal benefit systems, including social security, are based on a minimum benefit indexed for inflation—the primary program for children, AFDC, has neither a national minimum benefit nor protection against inflation.

A national minimum recognizes that benefits by and large are too low, but does not take into account the very different living costs experienced from one region of the country to another. The commissioners recommended the family living standard approach based on the pragmatic assessment that, while benefits should be raised and should be based on need, they should also be specific to a given geographical area to take living cost differentials into account.

Among the other proposals, the Evans bill would establish a national federal minimum benefit equal to 50 percent of the federal poverty line, to be increased by 2 percent each year and capped at 90 percent of the poverty line. The Babbitt report took the same approach, but proposed that benefits equal 65 percent of the poverty line in fiscal 1988 and increase more rapidly in subsequent years.

The House Ways and Means Subcommittee on Public Assistance and Unemployment Compensation took a different tack. Recognizing the need to increase benefits, lawmakers proposed to tie cash assistance to the state median income so that benefits would equal at least 15 percent of the state median income by fiscal 1993, with an increased federal share paid to states that raise benefits beyond that amount.

When the bill was considered by the full Ways and Means Committee, the minimum benefit provision was dropped. Representative Tom Downey (D-N.Y.), acting subcommittee chair, recommended the deletion of the provision based on the political judgment that southern Democrats would not support a bill retaining the minimum benefit provision. Making a similar judgment about what he believed he could sell politically, Senator Moynihan did not include benefit improvements in his bill.

One reason commissioners and many others feel so strongly about changing and improving the welfare benefit levels is this: we are serious about self-sufficiency for welfare families. It is not realistic to expect poor parents to seek and obtain education and training, to master a marketable skill, if they must constantly worry about putting bread on the table for their children. Middle-class parents do not, for example, send their children to college and expect them to make the Dean's List without paying the bill for their room and board. One cannot make the difficult journey to independence without a stable economic base, a level of stability that current benefits, in far too many cases, simply do not provide.

The Cost of Reform. The bottom line is another area in which there is not yet consensus; how do we pay for the changes proposed, particularly elements of the work training program and benefit increases? The legislative process to date has seen benefit improvements fall victim to worry over cost and a lack of political will to allocate the necessary resources. Seeking program improvements in an era of severe budget restraint poses the single, biggest roadblock to significant welfare reform. But it is not insurmountable.

THE EMERGING LEGISLATION

The legislation that has been on the fastest track in Congress was proposed by the House Ways and Means Subcommittee on Public Assistance and Unemployment Compensation. The full Ways and Means Committee approved H.R. 1720 on June 10, 1987, after two days of closed drafting sessions. Approval came on a straight party-line vote, with Democrats supporting the measure and Republicans opposing.

As approved by the full House in December 1987, the bill's key feature is the "national education, training, and work (NETWork) program," which requires states to create comprehensive welfare-to-work programs for AFDC recipients. Participation in the program would be required of parents with children age three and over. States could, however, require part-time participation of parents with children under age three but over age one. Participation required of parents with children under age six would be part-time and child care would have to be provided.

The federal government would fund NETWork at a 65 percent open ended rate. States would be required to have the program in place by October 1, 1989, but could implement it earlier. Recipients leaving welfare for employment could continue to receive transitional child care for up to twelve months.

As with the proposals put forward by APWA, the NETWork program is based in large part on the successes states have had in moving welfare recipients into nonsubsidized jobs through the work incentive (WIN) demonstration programs. One additional wrinkle in the welfare reform debate has been the need to maintain federal support for the WIN program until a new welfare-to-work program can take effect. As this goes to press, the congressional appropriations process includes very limited funding for WIN in fiscal 1988 on the assumption that a welfare reform bill will be enacted, providing funds for a new work program starting in fiscal 1989.

The Ways and Means Committee bill also provides new work

incentives, starting in fiscal 1988, by allowing the first one hundred dollars in earnings and an additional 25 percent of earned income to be disregarded when computing benefits.

The bill mandates coverage of two-parent families in all states by January 1, 1990 and would provide states with an enhanced federal matching rate when states raise welfare benefits. The legislation also calls for a two-year National Academy of Sciences study of the APWA-proposed family living standard and minimum benefit approaches.

The legislation includes proposals made by APWA and the nation's governors to require an agreement between the client and the agency detailing the responsibilities of both under the welfare-to-jobs program, and requiring case management services to families in the program.

The legislation, S. 1511, introduced in the Senate by Senator Moynihan is similar to H.R. 1720 in some respects; but does not go as far, particularly in terms of comprehensiveness. As approved by the Senate Finance Committee, the welfare employment program (Job Opportunities and Basic Skills Training, or JOBS) is mandatory, but funded as a capped authorization rather than an open-ended entitlement. It also allows a state to limit the coverage of children in a two-parent family to six months in a twelve month period.

The Moynihan bill includes a version of the proposal made by the White House to grant waivers to states to conduct five-year demonstration projects designed to test alternative ways of delivering services to poor families. The White House proposal sought wide authority for states to consolidate and reallocate the low-income assistance dollars coming into a state. The provision in S. 1511 limits the waivers to fifty state or local administrations, and limits the programs eligible for consolidation to those within the jurisdiction of the Senate Finance Committee. In addition, it would allow states to continue operating programs as entitlements and would prohibit states from reducing benefits for recipients who participate in the demonstration program. In effect Senator Moynihan sought to gain Republican support by adding a White House proposal to the bill; but he added numerous protections to the demonstration authority in order to meet objections voiced by advocacy groups to the initial administration proposal.

Senator Moynihan succeeded in gaining Republican sponsorship for his legislation, and when it was introduced on July 21, 1987 the twenty-six original cosponsors included five Republicans. By the time the full Senate Finance Committee held a hearing on the legislation in mid-October, the sponsors numbered more than half of the Senate as well as a majority of finance committee members. Although he held numerous meetings with White House officials and delayed introduction of his bill pending White House endorsement, Senator Moynihan did not succeed in lining up administration support prior to the July 21 introduction of his bill.

In August, however, the White House signaled possible support for legislation that goes beyond the kind of demonstration program approach unveiled in the welfare task force report, *Up From Dependency* (U.S. Executive Office of the Present 1986), released in December 1986. That report was a disappointment to many who heard President Reagan speak in his 1986 State of the Union Address about sweeping change in the welfare system. The piece-meal approach reflected in the December report, and in legislation that followed, fell far short of the expectations raised by his rhetoric.

At an August 6 meeting with congressional Republicans, President Reagan indicated support for an alternative welfare bill introduced by the House Minority Leader Robert Michel (R-Ill.) and Representative Hank Brown (R-Colo.), ranking GOP member of the Ways and Means Public Assistance Subcommittee.

That legislation, the AFDC Employment and Training Reorganization Act of 1987, H.R. 3200, would provide $500 million for an education, training, and employment program, including stringent participation rates and a 50-50 federal-state match. It would allow, but not require, use of client-agency agreements and case management, and include stronger child support enforcement and transitional support for child care. It would provide broad waiver authority to states for demonstration programs. Absent from the House Republican bill are the mandatory AFDC-UP (AFDC-Unemployed Parent) coverage, medical transition benefits, improved income disregards, enhanced matching rate for states that raise benefits, and the study of the family living standard—all contained in H.R. 1720.

THE PROSPECTS; THE CHALLENGE

One of the biggest challenges facing anyone working in Washington's environment today is forging consensus among political leaders on both sides of the aisle. The experience of the American

Public Welfare Association over the last three years has shown that it is possible to forge a comprehensive welfare reform package that can withstand the political heat.

The human service commissioners who worked on our welfare reform proposal and are now tackling the equally difficult issues of health care and housing for poor families come from a variety of political backgrounds. They work for and represent Republican and Democratic governors; they come from rural and urban states; they are liberals and conservatives; and because *they* were able to draft a comprehensive, pragmatic, and compassionate package of proposals that were well-received by the governors and members of Congress, I am optimistic that others can do the same. The "others" I refer to are members of Congress and officials in the Reagan Administration. There has not been as much bipartisanship on welfare reform in Washington as the subject merits. Poverty is not a partisan concern. The children born into poverty today are not Democrats or Republicans; they're *poor.*

If welfare reform legislation is enacted in the 100th Congress it will not close the chapter on what is needed in the way of national policy to reduce poverty among America's citizens. Even if the most far-reaching of the bills is enacted, it is merely a first step toward a more humane, more coherent welfare system. There will be implementation questions to be answered: if welfare departments are to become *self-sufficiency* departments, what does that mean in terms of the case worker's role? The mutual obligations to be reflected in the new client-agency agreement raise capacity concerns—how can quality, affordable child care be assured in the communities where it is needed?

From the perspective of the national policy maker there will be many other questions to resolve. None of the bills now before the 100th Congress contains benefit improvements. Implementing the family living standard, once the National Academy of Sciences has completed its study, will require further legislation.

Even more broadly, reforming the welfare system alone will not end poverty. Many other "systems" need attention. The education system must serve poor children better, so that they have the best possible chance to escape intergenerational dependency. The health care system must provide access to better health for all of our citizens, particularly poor children. As a country we have largely abandoned the idea of a national housing policy that ensures not just emergency shelter but decent, affordable housing for families with children. Partnerships across jurisdictional lines and between the public and private sector offer the best hope for addressing the complex questions associated with poverty in this country. National welfare reform is one step, and a necessary step. Other steps must follow.

EPILOGUE

On October 13, 1988, President Reagan signed H.R. 1720 into law, renamed the "Family Support Act of 1988." The bill established comprehensive state education, training and employment programs; transitional child care and medical assistance benefits; mandatory coverage for two-parent families at least six months a year; and stronger child support enforcement. The question of benefit levels and the reforms of other "systems" remain on the agenda facing the nation's policymakers.

BIBLIOGRAPHY

American Public Welfare Association, and the National Council of State Human Service Administrators. 1986. *One Child in Four.* Washington, D.C.

Babbitt, Bruce, and Arthur Flemming. 1986. *Ladders Out of Poverty, A Report of the Project on the Welfare of Families.* Edited by Jack Meyers. Washington, D.C.: American Horizons.

Harris, Fred. 1967. *Alarms and Hopes: A Personal Journey, A Personal View.* New York: Harper and Row.

Margolin, Ilene. 1986. *A New Social Contract: Rethinking The Nature and Purpose of Public Assistance.* Report of the Task Force on Poverty and Welfare submitted to Governor Mario Cuomo, New York.

National Governors' Association. 1987. *Policy on Welfare Reform.* Washington, D.C.: National Governors' Association.

U.S. Executive Office of the President. 1986. *Up From Dependency: A New National Public Assistance Strategy.* Washington, D.C.: Office of Policy Development.

9

Policy on Welfare Reform

National Governors' Association

JOB ORIENTED WELFARE REFORM

We believe that public assistance programs must foster the creation, strengthening and preservation of a solid family structure in which parents can do productive work and raise healthy children. They must provide incentives and opportunities for individuals to get the training they need and to seek jobs. It is our aim to create a system where it is always better to work than be on public assistance.

The governors are convinced that the provision of genuine employment opportunities represents the surest route out of poverty for our nation's poor families and children. For this reason, the current system must be refocused to place primary emphasis on the placement of recipients into jobs and the removal of existing barriers to economic self-sufficiency.

Our approach to welfare reform is grounded in the notion that we can and must *prevent* dependency on welfare by strengthening the family and by aggressively providing opportunities for work. This preventive approach reflects our belief that investment in human development is a critical part of any agenda for economic growth. The initial costs of this investment may be somewhat higher than current expenditure levels, but we believe that public expenditures will eventually be lowered if we can target resources on programs that will reduce the need of children and their families to resort to the welfare system.

The federal government and the states must be prepared to invest in programs that address the many recognized needs which are factors in welfare dependency. A major National Governors' Association (NGA) effort, entitled "Bring Down the Barriers," is currently identifying strategies to help us address these problems at the critical stages of childhood and adolescence. Initial steps have been taken with public and private sector funds; but we must strengthen and further develop initiatives to reduce the incidence and consequences of teen pregnancy, increase the rate of high school completion and adult literacy, increase access to prenatal and primary health care for children and their families, increase the collection of child support from absent parents, improve parenting skills, and reduce alcohol and drug abuse. Sound preventive initiatives in these areas will pay off, we are convinced, in a reduced need for welfare assistance in the future.

The governors' aim in proposing a welfare reform plan is to turn what is now primarily a payments system with a minor work component into a system that is first and foremost a jobs system, backed up by an income assistance component. This must be the first step in any serious attempt to reform the welfare system. In addition to this immediate reform goal, our plan envisions an income assistance system which provides more adequate financial support for those unable to work, as well as for those taking the necessary steps to increase their employability.

To achieve these goals, the governors strongly believe that public assistance must be formulated in terms of a contract between government and the individual. Responsibility must flow in two directions in this relationship. The individual must be committed to undertaking a number of specific actions to prepare for and seek a job, with the objective of achieving self-sufficiency. In return, government must commit itself to investing in the employability of the individual and to providing adequate income assistance.

This notion of a social contract recognizes that the welfare system serves individuals with a wide range and variety of needs. We cannot expect that uniform treatment of "caseloads" will meet individuals' circumstances with satisfactory results. The governors believe that there is substantial gain in the notion of services and contracts tailored to individual families.

The major obligation of the individual in the public assistance contracts we propose is to prepare for and seek, accept, and retain a job. The governors recommend that all employable welfare recipients must participate in an education, job training, or placement program and accept a suitable job when it is offered. Employable recipients include those with children age three or older.

In this way, we hope to prevent long-term welfare dependence by bringing into the employment stream parents who have been welfare recipients for relatively short periods of time. We also believe that this recommendation reflects current social and economic realities. As affordable, quality child care for younger children becomes available, we believe that recipients with children age one or older can successfully participate in an education or jobs program.

The governors believe it is critical to give high priority to young, first-time mothers. Studies show that over 60 percent of AFDC mothers under age thirty had their first child as teenagers. In many cases, it is easier to train and find jobs for those individuals than for long-term recipients. For a relatively modest investment, there is the potential for substantial savings if these individuals can be diverted from the welfare system into the job stream. This would also tend to reduce the incidence of a second or third birth.

At the same time, the governors believe that the employment needs of long-term welfare recipients must be addressed. As indicated by successful state employment and training initiatives, long-term welfare recipients can achieve self-sufficiency if given the necessary training and support services. Therefore, in designing our employment and training programs, we are likewise committed to helping these individuals reduce their dependence on welfare.

The principal responsibility of government in the welfare contracts is to provide education, job training, and/or job placement services to all employable recipients. These services must be carefully structured so that they suit the employment needs of individual participants.

Government also has the obligation to provide adequate support services to individuals participating in the program, particularly the critical supports of child care and health care coverage. Parents cannot be expected to give up welfare if the loss of Medicaid jeopardizes access to health care for their families. Once a participant has found a job, support services should be provided for a transition period. The governors support the development of initiatives through which people who are not covered by Medicaid and whose jobs do not provide health coverage can be provided health services, and we are ready to work with the Administration and Congress on this issue. For example, in our policy on "Health Care for Uninsured Individuals" we recommend an expansion of pooling arrangements, tax exemptions for health care premiums paid by unemployed workers for continuation coverages, and changes in tax policy such as equitable treatment for health care coverage of unincorporated businesses.

The governors also recognize that unpaid child support represents a sizable resource for low-income families and we will continue to strengthen current enforcement efforts. Toward that end, we are committed to full implementation of the 1984 federal child support amendments. Moreover, the governors will continue to explore other proposals, such as increased interstate cooperation and enforcement; extension of employment and training to noncustodial parents; and implementation of equitable support guidelines, to help ensure that individuals fulfill their basic parental responsibility of income support for their children.

The contract, in addition to expressing a key conceptual tenet of our approach to welfare reform, must be a central mechanism for implementing our recommendations. The contract implies a level of specificity generally not found in public assistance programs. Indeed, the governors believe that job oriented welfare reform cannot succeed unless it is "customized" to take into account the circumstances and needs of individuals and their families.

The most promising approach for implementing the contract is case management, in which the responsible government agency and caseworker broker and coordinate the multiple social, health, education, and employment services necessary to promote self-sufficiency and to strengthen family life. Several states have shown that we can personalize the bureaucracy through this approach, and that the one-to-one relationship provides enormously important incentives for both parties to succeed.

Finally, the contract must be enforceable. If the recipient does not meet his or her obligations under the contract, then the adult's portion of the assistance payment should be eliminated until he or she meets the terms of the contract. Support for the child would be preserved. Similarly, if government does not fulfill its obligations, then the contract would not be enforceable and full assistance to the entire family would continue.

The governors believe that it is the proper role of the federal government to structure funding so that the governmental obligations of the welfare contract can be met. Funding for the education, job training, and placement programs for welfare recipients should be primarily federal, but retain a significant state contribution.

Under the current system, federal spending devoted specifically to the training and placement of welfare recipients represents substantially less than 1 percent of the amount spent for AFDC benefits. Nothing could indicate more dramatically the lack of jobs focus in our current program.

In implementing our welfare reform plan, it is critical that federal matching funds be made available for all services which are extended to recipients who are required to participate in the jobs program. Further, the emphasis on jobs should be reflected in the federal matching rate. Ultimately, we believe that there should be a higher matching rate for the jobs program than for the income assistance program.

We are willing to be judged on our performance in spending federal and state funds on job training and placement programs. We are willing to work with the federal government to devise standards which reflect real measures of outcome—e.g., how many clients are getting into lasting jobs, and to what extent is welfare dependency reduced? But we oppose federal requirements that tell us how to implement job related services. There is no one solution to the challenge of employability and job placement. The leading innovations have come from the states in this area, and the states must have maximum flexibility in designing their education, training, and employment programs for welfare recipients.

REFORM OF INCOME ASSISTANCE

The immediate goal of the governors is to put into place the preventive initiatives and the jobs programs recommended above. As these begin to take effect, reducing dependency on welfare and restraining public spending on public assistance, we believe that reform of the basic cash assistance program, Aid to Families with Dependent Children (AFDC), must be undertaken. It is our intent that the reforms in the income assistance program will be funded with savings realized through our preventive initiative and through our jobs program.

It is our equally important, if longer-range, goal to provide adequate income support for families in which no individual can work.

In some areas of the country and for some recipients, benefit levels are not adequate to meet minimal requirements. There is no systematic nor uniform way of setting benefits, and levels are determined with little regard for the cost of meeting the basic requirements of supporting a family.

The governors recommend that income support should be based on a measure of family need, or family living standard. This standard would represent the cost of purchasing family essentials—food, housing, clothing, health care, etc. It would be determined on a state-by-state basis, using a nationally consistent methodology. Support should be provided for current AFDC recipients plus two-parent families where that option is now available. Coverage should be increased gradually to all families living below the family living standard.

Given limited federal and state resources, this new income support payment must be phased in gradually. Initial payments should be set at a national minimum percentage of each state's family living standard. This percentage should be increased over time, as resources allow, with the goal being the payment of the full family living standard. Funding of the national minimum percentage should be primarily federal, but retain a significant state match. If a state supplements payments above the national minimum, the federal match should start at current AFDC matching rates and increase as the supplement increases.

It is critical that benefits in this system be structured so that it is always financially better for the recipient to work than to receive cash assistance. The system must be designed carefully, so that there are no disincentives for employers to provide wages above the minimum or to reduce or eliminate health care coverage.

We recognize that changes of the magnitude we have recommended may not be accomplished overnight. We also realize that our goals can be achieved in numerous ways. We are prepared to work with all of our partners in government and in the private sector to develop sound plans which will prevent and reduce the dependence of families on the welfare system.

10

Changing Welfare: An Investment in Women and Children in Poverty

The Proposal of The National Coalition on Women, Work and Welfare Reform

THE PRINCIPLES

The National Coalition on Women, Work and Welfare Reform came together in 1985 out of our conviction that the emerging debate on welfare reform must address the needs of poor women and their children. We are now more than twenty-five national organizations which share a long standing concern for the dramatically disproportionate levels of poverty experienced by women-maintained families in this country. In August, 1986 we published our recommendations to guide the development of state-level welfare employment programs in *Perspectives on Women and Welfare Employment* (National Coalition 1986). Building on this work and grounded in the varied perspectives and knowledge of coalition members, we have now prepared a welfare reform proposal. The proposal has been guided by the following principles:

- The *problem* is poverty, not welfare. The *solution* to poverty is not to reduce the welfare rolls, but rather to transform the welfare system into one which enables recipients to become economically self-sufficient.
- Effective welfare reform cannot be revenue-neutral. Only a se-

rious and thoughtful investment of time and resources will enable low-income citizens to participate more fully in our economy. This investment is primarily the responsibility of the federal government, although it will require support from a broad spectrum of public and private groups as well.

- Welfare reform should result in a structure that respects the dignity of welfare recipients and strengthens their capabilities for determining choices for their own lives. In short, the welfare system should be "user-friendly." Recognizing that most welfare recipients want to work outside the home, voluntary education, employment, and training programs are the most efficient as well as effective approach.

- While flexibility and community involvement are extremely important in shaping programs at the local level, the federal government must continue to exercise its responsibility in the areas of performance standards, civil and other rights protections, technical assistance, uniformity of standards, guarantee of entitlement, and data collection.

THE CONTEXT

If welfare reform is to ensure a transition towards economic self-sufficiency and an end to poverty, it must address:

- the current unacceptable lack of basic income support for poor families in many states;
- the dearth of jobs in many areas of the country, and the shortage of jobs that pay wages and benefits adequate to support a family;
- the widely varied needs and situations of welfare recipients for education, training and employment services, health care, and vocational rehabilitation and counseling;
- the contrast between the depth of support services needed and their availability and affordability for most families; and
- the continuing presence of race, sex, and age discrimination which limits the access of women and minorities to such areas as education, housing, employment (including pensions, health insurance, and benefits).

THE FOCUS: SCOPE OF THIS PROPOSAL

Our recommendations reflect an ongoing tension between the necessity to focus on welfare recipients directly, and our deeply held conviction that the problem of women's poverty, and therefore its solutions, are much broader than that which can be subsumed under even a comprehensive welfare reform proposal. The choice to focus on poor families with children becomes painful when it excludes, for example, displaced homemakers who no longer have dependent children.

Likewise, coalition members believe that the fate and effectiveness of welfare reform will be greatly affected by public policy changes in other areas, particularly housing, education, affirmative action, and the minimum wage. Without real gains in each of these areas, there will not be a substantial reduction in poverty, which is the true object of welfare reform.

THE PROPOSAL IN BRIEF

Our proposal consists of four distinct elements that form an integrated and interdependent whole. None are sufficient alone. All are necessary. In a time of fiscal constraint, we recommend gradual implementation of the proposal as a whole, rather than selecting from among these elements.

The four elements of this proposal are: 1) initiatives to achieve an *adequate income maintenance system* which guarantees that all needy families will receive benefits equal to at least the federal poverty level;   2) establishment of voluntary and adequately funded comprehensive education, employment, and training programs which prepare welfare recipients for employment with incomes and benefits adequate to support their families;   3) provision of support services and subsidies, which assure the availability and affordability of child care, health care, and other training and work related expenses necessary for welfare recipients who are making the transition from welfare to employment; and   4) effective child support enforcement to enhance the collection of support payments from noncustodial parents.

PART I: INCOME MAINTENANCE

The National Coalition on Women, Work and Welfare Reform supports federal welfare reform legislation that will improve assistance to welfare recipients and their families and provide support in increasing their long-term economic self-sufficiency. While this statement addresses only our concerns with respect to needy families with children, we support the provision of income maintenance benefits to all those in need without regard to age, family status, or other categorical limitations. We recommend:

- establishing federally supported income maintenance benefits equal to at least 100 percent of the federally established poverty level;
- increasing the Earned Income Tax Credit (EITC) to reflect differences in family size;
- extending income maintenance to all needy families with children;
- basing income tested eligibility and benefit determination only on income actually and currently available to the family for use in meeting its basic needs;
- providing adequate income disregards in income tested programs: including among other things disregard of some of a family's earnings, child support receipts and social security benefits, and establishing adequate resource levels;
- ensuring that income maintenance benefits are provided without the attachment of any mandatory educational, employment, or training requirements;
- establishing appropriate measures of state performance in federal/state programs that focus on identifying the reasons for poor performance and on finding cures, rather than on just imposing penalty reductions in federal funding; and
- establishing methods for the determination and provision of aid which make benefits accessible to all who are eligible and which respect their dignity.

These goals could be accomplished within the existing federally supported income maintenance systems for families by adopting the changes described below.

Increasing Income Maintenance Benefit Levels and the EITC. A federal floor should be established to assure that benefits equal the difference between food stamps and 100 percent of the federally established poverty level. This should be done without any diminution of federal funding for AFDC benefits that exceed this minimum. To the extent that resources do not permit immediate attainment of the 100 percent level, any phasing-in should begin at a high enough level to provide significant relief to a substantial number of those who are now living in the subpoverty of AFDC and should be geared to attain 100 percent in the foreseeable future. In addition, the EITC should be adjusted for family size.

Extension of Coverage to All Needy Families with Children. Since the food stamp program covers needy families with two parents in the home, full provision of federally supported income maintenance to such families could be obtained by also covering them under AFDC. This goal could be achieved in stages by initially mandating AFDC-UP coverage of needy two-parent families in which a parent is unemployed or underemployed. This extension should be accompanied by modification of three features of the unemployment/underemployment test. First, a family should not be denied aid because only its secondary wage earner, typically the female parent, has suffered the loss of employment. Second, underemployment should be recognized as anything less than full-time hours. Third, aid should not be denied to the long-term unemployed or those who have never been able to obtain and/or retain "on the books" employment long enough to amass sufficient quarters of work to meet the labor force attachment test.

Limiting Consideration to Actually Available Current Income. To the extent that benefits are means tested, they should be calculated only on the basis of income which is actually and currently available to the members of the family seeking assistance.

Benefits should be provided on the basis of current needs so that benefits provided to cover needs during a particular time period are based, as closely as possible, on income that the family can reasonably be anticipated to have available for use during that period.

Income which is not actually available to meet the basic needs covered by the income maintenance grant, (e.g., amounts withheld from wages for mandated contributions such as taxes, amounts that have to be spent for expenses attributable to involvement in employment or self-employment such as child care costs, proceeds of bona fide business loans), should not be counted against the family in determining eligibility for assistance. This requires modification of the allowances for work expenses and elimination of the 185 percent cap on eligibility.

Lump sum payments received by families should be treated in the same way as lump sums are treated in the Supplemental Security

Income (SSI) program. Families who receive such amounts should be allowed to retain the proceeds of such receipts up to the applicable resource limits. To the extent that the proceeds make them ineligible; ineligibility should continue only as long as the proceeds are still available to them.

A family should be free to seek aid only for its needy members, so that income that is the specific property of one child in the family cannot be assumed to be available to meet the needs of siblings. Similarly, it should not be assumed that a child is receiving income from grandparents or step-parents who have no enforceable duty to support her.

Opportunities for Voluntary Participation in Education, Employment, and Training Activities. As expressed in our statement on education, employment, and training opportunities for poor families, conditioning the receipt of benefits on work tests or work requirements undermines the goals of both education, employment and training programs and income maintenance programs. Our views on how education, employment, and training opportunities can best be provided are set out fully in part two of this proposal.

Disregarding Income and Increasing Resource Limits. Low-income families should not be forced to take jobs which would leave them less well off than receiving welfare. The earned income disregard which currently applies to the first thirty dollars of income earned per month and one-third of the remaining earnings should be liberalized, should apply to all earnings regardless of the source, and should not be time limited. The EITC should not be considered income for the purposes of calculating gross income. At least one hundred dollars of child support and social security benefits should be disregarded in all cases, with additional disregard of any amounts needed to meet the special needs of the beneficiary of the payments. All work related expenses should be disregarded or reimbursed. Resource limits should be increased, including provisions (as exist in SSI) for excluding assets necessary for fulfillment of a self-support plan, and families should be able to accumulate resources while receiving aid so that a family can retain some monies to, among other things, invest in its future.

Appropriate Measures of State Performance in Federal/State Income Maintenance Programs. Fiscal sanctions should not be associated with quality control programs. Quality control programs should be designed to identify as clearly as possible the causes of errors in program administration and to establish and implement well-designed corrective action plans. There should be no incentive for reviewers to overlook errors or for administrators to bias administration in favor of underpayment, and/or wrongful denials and terminations to avoid the fiscal risks of overpayments.

Administrative Policies and Procedures. Administration of an income maintenance system must give equal consideration to efficiency and the needs of the people it is designed to serve. It should function to assure fair treatment and prompt and accurate payment of benefits. All people who come into contact with the system should be treated with respect and dignity and should be given whatever help they need to meet the procedural and verification requirements that attach to the receipt of aid, including the payment of any fees required to obtain documents. Verification of eligibility should be done in the least intrusive manner possible. Monthly reporting requirements should be eliminated, and there should be provision for immediate reinstatement of benefits where failure to comply with other reporting requirements is cured within the month following the date of default.

PART II: EDUCATION, EMPLOYMENT, AND TRAINING

Introduction. The National Coalition on Women, Work and Welfare Reform recommends the development of a new federal and state initiative to support education, employment and training for welfare recipients that will enable them to achieve economic self-sufficiency. The new initiative should lead to occupations with demonstrated labor market demand; provide access to jobs which pay wages above the minimum wage and benefits resulting in a new economic gain for the recipient and her family; and develop generic occupational and life skills which enhance long-term employability.

Five key elements guide the education, employment, and training component of our proposal:

- the delivery of services within the existing education, employment, and training systems, rather than the development of education, employment, and training programs within the income maintenance system;

- flexibility for states to develop comprehensive strategies which are responsive to the economic realities of their locales, with incentives to involve employers, community based organizations, and educational institutions in a cooperative and coordinated effort;
- the voluntary participation of welfare recipients in any education, employment, and training program and the elimination from federal law of provisions which require or permit states to mandate the participation of welfare recipients or risk loss of benefits;
- performance standards which provide incentives for states to develop innovative programs consistent with these principles and which discourage "creaming" or the provision of low-cost/low-impact training; and
- a strong federal role in research, oversight, technical assistance, and data collection to document success and facilitate replication. The privacy of individuals must be protected in any research or data collection efforts.

We propose the development of a new federal/state initiative to support education, employment, and training services for welfare recipients. The following recommendations should be used to develop this initiative.

Allowable Uses of Funds. Federal funds appropriated for this initiative should be used to purchase or otherwise provide the supportive services required by participants. It is expected that 30 to 50 percent of participant costs may be used to cover these services. States must provide:

1. outreach to eligible participants;
2. individualized assessments of all program participants' educational levels, job skills, barriers to employment, and supportive services needs. These assessments will be used to develop an individual employability plan in which each participant determines the education, employment, training, and supportive services desired and needed to gain economically sustaining employment or self-employment;
3. job readiness and career counseling;
4. educational remediation, including high school equivalency certification, literacy, and English as a second language;

5. short-term training and postsecondary education in fields with demonstrated labor market demand;
6. job placement and job development services;
7. short-term workplace internships in occupational areas with a good prospect of permanent employment providing on-the-job (no more than twelve weeks) experiences, references, and stipends to cover the costs of participation; and
8. appropriate support services.

This mix of services must be available to participants served in this initiative, with participants choosing which elements should be part of their service package based upon their skills, interests, needs, and employment goals.

Federal funds—including incentive funds—appropriated for this initiative could be used for other approaches, including self-employment or enterprise development, job creation, nontraditional training, work supplementation, or other approaches which might increase the prospect for economic self-sufficiency.

Federal funds—including incentive funds—appropriated for this initiative could also be used for experimental approaches which enhance the prospect of self-sufficiency for target groups of welfare recipients with especially severe barriers to employment.

Federal funds appropriated for this initiative may *not* be used to support any program of:

- mandatory assignment to employment, training, or education;
- unpaid work assignments of more than twelve weeks in duration or required public or private employment;
- mandatory job search efforts;
- providing services to welfare recipients under threat of a sanction if they fail to participate; or
- training or services which result in net economic loss for welfare families;
- employment or training that does not assure employee rights, such as health and safety protection, worker's compensation, the applicable minimum wage, and protection against displacement of current workers or trainees.

Administration. The administration of education, training, and employment programs for welfare recipients should be placed in one federal agency to avoid duplication and counterproductive bureaucratic competition. The U.S. Department of Labor is preferable because it has responsibility for other employment training programs. For the same reasons, the administration of programs on the state level should also be clearly placed in one state agency. The state agency should be required to utilize existing education, employment, and training programs so that welfare recipients are served by the same programs as nonrecipients. Educational institutions, JTPA agencies, community based organizations, vocation/technical schools, employment service, and other existing delivery systems are the appropriate vehicles for delivering these services.

State Plans. Each state should create a plan for the delivery of services which should be reviewed by a state council developed for this purpose or a subcommittee of the State Job Training Coordinating Council. Council members should include training, education (including remedial, postsecondary, and higher education), and welfare state administrators, employers, unions, community based organizations, and representatives of welfare recipient groups. The state plan would then be reviewed by the governor and submitted to the secretary of labor for approval. The state plan should outline the procedure for administering, allocating, and matching funds. Within the state, monies should be distributed through a request for proposal process, based on the following factors:

- demonstration of capacity to serve recipients with greater barriers to employment;
- demonstration of coordination among welfare, training, education, and economic development agencies, community based organizations, and employers in delivering the services;
- demonstration of plans for meeting the literacy and basic skills needs of recipients;
- demonstration of plans to train in high-demand occupations with a good prospect for placement in jobs with good wages and benefits;
- capacity to add funding or in-kind services to the federal/state funding of the program; and
- demonstration of a comprehensive plan to provide needed supportive services.

Eligible recipients of the funds would include local private industry councils, service delivery areas, education agencies, community based organizations, local governments or consortia of such agencies.

Financing and Federal Allocation of Funds.
1. Funds for this initiative should be provided through the federal government, with a state match developed so that poorer states are not penalized. Financing should come from current WIN dollars, new federal dollars, and the state match. Communities where programs are being operated should also be encouraged to provide additional support.
2. Funds should be allocated to states based on a funding formula, taking into account the relative number of AFDC recipients in a state compared to the number nationally, and the relative number of AFDC recipients who have received AFDC for two years or more who live in the state as compared to all other states.
3. A percentage of the total appropriation of federal dollars for the initiative would be retained by the U.S. Department of Labor for three purposes: training and technical assistance; research and data collection; and incentive bonuses to states (whose plans included and who subsequently successfully carried out innovative programs and performed well according to the performance standards).

AFDC Adjustments. Adjustments to AFDC law must be made to ensure that no welfare recipient could experience a net loss in cash assistance or welfare benefits for participating in the education, employment, and training initiatives designed in this program, including longer-term education, training, or enterprise development activities.

Performance Standards. Federal legislation developed to implement this initiative should contain performance standards of two types: standards designed to address the program components developed by states for participants; and standards designed to measure the outcomes for participants of such programs. States should be held accountable for both types of performance measures by the U.S. Department of Labor, with incentives available to states for meeting the standards.

Program Standards.
- targeting welfare recipients with greatest needs and providing serial services to such participants as needed;
- providing additional matching monies to expand the program;

- involving the full spectrum of employers, community based organizations, education and training providers in the delivery and coordination of services;
- demonstrating the delivery of appropriate supportive services before, during, and throughout the program and the transition to self-sufficiency; and
- developing innovative service delivery and targeting strategies consistent with the goals of the program.

Outcome Standards.
- achieving participant placements in jobs with wage above the minimum wage and full health benefits such that the family experiences a net economic gain;
- achieving participant educational gains; and
- achieving job permanence, through demonstration of job retention after one year.

PART III: SUPPORT SERVICES

The National Coalition on Women, Work and Welfare Reform recognizes that support services including child care, health care and transportation are vital for families to achieve economic self-sufficiency. These services must be provided both during any education, employment, and training program and during a transition period after placement into a job. In addition, are other support services—such as dependent care for adult family members—which are also essential, but are not addressed in this proposal. While welfare reform proposals must primarily deal with public assistance recipients, they should move towards a goal of providing these support services to all families living below the poverty line.

Health Care. Since 75 percent of the uninsured in America are workers in paid employment and their families, it is clear that moving from AFDC into a job does not guarantee that a worker will also move from public to private health insurance. The provision of subsidized health care can help to remove this barrier to economic self-sufficiency. Additionally, equity mandates that working poor families who are not presently eligible for Medicaid also be given assistance. We recommend that:
- The federal government guarantee Medicaid coverage for at

least eighteen months after the recipient enters employment and the family leaves the welfare rolls. An optional six-month extension of Medicaid coverage should be provided if the family will otherwise lose health coverage. If the family will lose more comprehensive coverage, states should fill the gap between the services provided by the employer's plan and the services provided under the state's Medicaid plan. This extension should be automatic and should not depend on reapplication by a family losing its welfare benefits.

- States be required to extend Medicaid coverage to all families of workers with total incomes below the poverty line. Additionally, states should develop plans to phase-in Medicaid for all uninsured poor families.

Child Care. Addressing the child care needs of low-income families is a high priority for the coalition. This requires consideration of the needs of parents as well as the developmental needs of children. High-quality child care must be available to ensure that low-income children are not subjected to a separate and inadequate system of care. We recommend that:

- Fully subsidized child care be provided for welfare recipients who participate in education, employment, and training programs and should continue to be provided for at least twelve months after the recipient enters employment and the family leaves the welfare rolls. Thereafter, families would contribute to the cost of child care on a sliding fee basis.
- Subsidized child care be provided for all workers' families whose total income is below the poverty level, except in two-parent families if one parent chooses to remain at home to care for children.
- Parents be allowed maximum flexibility, in accordance with adequate standards that will ensure quality and safety, to select the child care that meets their needs and those of their children.
- Child care for education, employment, and training participants be paid for at market rates to ensure that low-income families have access to quality care. Since there is no national standard, market rate would be determined in each community.
- States be required to establish information and referral systems to help parents acquaint themselves with the available child care and subsidies.

Transportation. Adequate transportation is an integral component of a support services package which will enable low-income families to take advantage of education, employment, and training opportunities. These families often live in areas where public transportation is either very expensive or nonexistent. We recommend:

- A flexible approach which allows communities to combine existing transportation services and develop new services as needed through the use of public, nonprofit, and private sources.
- Subsidies and vouchers as methods to reimburse welfare recipients for transportation costs while participating in education, employment, and training programs (including those necessitated by child care).

PART IV: CHILD SUPPORT ENFORCEMENT

The National Coalition on Women, Work and Welfare Reform supports welfare reform that will improve the enforcement and collection of child support. Any proposal for reform must recognize that, even at its best, child support enforcement will not eliminate poverty among women and children. Hence, improved child support enforcement, so critical to the economic well-being of poor women and their families, must be pursued in combination with strategies that improve benefit levels and employment opportunities. We recommend:

- changing the method of distribution of support collected for children receiving AFDC to assure that a significant portion of every collection is passed through to the child without affecting her or his eligibility for aid;
- increasing limitations on a state's right to pursue arrears on its own behalf to assure that such right is always secondary to a family's right to current support payments;
- making changes in the paternity determination process to ensure effective and timely assistance to caretakers seeking to establish the paternity of their children;
- requiring improvements in the management of child support enforcement agencies (IV-D agencies);
- improving the use of state established guidelines for child support awards; and
- improving interstate child support collection services.

Emphasizing Collection of Current Support Obligations and a Pass-through for Children Receiving AFDC. The current federally mandated passthrough of fifty dollars of monthly child support collections on behalf of children receiving AFDC should be increased. The passthrough should apply to all collections of amounts representing monthly obligations whether the amount collected is a current payment or payment of an arrears and regardless of when the payments are made or whether they are made to an agency in the state of the custodial parent's residence or in another state.

Provisions giving precedence to the collection of current support obligations for children who are currently receiving AFDC or who formerly received it should be improved to assure that the child's right always takes priority over the state's right to collect arrearages owed to it under the AFDC assignment.

Ensuring Effective and Timely Establishment of Paternity. The legal and administrative barriers which severely limit the number of paternities established by state child support agencies should be removed. Such an effort would include:
- requiring states to set up civil procedures with appropriate due process protection under which paternity can be established or voluntarily acknowledged;
- requiring states to permit HLA blood tests, and other tests with equivalent reliability, to be admissible as evidence of paternity in legal proceedings; and
- improving state procedures for the interstate establishment of paternity.

Requiring State Child Support Agencies to Provide More Timely and Efficient Services. Better management of resources should be assured by requiring states to establish automated tracking and monitoring systems. More timely action should be assured by requiring federally established timelines and performance standards for states which govern all aspects of child support enforcement, including establishment of paternity and establishment and enforcement of support awards.

Improving the Use of Guidelines in Establishing Child Support Awards. States should be required to apply their state established guidelines as a rebuttable presumption in establishing child support awards. The guidelines should be periodically reviewed and updated. Awards also should be periodically updated in conformity with the guidelines, if appropriate, with notice to and appropriate due process protection for both parents.

Improvements in the Procedures Governing Interstate Child Support Services. State procedures should be made more uniform and the tools available for application in interstate cases should be expanded. This would include:
- the establishment of a commission to study and recommend solutions to the full range of problems plaguing interstate enforcement;
- the development of timeliness and performance standards for states in interstate as well as intrastate cases; and
- the expansion of location and enforcement tools currently available in intrastate cases to make them more effectively available in interstate cases.

Ensuring Adequate Resources at Both the Federal and State Level. There should be assurance of sufficient funding for the requisite improvements in the child support enforcement program by:
- maintaining current levels of federal funding for child support;
- retaining the special federal funding for the development and implementation of automated systems; and
- considering additional financial incentives for states to improve their performance in areas such as the establishment of paternity, where current efforts are conspicuously and woefully inadequate.

BIBLIOGRAPHY

National Coalition on Women, Work, and Welfare Reform. 1986. *Perspectives on Women and Welfare Employment.* Washington, D.C.: National Coalition on Women, Work, and Welfare Reform.

IV
Southwestern
Case Studies

11

Welfare Reform in a Society in Transition: The Case of New Mexico

Tomás Atencio

The origins of the American welfare state have been attributed to industrialization; the precipitating condition was clearly the Great Depression triggered by the stock market crash of 1929. Institutionalized in the Social Security Act of 1935, the first American welfare state programs were soon overshadowed by a World War II economy, which temporarily minimized their need and importance. Since the war, however, welfare programs have grown incrementally, evoking fears that the welfare state has run amok. Expansions, however, have been in noncash programs while cash supplements for the poor and guaranteed income proposals have received less attention (Browning 1986, 170–71).

Welfare programs were introduced to New Mexico at a time when the subsistence agricultural economy was in the early stages of transition to a modern industrial society. Modern economic foundations were yet to be fully established, and most of the region's Hispanic inhabitants were partially dependent on the subsistence agricultural economy and reflected in their values and world view that preindustrial mode of subsistence. As a result, they were rendered impoverished and politically impotent within the larger sociopolitical world. Into this scene entered New Deal programs of work relief and income maintenance, along with others in education and training, land use, and community development. These programs were the first direct economic benefits of industrial society which many Hispanic village dwellers could enjoy without having to leave their communities; they were the first income-producing activities within an industrial context in most of the villages themselves. Despite community development and land use efforts, relief and income maintenance programs filled an economic development vacuum and formed for posterity a significant part of the region's economic foundations.

One goal of this paper is to examine the history of welfare in New Mexico to discern those factors that caused emergency welfare programs to become institutionalized and result in an economic prop for part of northern New Mexico. The second goal is to examine current welfare reform proposals within the context of New Mexico's welfare history to discern any historical continuities and assess their relevance to the region and its current needs.

I attempt, therefore, to analyze the role of the welfare state in a society in transition by examining the part of New Mexico society that was served by welfare at the inception of New Deal programs, during the post-World War II period, and through the Great Society and the War on Poverty era. This historical narrative provides the backdrop against which I will examine the present state of welfare reform in New Mexico.

Although this discussion focuses on rural New Mexico, it is intended to raise questions about the general applicability of the United States' model of welfare to traditional societies in transition. Consequently, this analysis should at least provide food for thought for those concerned with other rural societies in the United States and with developing Third World countries that are creating their welfare programs.

HISTORICAL CONTEXT

The area of New Mexico discussed in this paper is characterized by small villages along the Rio Grande and its tributaries. Initially, these villages were within land grants issued to settlers by the Spanish and Mexican governments.[1] The village pattern of settlement drew groups of families and, in isolated cases, single extended families around a *plaza* or town square where houses were constructed contiguously. Land beyond the village was held in common by the land grantees for livestock grazing. But the principal mode of subsistence was small-scale farming fed by water from the creeks conveyed through gravity flow canals, *acequias*, dug and maintained by the small farmers. Water distribution was, and still is, administered by a commission elected by the water users. A form of mutual aid, the water distribution mechanism comprised the quasi-governmental jurisdiction closest to the community itself.

Although small-scale village farming was the mainstay for a subsistence economy, sheep raising by a few semi-autonomous farmers and wealthier ranchers and their sharecroppers, *partidarios*, engaged in commercial agriculture supported a primitive but viable textile cottage industry that endured into the late colonial period (1790–1821) (Ríos-Bustamante 1976). Blankets woven in New Mexico were exported, mainly to northern Mexico. In addition to weaving, moccasin, *tegua*, manufacturing also provided limited revenue for the region. These were the principal avenues for economic development. Subsistence agriculture, of course, generated no surplus. Communities engaged in barter of produce and other goods among themselves.

The laws of the colony derived from Spain. The most significant for this analysis concerned taxation and care of the indigent. Taxes were levied on the product of the land and not on the land itself. In regard to the indigent, a semi-feudal, mercantilist-like policy placed responsibility for caring for the disabled indigent on the state rather than on the family (Ellis 1948).

The beliefs and values of the New Mexico Hispanic community reflected the patterns of existence based on kinship networks in small villages, subsistence agriculture, and a balanced ecological relationship in a semi-arid environment. These traditional values and beliefs inter-twined with Catholicism, which in turn melded with Indian world views. Values that guided behavior in this region were harmony with the environment, reciprocity and sharing, respect, *vergüenza* (a belief that communal solidarity superseded individual accomplishments), mutual aid, and a commitment to the idea that the supernatural could be influenced to placate its wrath and to enhance its bounty. This pattern endured in the isolated region and resulted in a sense of solidarity and a class and ethnic consciousness that manifested itself in various resistance movements (Atencio 1985, 40–42 and 77–79).[2]

These values were reflected in the communities' indigenous welfare organizations. Most villages had mutual aid societies organized around the village patron saint. A *síndico*, the treasurer of the alms of the poor, was chosen to administer the granting of assistance, usually through loans or "seed" in-kind resources to help a young couple start their subsistence plot or to assist a family facing hardship. These were loans and were to be paid in-kind. In this traditional society there was no public education for participation in a wider industrial society.

Independence from Spain in 1821 did not significantly affect the life of middle Rio Grande residents. Annexation of New Mexico to the United States in 1848 did, however. A new social and economic order was introduced. One scholar describes the principal problem at that juncture as the United States territorial government failing ". . . to recognize the political and legal rights of the rural Hispanic corporate communities where the bulk of the population resided" (Van Ness 1980, 5). Villagers were viewed as interlopers in their own lands, which had to be measured and adjudicated according to United States standards and laws. This, coupled with "unscrupulous transactions . . ." (Dinwoodie 1986, 300) and American law which required payment of taxes on the land rather than on its produce, caused Hispano villagers to loose over 90 percent of their land.

Anglo newcomers reflected different cultural values. In expansive river valleys such as the middle Rio Grande from Albuquerque southward or in the mountains of northern Rio Arriba County, settlement patterns that had guided Spanish settlers were disregarded by Anglos who established residences constructed as individual dwellings along roads. Instead of irrigation and small-scale farming, they raised livestock commercially and introduced dry farming. Those who engaged in irrigated agriculture did so commercially. Commercial enterprises in search of higher profits led to competition for scarce water resources; commercial stock raising led to over-grazing and a resulting imbalance in the region's natural ecology.

This trend accelerated in 1880 when the railroad passed through New Mexico. Railway transportation incorporated the region into the national and world economy, bringing the New Mexico subsistence agricultural community into the wage labor and cash income arena (Weigle 1975). This development altered the occupational structure as many men were pulled away from their villages to become sheepherders, railroad workers, and miners, as well as seasonal farm workers in other states. By 1929, ". . . on the average of one person per family went out to work for 4 to 7 months at wages averaging from $40 to $100 per month" (Weigle 1975, 36). These men were at the fringes of industrial society and did not possess the conciousness of the wage-earning proletariat. For even as they worked at itinerant migrant jobs, these men and their families were responsible for farming the small three-to-five-acre plot of land which had been inherited from the subsistence farming era.

Summarizing these trends, Harper, Córdova, and Oberg wrote in the late 1930s: "Life in the Rio Grande Valley north of Albuquerque at the end of the Spanish-Mexican era was dominantly peasant in character, with a strong accent upon the small, individual owned tract of land for farm and home, and upon free acreage of community-owned pasture and grazing land" (1943, 58). Hispanics were "running a race with the most recent newcomers, the Anglo Americans. This is one reason why the limited resources of the middle Valley are subject to such severe competition." (Harper et al. 1943, 16).

By 1930 the few northern New Mexicans who had adapted to the dramatic changes introduced by the new social and economic order and held on to their land lived a comfortable life as ranchers and farmers (Sánchez 1967). And by 1940 only 30 percent of the population was dependent on farming operations. Of these 30 percent in agriculture only 10 percent totally depended on the land for a livelihood (Harper et al. 1943, 58–69). Some who had taken advantage of the extremely limited educational opportunities were employed in state and federal government jobs. The majority of Hispanic New Mexicans, however, wrote George I. Sánchez, were "a severely handicapped social and economic minority" (1967, 27). According to Sánchez, lack of educational opportunities was a principal contributing factor to this condition. On the other hand, the dramatic impact the new society had on land tenure and ownership of the native community cannot be ignored as a factor contributing to these dismal social conditions. Industrial jobs pulled many away from the villages, but "the depression had destroyed this migrant livelihood for most of the workers, and since the land could not support them, they turned to the government's new relief programs" (Dinwoodie 1986, 300–01).

WELFARE STATE IN A TRADITIONAL SOCIETY

Welfare in New Mexico has some politically and culturally unrelated antecedents. Native Americans by virtue of their cosmology, beliefs, and social organization, for example, had an inherent system where family and clan assured the human welfare of those in need due to misfortune. New Spain as well as Mexico promulgated semi-feudal policies where the state rather than the family was responsible for the indigent. The territorial welfare laws after 1848 shifted responsibility for the "unable-bodied" indigent from the state to the family. In 1919 the Bureau of Child Welfare was created to administer programs to care for and protect children. In 1931 the bureau turned to the needy as a category at the request of the governor to conduct a survey of relief needs. Later that year the bureau was placed in charge of the federal relief funds allocated to New Mexico. The New Mexico Department of Public Welfare was created in 1937 in response to the Social Security Act of 1935 (New Mexico Department of Public Welfare 1947).

The new Department of Public Welfare took administrative charge of Old Age Assistance (OAA), Aid to Dependent Children (ADC), Aid to the Needy Blind (ANB), and general assistance (GA). In addition to its role in administering public assistance the agency was responsible for certification and referral to relief work or work relief agencies. This last activity became the main service function of welfare workers. Between 1937 and 1942, the agency referred to the Civilian Conservation Corps a large number of youth who because of their status generated a monthly allotment to their parents. The Works Project Administration and work relief also brought income directly into the villages; the worker or recipient did not have to leave the home area (New Mexico Department of Public Welfare 1947).

As in other parts of the country, the welfare system in New Mexico had an enormous task before it. Jobs away from home during the previous three decades ended with the Great Depression. Before the Depression, an average of one individual out of every family was employed out-of-state. After 1929 only two or three out of 100 to 150 people were employed outside their communities. The rest returned to their marginal subsistence farming plots, which they had left behind during the last three decades. As already mentioned, the land could not sustain them so they turned to government emergency relief programs. Recognizing the relationship of the economic picture to land as a traditional source of subsistence and in response to political pressures by Hispanos, New Deal officials made an effort to maximize use by local villagers of land then under the management of the federal government. It had been available only to large commercial livestock operators (Dinwoodie 1986, 301–03 and 310).[3]

Regardless of the help from these and other efforts directed at building the foundations of a land based economy, 60 to 70 percent of the region's residents continued to depend on relief orders or were on the relief rolls (Weigle 1975).

The number of recipients climbed gradually during the first year of welfare operations. By 1943 costs were getting out of control; thus, ceilings were placed on OAA grants. Eventually funding leveled off and federal policies brought the state income support consistent with national standards.

By the early 1940s it was clear that welfare had assumed an economic development role in northern New Mexico. Harper et al. summarized the alternatives to the economic conditions as follows: Either attack the problem by "contributing to relief appropriations through taxation" or by endorsing "a program of redistributing the use of publicly owned resources in order to allow an underprivileged section of the population access to a livelihood" (Harper et al. 1943, 102). Other students of the region recommended a comprehensive program such as the Tennessee Valley Authority (Ellis 1948, 15). Relief appropriations continued; land distribution, addressed above, was a small part of the New Deal and opened avenues for grazing among small subsistence farmers; but it had no impact on the New Mexico land grant issue. The fundamental question of developing a sound economic base by way of land redistribution that took relief programs into account only as intermediate emergency measures and not as a permanent economic foundation was too radical an idea; it floundered and died in the face of conservative forces in Congress. Individual farm ownership won over communal land-use programs (Dinwoodie 1986, 314). Relief programs became the "safety net."

In the preventive arena community education, small scale agricultural projects, medical care, and nutrition and crafts programs were implemented in a few northern New Mexico counties. These endeavors seemed to have been grounded on an understanding of the region's conditions. As the war economy minimized the importance of welfare in general, however, it affected the northern New Mexico community by luring residents away and diminishing the importance of the community development programs.[4]

Amendments to the Social Security Act of 1935 led to a growth in welfare caseloads in New Mexico; in 1953 the first organized public reaction to increased welfare dependency and costs was organized by the Taxpayers Association of New Mexico. In a report prepared for the state legislature the Taxpayers Association (1953) called for lien laws to recover the cost of assistance from the client's estate and for the enactment of relative responsibility laws, which placed partial responsibility on relatives for assistance to the needy. This proposal made clear that Old Age Assistance was not a pension, as many Hispanics had been accustomed to calling it. In the 1955 legislative session, both a lien law and a relative responsibility law were enacted.

The 1955 legislative session was confronted with a deficit appropriation request due to declining earmarked revenues and the dramatic rise in cases. In response, a special legislative session was called in 1955; it authorized the formation of the Welfare Investigating Committee. Following a series of hearings throughout the state, the committee prepared a report that underscored the seriousness of Public Assistance programs (Committee and Staff Reports 1957). It recommended that a concerted effort in economic development planning be undertaken and that public assistance be administered separately from social services and have a director under the governor. The committee also recommended abolishing the lien and relative responsibility laws, which had not been in operation long enough to be evaluated.

Little had changed by 1956, despite efforts by a combination of federal and state agencies concerned with rural development. Scarcity of employment in the village enclave, small-scale subsistence farming as an adjunct to seasonal employment, conflicts over land and water, inadequate educational opportunities, and other poor socioeconomic conditions persisted. A sample survey of north-central New Mexico by the Agricultural Experiment Station of New Mexico State University in collaboration with the Agriculture Research Service of the U.S. Department of Agriculture in 1956 reported that "Of 135 household members who reported as available for employment, only 58 per cent indicated that they were actively seeking employment. Of 69 household members who said they were willing to leave home to get work, nearly a third had no plans to do so." Of those reporting they were employed, most worked at semi-skilled or manual labor jobs that required very little formal education. ". . . [N]early one-fifth were receiving public welfare assistance. About 30 percent were receiving either unemployment compensation or public welfare payments or both" (Agricultural Experiment Station 1960, iii–iv).

The Department of Public Welfare conducted its own study in 1956 (Ellis 1957, 35–40) that compared the rates of dependency on welfare between San Miguel (a north-central New Mexico county) and Lea (a southeastern New Mexico county) at that time enjoying the benefits of the oil and gas boom. A random sample of 10 percent of all ADC active cases in San Miguel and 20 percent of all active ADC cases in Lea was selected. The study revealed what is obvious to those familiar with patterns of ethnic stratification in the state. San Miguel ADC payees were overwhelmingly Hispanic. The majority in Lea were black.[5] In San Miguel, 38 percent were over age forty; while in Lea the majority ranged from ages twenty-one to thirty-nine.[6] The characteristics that qualified clients for assistance were as follows: the majority of cases in San Miguel met eligibility because of physical disability; the second stated reason was social breakdown, such as family problems and cultural factors, including language barriers and "customary traits."[7]

The extremely limited educational opportunities in the 1930s discussed by George I. Sánchez (1967) had improved somewhat by the mid 1950s, yet "educational retardation" among Hispanic recipients was a significant finding of the Department of Public Welfare study. Over 80 percent of the San Miguel AFDC payees had less than an eighth grade education, as compared with 70 percent in Lea County. Almost 70 percent had no employment history before receiving ADC, as compared to 31 percent in Lea county (Ellis 1957).[8]

The recommendations of studies by the Agriculture Department and the Department of Welfare were similar. The former urged "a program to induce outmigration . . . [of] the younger age groups, . . . improved education programs that would emphasize specialized training. . . . [and] a reappraisal of public programs, such as welfare assistance, to determine if some adjustments might improve the situation" (Agricultural Experiment Station 1960, 28). The Department of Welfare study emphasized the educational dimensions, including the need to conduct ". . . fundamental research in educational retardation; the. . . . enforcement of compulsory school laws; and the need for teaching vocational skills." One recommendation focused on "the need for jobs at a living wage especially in counties similar to San Miguel." This was the only specific mention of employment with equitable remuneration. A final recommendation specified "the need for integrated community services which enable young people to acquire linguistic, recreational, vocational, and social skills and a sense of civic and moral values befitting a free citizenry" (Ellis 1957, 40).[9]

Although some of the administrative recommendations were implemented in the mid-sixties with the reorganization of the New Mexico Department of Public Welfare and Department of Public Health into a Department of Health and Social Services, public assistance has never been placed directly under the governor. In another reorganization of state government a decade later a Department of Human Services was created at a state cabinet level. Public health functions were placed under the Department of Health and Environment. The relative responsibility and lien laws were abrogated in the 1956 session of the legislature. None of the substantive recommendations was implemented until other federal programs were brought to the region years later under the Economic Opportunity Act of 1964 (EOA) and other legislation on the Great Society initiative. These programs will be discussed under the section of the Great Society.

In the early 1960s, the Area Redevelopment Administration (ARA), through various agencies of the federal government working in rural development, offered economic development support for the region. Resource development projects availed low-interest loans to rural area entrepreneurs to encourage tourism and rekindle an interest in small-scale agriculture for the production of traditional Spanish foods. Since the target of ARA projects was the small entrepreneurial sector, the impact on present or potential welfare recipients was probably minimal. Beneficiaries of ARA loans were local businessmen and those heirs of the native farmers and ranchers who had survived the dramatic changes occurring since the turn of the century and had thrived as independent small farmers. In any case, these new initiatives coincided with a resurgence of land grant claims by native Hispanics which resulted in violence in Rio Arriba county.[10]

GREAT SOCIETY PROGRAMS

In 1965 the War on Poverty spawned by the EOA of 1964 came to New Mexico. Hispano politicians reacted with suspicion to the principle of "maximum feasible participation," a hallmark of the act, as community activists got the most out of it in their attempts to empower the impoverished community through the Community Action Program, VISTA volunteers, and migrant programs.[11] Meanwhile, in 1964 The Food Stamp Act was enacted, which benefited many northern New Mexicans by virtue of their unemployed status. In 1972 the Supplemental Security Income program was instituted, bringing many people receiving public assistance under the new program and leaving AFDC to carry the brunt of criticism leveled against welfare.

Between 1965 and the mid-1970s the EOA generated a host of training projects sponsored by the U.S. Department of Labor. These programs offered stipends to students attending Northern New Mexico Normal at El Rito (now Northern New Mexico Community College in El Rito and Espanola) and vocational schools in Santa Fe as well as in Albuquerque. New careers programs promised to move persons from clients to service providers as para-professionals. AFDC recipients were required to participate in Work Incentive Programs (WIN). Many beneficiaries of these programs viewed the stipend as a wage, a suggestion that government welfare programs were perceived as legitimate employment activities. As in the New Deal era, people "earned income" in their own communities.

Amendments to the EOA created the Special Impact Program that authorized Community Development Corporations (CDC). CDCs were designed to stimulate economic development in the community and increase employment opportunities. As capitalist ventures they were undercapitalized, but some continued in existence after government support was curtailed by the Reagan Administration. A northern New Mexico CDC endures in 1988, a decade after government funding discontinued, and offers alcoholism treatment services under contract with the state's Health and Environment Department; it is building an economic base with its own investments by purchasing land.[12]

THE WORKFARE TREND: WELFARE REFORM IN THE 1980S

The demographic picture for northern New Mexico remains relatively unchanged at the time of this writing. Mora, Rio Arriba, San Miguel, Santa Fe, and Taos counties' populations are over 50 percent Hispanic, with Mora the highest at 86.6 percent and Santa Fe the lowest at 55.6. The socioeconomic picture according to the 1984 *New Mexico Statistical Abstract* was not encouraging. In Mora county the median family income was almost half that of the state's median family income. All other northern New Mexico counties, with the exception of Santa Fe, are below the state's median family income. Unemployment rates for Mora county are 31.6 percent, for Rio Arriba 20.4 percent, and for San Miguel 12.6 percent, compared with 9.2 percent for the state overall (Bureau of Business and Economic Research 1984).[13]

Within the welfare domain, the aggregate picture also remains relatively unchanged. Of those qualifying for food stamps, approximately 57 percent of household heads are Hispanic and 16 percent Native American, accounting for almost three-quarters of the population (New Mexico Department of Human Services 1986).

In the AFDC program, New Mexico saw an increase of one thousand new cases in 1985–1987. The Department of Human Services anticipates that by 1990 the present (1987) figure of 19,000 families now participating in AFDC will have risen to over 21,000, and total costs will have climbed from the present (77th fiscal year request) $54.9 million to $70 million (New Mexico Department of Human Services 1987).

Closer scrutiny of the traditional Hispanic counties' eligibility for food stamps reveals the following: Rio Arriba, Mora, and Taos have more male than female heads of household who are eligible; in the rest of the participating counties more women heads of household are eligible. In more urbanized counties, including San Miguel, which historically has had a high dependency rate, women heads of household outnumber men. This suggests that socioeconomic conditions are so very poor in the traditional rural Hispanic counties that the male head of household, rather than the single female head of household as in the rest of the state, is at risk.

A consistent pattern emerging since the beginning of welfare programs in New Mexico seems to continue into the present. Employment opportunities for men are extremely limited. Yet some individuals and their families have a small plot of land and a limited number of livestock; they haul their own wood for heating and survive at a subsistence level. While this mode of existence offers certain informal social props it is not sufficient to sustain an adequate standard of living from an economic perspective; thus most men and their families living under these conditions are eligible for food stamps. They become candidates for residual welfare programs since lack of steady, covered employment denies them Old Age, Survivors, and Disability Insurance.

Despite the limited employment opportunities in this region and the bleak socioeconomic picture, work incentives for welfare recipients are the first line of offense in the current (1987) welfare reform strategy. Building on the legacy of the AFDC Work Incentive Program (WIN), the Community Work Experience Program (CWEP), and the Food Stamp Job Search Program, the New Mexico Department of Human Services has implemented the first phase of a comprehensive reform plan directed at full employment of its food stamp recipients. Titled "Project Forward" (New Mexico Department of Human Services 1986), the program consolidates work incentive and training programs into a comprehensive project that determines eligibility of food stamps recipients. It issues food stamps to applicants who accept employment counseling and seek a job. The jobs are expected to be found in the private sector.

At this writing, "Project Mainstream" (New Mexico Department of Human Services 1987), the current administration's (Governor Carruthers') welfare reform package was recently enacted into law in the 1988 legislature. Most of the governor's requests were passed. The proposal in its original form included reforms of income maintenance as well as noncash programs administered by the Department of Human Services. "Project Mainstream" reflects the optimism of projected growth in the number of jobs in the service and sales industries; consequently, like "Project Forward," "Mainstream" aims at full participation in the economic system of the welfare population that is able to work. Its goals are stated accordingly: "1) to make parents better able to support their children; 2) to control the long-term cost of the AFDC program; and 3) to break the welfare cycle" (1).

The objectives of "Mainstream" include a combination of work requirements for clients and an adjustment in attitudes so that eligible recipients place value on the concept of work and develop personal responsibilities in the management of their affairs.[14] These individual objectives will be enhanced by the county level welfare agency, which will strive to create opportunities for self-reliance through education, training, and enterprise. Among other structural supports built into the proposal's design are the provision of incentives to work, the elimination of barriers to full-time employment, the increase in efforts to enforce child support, and the increase in efficiency of service delivery, as well as other efforts that will diminish the need for public assistance.

Under the proposed reform the private sector is expected to be-

237

come a full partner with federal and state agencies in implementing this plan and assuring its success. The administration of the program itself is composed of a constellation of functions including social services counseling, enforcing child support payments from absent parents, ensuring that parents assume responsibility for their daughters' sexual behavior by requiring them to support any offspring born out of wedlock, and providing job placement, support, and special services to youths receiving AFDC payments. Meanwhile, welfare rolls are expected to be reduced by a requested change in federal regulations. New Mexico's plan intends to lower the dependent child's age that exempts mothers from participation in work training from age six to age one. In New Mexico the majority of children participating in AFDC are older than the recommended age for exemption. Failure to comply with the work training and employment requirements, even if it means relocation to another town, will be cause for denial of assistance.

Of these proposals, the grandparent responsibility clause for the unmarried daughter's child was defeated; the floor of the dependent child's age for exemption of the mother from work training was lowered from age six to age three. According to the welfare reform task force convened to evaluate the governor's plan, it is doubtful that the federal government will accept that change. The counseling provisions were not included in the legislative package since they are operational procedures rather than policy. All child-care-related proposals and income retrieval from absent fathers plans were passed. But, despite the concern of the task force over the effect of work requirements on AFDC recipients living in rural areas, all provisions associated with workfare were enacted into law.

The principal defining features of New Mexico's 1986–1988 welfare reform proposals are related to employment in the private sector. The secondary characteristics focus on the client's personal responsibilities. Neither of these two emphases is New Mexican in origin, although both are compatible with the goals of current state administration officials who are endorsing them. These objectives reflect the attitudes and values of national policy planners and are directed at urban communities where employment alternatives are greater. Welfare reform is founded on the availability of jobs; these jobs are not in the rural northern New Mexico counties. The legislative task force addressed this issue, citing that by the governor's own admission, most of the projected job growth will be in urban areas. The proposed work requirements, the task force concluded, would draw AFDC families from the rural areas, severing their existing informal support systems. Settlement of these families in urban areas would add undue burdens because of the higher cost of living, and their presence there would add stress to the already critical public housing scene. This analysis was evidently disregarded by the legislature and the governor.

Thus, another chapter in the history of welfare in New Mexico begins, suggesting at the very outset that it will incorporate historical continuities into its program, as well as current prejudices and visions. The recurrent themes in the state's welfare past that may help explain the role of welfare as an economic foundation, and the shortcomings of the various reform measures throughout the history of welfare in New Mexico are summarized below.

SUMMARY OF ANTECEDENTS, WELFARE PROGRAMS, AND REFORM

1. New Mexico Hispano society was supported by a subsistence mode of production based on large land grants used for stock raising and smaller subsistence plots around villages where people lived. After annexation to the United States the Hispano community lost 90 percent of its lands. The railroad drew subsistence farmers into wage labor and through the years the gradual erosion of existing land holdings continued, eventually transforming the life style into one of itinerant wage labor and part-time subsistence farming and stock raising. The Depression displaced itinerant wage labor, forcing the marginal workers to return to the subsistence plots that could no longer support them. At this point the New Deal entered. Two significant programs were introduced: land use and emergency relief. While some gains were made in communal use of public lands, the land question was not addressed fully due to the ideology of the dominant forces in Congress; in time emergency welfare relief became institutionalized and land reform was no longer a goal of the New Deal.

2. Sustained economic development programs of an industrial nature were never introduced to rural areas; thus welfare filled the vacuum and became an economic prop for the region. The literature on welfare in New Mexico does not identify welfare

as an economic foundation, rather the situation is viewed from the perspective of the client: he or she became *dependent* on welfare. According to the dominant view, the client is responsible for the dependency, not the social conditions as outlined here. That being the case, reform programs and welfare goals have been geared to changing the individual rather than the social conditions.

3. With the growth of welfare as a mode of subsistence for the population of northern New Mexico, one of several recommendations to alter this relationship and break the growing dependence encouraged out-migration by the younger generation. The 1988 welfare reform package by implication includes these recommendations; job requirements in areas that have no jobs encourage out-migration from the villages, since people must move in order to qualify for training or assistance.

4. The various studies in the past describe the problems of welfare dependency as deriving in part from "educational retardation." Again, the problem is with the individual and not the system or the institutions, leading to reform measures that offer job training. Job training in rural Hispano counties where jobs are scarce is largely irrelevant. On the other hand, implicit in this requirement is support of out-migration, its consequences and impact on rural clients already having been discussed.

5. The values of a preindustrial society endure among many villagers in northern New Mexico. Some are detriments to modernization. On the other hand, aspects of a subsistence agricultural society offer informal supports. Their absence would render village dwellers destitute and alienated in their own villages or urban migrants if they are forced from their rural homes. Previous efforts, as well as current reform proposals, offer casework services to clients and potential clients on assumptions that because of their enduring cultural traits they do not embrace the concept of work and therefore cannot find employment. It is also assumed that potential clients are not responsible for the management of their affairs. Accordingly, the client is the focus of the reform and not the system.

Viewed within the historical overview presented here, current reform efforts are shortsighted and far from reform. The concluding section offers brief reflections on the past and on the prospects for the future.

CONCLUSIONS AND RECOMMENDATIONS

This historical overview of welfare in the middle and northern Rio Grande region of New Mexico shows that welfare, an institution developed and nurtured by industrial society, was imposed on a traditional subsistence agricultural society whose resources had been depleted in the course of political changes. It has relieved misery and suffering throughout its existence. It seems, however, that the institution of income maintenance was not an organic part of other New Deal programs of community development and land reform. Consequently, income support programs missed the importance of the social and cultural antecedents of the region taken into account by the land use endeavors, and eventually because part of the area's economic foundations.

In summary, welfare became industrial society's legacy in northern New Mexico, which resulted in perpetual dependency on welfare programs among a few of northern New Mexico's Hispanic residents. This trend has led to strong stereotypical criticisms of welfare dependency among northern New Mexicans, placing the responsibility on the individual while ignoring the historical and social background. Disregard for the macro conditions detours efforts that might attack the problem at its roots. The latest welfare reform proposals, as others before them, have singled out "cultural traits," attitudes about work, and inadequate social and educational preparation of the region's inhabitants. The current plans with emphasis on employment seemingly ignore the fundamental socioeconomic conditions and cultural systems of the area and focus on altering the client's life ways instead.

Specific alternative proposals to welfare reform are beyond the scope of this paper. But the summary above raises significant questions for critical reflection. Such reflection is particularly important as we move from the industrial society that gave birth to the welfare state to a post-industrial society that promises to usher out the welfare state as we know it. Furthermore, as this trend gains momentum the region attracts more people, placing more stress on limited natural resources and bringing attention once more to the land and water issues.

Redistribution of lands among its historical heirs is not a dead issue in New Mexico. In response to political pressure from grass roots Chicano and Indian people, the governor of New Mexico has agreed to appoint a commission that will investigate land, water, and human rights issues affecting the indigenous peoples in the state. Welfare and social services administrators should consider the relationship of the role of this commission to issues of poverty and social adjustment in a society in transition.

Land distribution, a topic that is clearly related to welfare in rural New Mexico, should be of interest to Third World countries now in the process of modernization and implementing their own welfare programs.

In the broader economic development scene, northern New Mexico is not receptive to industrial projects in the traditional sense as they would mar the landscape and affect adversely the region's tourist potential. Accordingly, tourism is offered as a "clean" industry. The development of tourism for economic development is intimately related to land and water issues and the villager's traditional life style. Social service and welfare administrators should participate in overall tourist development plans in the northern region and be aware of the meaning to villagers of the "Old Townization" of villages, or the turning of traditional communities into tourist attractions.

More to the point of social change and appropriate preventive prescriptions, many northern New Mexico communities are at the point of transition from a pre-industrial to a post-industrial society, having missed the middle stage—industrial society. In an information society, one toward which the developed world is rapidly moving, labor and employment change. Service industries replace manufacturing and the workplace is modified. Accordingly, the information society offers both a threat and an opportunity to the northern New Mexico community. If it does not adjust and accommodate to this trend Hispano New Mexico will suffer and its future citizens will do the menial jobs of the service industries—welfare of the future. Consequently, the greatest possibility for preventive programming lies in the area of education and training (an area of ongoing concern for welfare reformers). They should join with education planners and communication specialists to link rural schools in northern New Mexico with communication networks, and usher the region into the twenty-first century appropriately. Excellent programs should be established in rural areas and barrio schools for basic education, sciences, humanities, and the arts, all revolving around computer literacy for the young generation. Their parents, if in need of income support, should receive a guaranteed income similar to the Family Assistance Plan recommended by the Nixon Administration.

The last recommendation is a radical preventive measure. The implementation of such a program at this time is as significant to the future of rural Hispanic New Mexicans as having the land question fully and equitably addressed shortly after annexation and during the early days of the Depression would have been for them then.

Finally, the underlying values about welfare should view all income support programs as truly "social security"—human and social investments—rather than as the last line of defense for the impoverished. If a plan guided by these values were to emerge, the focus would be on the economic structures and institutions as well as on the individual. Social work, instead of counseling to readjust ideas about work in clients, would be a process of consciousness-raising about the past, which more than likely defines their client's current situation; from there a responsible path to the future can be discerned.

NOTES

1.   New Mexico was settled in 1598 by Juan de Oñate who led a group of soldier-citizens and Spanish settlers to the northern Rio Grande Valley near present-day San Juan Pueblo. Indians took an oath of allegiance to the Crown of Spain and became vassals under a semi-feudal institution called the *encomienda*. Those who administered the encomiendas utilized Indian labor and extracted tribute from the Pueblo natives. Native religion was denigrated and religious leaders were persecuted. In 1680 Pueblo Indians revolted and drove the Spanish governmental and ecclesiastical apparatus to El Paso del Norte in present-day Juarez Mexico. New Mexico was reconquered in 1692, marking the beginning of Spanish presence in this region. The encomienda system was abolished, and a policy of issuing land grants to prospective settlers was implemented to encourage settlement of the region. Land was issued to soldier-citizens, ordinary citizens wishing to establish a community, to entrepreneurs, and to Pueblo Indians who already occupied the land. Governed by the Laws of the Indies promulgated in 1680 to protect Indian rights in all of *Ibero* America, community and Indian lands were held in common by the grantees. For a good review of New Mexico settlement, the Pueblo Revolt, and land grant issues, the following books are recommended: *Albuquerque* by Marc Simmons (1982) and *Mercedes Reales* by Victor Westphall (1983).

2. The foundations of traditional New Mexico Hispanic society and culture were laid between 1692 and the 1820s when the mixture occurred between Spanish, Mexican mestizos (Spanish and central Mexican Indian mixed bloods), and Pueblo and North American Plains Indians. From the amalgamation of races and the proximity of the various racial and ethnic groups emerged a consciousness that reflected both the Catholic religion and Native American world views. Most of the population that adhered to these emerging world views was composed of impoverished subsistence farmers and day laborers. Because of the Indian and mestizo influence and the lower-class status, the beliefs reflect both an ethnic and class consciousness, or *genízaro* consciousness—the consciousness of the detribalized and hispanicized Indians.

This consciousness is defined by four principal features discussed by Fray Angelico Chavez in *My Penitente Land* (1974): 1. Belief in Santos (carved wooden images of Catholic saints) as intercessors with the supernatural and social mediators, 2. veneration of la *Virgen de Guadalupe* (an Indian Blessed Mother), 3. belief in the sacred and healing powers of earth as symbolized by the Santuario del Potrero in Chimayo, and 4. the Pious Fraternity of Our Brother Jesus of Nazareth, known as the Penitentes. Penitentes served as the central spiritual group in the community and are believed by some scholars to have provided a network for political action and social movements.

The 1837 revolt in Chimayo and the 1847 revolt in northern New Mexico against American occupation that ended in Taos with the assassination of the first American governor were believed to have had genízaro and Penitente involvement. Others of the higher classes who stood to lose from annexation may also have been involved. Their consciousness of resistance would be covered under genízaro consciousness.

3. David H. Dinwoodie (1986) gives a full account of the New Deal's involvement in land reform and utilization of public lands by Indians and Hispano villagers. Tragically, the story Dinwoodie tells shows Indians and Hispanos fighting for the limited natural resources at a time when the national economic picture made the struggle for resources more critical. Both groups ended up winning something, but the commitment to go deeper into land redistribution ended when President Roosevelt failed to rearrange the Supreme Court and Congress killed its land reform measures.

Harper, Córdova and Oberg's recommendations of redistribution of natural resources suggests a link to the land grant question and the loss of land by native Hispanics after annexation in 1848. Redistribution of land would be a moral act as well as an economic initiative to solve the many problems encountered by the native people. For further elaboration on this question refer to Westphall (1983), Van Ness (1980), and Tijerina (discussed under Note 10 below).

4. J.R. Reid (1946) describes the kinds of community projects which followed the New Deal programs. They focused on community self-reliance, emphasizing the life-styles of subsistence agriculture. In addition to programs of community decision-making, these projects also improved conditions that were depleting and eroding the soil, worked at expanding grazing lands, organized medical services, and offered crafts training and technical assistance on production and marketing. These programs seemed to have taken the social and economic antecedents into consideration; but they were thwarted by World War II, which drew many rural residents away to war related industries. The economic problems were addressed by the war economy.

5. Ethnic background of ADC payees in San Miguel and Lea counties (Ellis 1957, 36).

Table 11.1   Ethnic Background of ADC Payees in San Miguel and Lea Counties

Ethnic Background	San Miguel		Lea	
	No.	Percentage	No.	Percentage
Anglo-American	2	3.8	3	18.8
Spanish-American	49	94.3	0	00.0
Negro	0	00.0	13	81.2
Other	1	1.9	0	00.0
Totals	52	100.0	16	100.0

6. Ages of Payees of Families Receiving ADC in San Miguel and Lea counties (Ellis 1957, 36).

Table 11.2   Ages of Payees in Families Receiving ADC in San Miguel and Lea Counties

Ages	San Miguel		Lea	
	No.	Percentage	No.	Percentage
Under 21	3	5.7	1	6.3
21 through 29	9	17.3	5	31.2
30 through 39	12	23.1	5	31.2
40 or more	20	38.5	4	25.0
No mother in home	8	15.4	1	6.3

7. The statement, "customary traits," refers to the value orientations of a traditional society, which encompass the extended family, work for meeting immediate needs and not necessarily employment with a long-term goal,

an aversion to geographical mobility and a permanent link to the region as homeland, and lack of interest in education to prepare for a modern, industrial society. These beliefs are perceived to be in conflict with the requirements of industrial society that undergird the welfare state where the individual is valued over the group, work is seen as employment, mobility is necessary, and education for employment and wage earning is fundamental for economic independence. See Octavio Romano (1968) for a penetrating criticism of the perspective that blames the victim.

8.   Educational Level of Homemakers in Families Receiving ADC in San Miguel and Lea counties (Ellis 1957, 36).

Table 11.3   Educational Level of Homemakers in Families Receiving ADC in San Miguel and Lea Counties

| | San Miguel | | Lea | |
Years of Schooling	No.	Percentage	No.	Percentage
None	4	7.7	0	00.0
1 through 3	12	23.1	0	00.0
4 through 6	11	21.2	3	18.8
7 and 8	15	28.8	5	31.2
9 and 10	6	11.5	2	12.4
11 and 12	1	1.9	3	18.8
Unknown	3	5.8	3	18.8

9.   The argument for instilling "civic and moral values befitting a free citizenry" is related to the issues discussed in Note 7 above.

10.   The land grant question in New Mexico has a long history. Land grants were first issued in the Colonial (1692–1921) and Mexican periods (1821–1846) to encourage settlement of the region as discussed in note one. Some of those grants were communal and (some believe) could not be sold by individuals. Many were sold and others were paid in lieu of legal fees in adjudication litigation following annexation. Harper et al. addressed the issue; their suggestions are covered under Note 4 above. Most land grant heirs remember with bitterness and resentment that part of their heritage, but litigation never yielded positive results for them. In the late 1950s Reies López Tijerina, an itinerant Pentecostal preacher and former farm worker from Texas, arrived in northern New Mexico to right the wrongs perpetrated on New Mexico land grant heirs. He mobilized a following and organized the *Alianza Federal de Pueblos Libres*. The alliance was composed mostly of the vestiges of subsistence farmers and heirs of landholding peasants who still adhered to traditional values. Conflict tactics were employed which eventually led to confrontations and violence in Tierra Amarilla in 1967. The

social movement that developed in the 1960s has been compared to the social banditry movements of peasant societies undergoing modernization. To some New Mexicans the movements was an embarrassment; to the impoverished victims of land dislocations it offered some hope for justice. For a detailed report of the movement see Reies Lopez Tijerina (1978) *Mi Lucha por la Tierra.*

11. The introduction of the War on Poverty programs to New Mexico were to some residents echoes of the New Deal programs. However, organizations spawned by the Area Redevelopment Administration and Department of Agriculture agencies sought to become the vehicles for community action. This led to a struggle with activist groups which resulted in the formation, under the sponsorship of the New Mexico Council of Churches, of the Home Education Livelihood Program (HELP) funded by the Migrant Division of the Office of Economic Opportunity early in the tenure of the OEO. HELP became the main force in the rural areas implementing stipended craft-oriented training programs and other economic development ventures that never fully blossomed.

12. Siete del Norte, the Hispanic northern New Mexico CDC, grew out of the HELP program. In theory it was to bring social services and economic development closer to the community. The service projects were funded directly by the federal government for noncash services, and the economic development dimensions were presented as "Brown" capitalist ventures that were sorely undercapitalized. While the ideas were sound in terms of the region's needs, both aspects failed to develop as real alternatives. For a good review of CDCs I recommend Lawrence F. Parachini, Jr.'s *A Political History of the Special Impact Program* (1980).

13. Conditions in northern New Mexico villages have not changed much since the 1984 report. A new trend is developing, however. Villages are taking an "Old Town" image, where they are becoming "art and culture" havens for non-Hispanics.

14. Counseling and social services aimed at value accommodation has been recommended since the mid-1950s and is part of the current (1987) reform platform. The value conflict approach criticized by Romano referred to in Note 7 above is applicable for critical review of this policy.

BIBLIOGRAPHY

Agricultural Experiment Station. 1960. "Rural People and Their Resources, North-Central New Mexico." (by Marlowe M. Taylor.) Las Cruces: New Mexico State University.

Atencio, Tomás. 1985. "Social Change and Community Conflict in Old Albuquerque, New Mexico." Ph.D. diss., University of New Mexico, Albuquerque.

Browning, Robert X. 1986. *Politics and Social Welfare Policy in the United States.* Knoxville: University of Tennessee Press.

Bureau of Business and Economic Research. 1984. *Statistical Abstract.* Albuquerque: Bureau of Business and Economic Research.

Chavez, Angelico. 1974. *My Penitente Land.* Albuquerque: University of New Mexico Press.

Committee and Staff Reports to the New Mexico Legislature. 1957. "Report of the Welfare Investigating Committee to the Legislature." In *Public Assistance and Social Services in New Mexico,* 7–10. Santa Fe: New Mexico State Legislature.

Dinwoodie, David H. 1986. "Indians, Hispanos, and Land Grant Reform: A New Deal Struggle in New Mexico." *The Western Historical Quarterly* 2:291–323.

Ellis, Helen Heacock. 1948. "Public Assistance in New Mexico." M.A. thesis. The School of Social Service Administration, University of Chicago.

———. 1957. "The Process of Aid to Clients." In *Public Assistance and Social Services in New Mexico,* 17–55. Committee and Staff Reports to the New Mexico Legislature.

Harper, Allan G., Andrew R. Córdova, and Kalevro Oberg. 1943. *Man and Resources in the Middle Rio Grande Valley.* Albuquerque: University of New Mexico Press.

New Mexico Department of Human Services. *Project Forward: State of New Mexico Employment Assistance Program.* Welfare reform program implemented in 1986. A proposal to reform the welfare system in New Mexico.

New Mexico Department of Public Welfare. 1947. "Annual Report, Fiscal Year Ending June 30, 1947." Santa Fe: Department of Public Welfare.

Parachini, Jr., Lawrence F. 1980. *A Political History of the Special Impact Program.* Cambridge: Center for Community Development.

Reid, J.T. 1946. *It Happened in Taos.* Albuquerque: University of New Mexico Press.

Rios-Bustamente, Antonio Jose. 1976. "New Mexico in the Eighteenth Century: Life, Labor and Trade in la Villa de San Felipe de Albuquerque 1706–1790." *Atzlán: International Journal of Chicano Studies Research* 3:357–89.

Romano, Octavio. 1908. "The Anthropology and Sociology of the Mexican-Americans: The Distortion of Mexican-American History." *El Grito* 1:13–26.

Sánchez, George I. 1967. *The Forgotten People: A Study of New Mexicans.* Albuquerque: Calvin Horn.

Simmons, Marc. 1982. *Albuquerque.* Albuquerque: University of New Mexico Press.

State of New Mexico, Human Services Department. 1987. *Mainstream: Economic Independence for Families.*

The Taxpayers Association of New Mexico. 1953. "Controlling Public Assistance Costs," A Presentation for the Legislature of New Mexico. Santa Fe, NM.

Tijerina, Reis López. 1978. *Mi Lucha por la Tierra.* Mexico: DF.: Fondo de Cultural Economica.

Van Ness, John R. 1980. "Introduction." In *Spanish and Mexican Land Grants in New Mexico and Colorado,* edited by John R. and Christine M. Van Ness, 3–11. Manhattan, Kan.: Sunflower University Press.

Weigle, Marta. 1975. *Villages of Northern New Mexico.* Santa Fe: The Lightening Tree.

Westphall, Victor. 1983. *Mercedes Reales.* Albuquerque: University of New Mexico Press.

12

Policy Making for Indigent Health Care in Texas: A Case Study in Welfare Reform

Philip K. Armour

POLICY TURNING POINT FOR A WELFARE LAGGARD

In an extraordinary special session, the 69th Texas Legislature passed legislation which broke with the Lone Star state's welfare traditions.[1] Of the bills passed the Texas Children's Defense Fund said, "It was like enacting a state version of Medicaid, WIC (Women, Infants and Children nutrition program), the (federal) Community Health Centers Program, and Title V Maternal and Child Health Block grant all at once" (Lanham 1985). The bills were passed in May 1985 in a highly charged atmosphere accompanied by rhetorical excesses on the parts of both advocates and opponents. Some curious and anomalous political alliances were forged in the processes of designing and enacting the legislation that defied conventional notions about Texas politics. The implementation of indigent health care programs altered historical institutions and patterns of state and local government. What makes all this so striking is that the primary beneficiaries of the program are a group that traditionally has had very few political allies in the state legislature and governor's mansion and that has been mainly neglected by these policy makers. This group is the medically indigent.

My objectives in this chapter are several: first, to describe and explain the process of enacting indigent health care legislation in

251

Texas; and second, to demonstrate the linkages between indigent health care initiatives, including Medicaid expansions, and related national welfare reform initiatives. Further, this analysis seeks to place these Texas policy initiatives within the context of the theory on and the history of welfare policy development in the United States and other advanced societies.

TEXAS SOCIO-HISTORICAL TRADITIONS IN THE CONTEXT OF THE WELFARE STATE

Texas represents a distinctive fragment of the Western societal traditions. It is the only state to join the Union as an independent republic, having secured its own independence from Mexico in a brief, heroic war led by fabled personages of the American frontier. Texas later seceded from the Union and was forcibly reunited, along with its sister Confederate States, to the United States. These nineteenth-century features, though seemingly remote from the present day political environment of an urban-industrial state containing three of America's largest cities, nonetheless create a context for interpreting Texas's historical hostility toward welfare and for understanding its fiscally conservative governmental posture.

Texas's Individualism, Free Enterprise, and Anti-statism. Applying Louis Hartz's perspective, Texas represents the rooting of distinctive fragments of European ideological and related institutional expressions of individualism, free enterprise, and anti-statism.[2] This complex is antagonistic toward notions of group dependence and collective responsibility, especially for the less fortunate in society.[3]

Harking back to the seventeenth-century Poor Laws of England, Texas's welfare policies are rooted in its post-Reconstruction Constitutions. Under the 1869 Constitution, counties are required to provide "a manual labor poor house for taking care of, managing, employing and supplying the wants of its indigent and poor inhabitants." In 1876 the legislature revised this section to make it permissive, and in a landmark 1886 case, Monghon v. Van Zandt County, the responsibility of the county commissioners court to provide medical services to indigents was affirmed. Counties were to provide "support," and as here used, "support" means more than supplying them with food and clothing and a house to stay in. It means "all that is necessary to bodily health and comfort, and it especially includes proper care, attention, and treatment during sickness." Reliance on local governments to provide for the poor has persisted in Texas's legislative and judicial history. Municipalities were given the authority to provide services in 1875. In general, local governments are charged with providing for the needs of the eligible poor within their domains, and they have had a great deal of discretion for determining the eligibility standards and the types and levels of services (or income support) offered. Local governments have provided health care through public hospitals, special hospital districts, health officers, and health departments.

In contrast to the early authorizations to local governments to provide care for the needy, the 1845, 1861, 1866, and 1869 state constitutions included a section stating that, "no appropriation for private or individual purposes . . . shall be made without concurrence of two-thirds of both Houses of the Legislature." This prohibition was strengthened in the constitution of 1876 which stated, "The Legislature shall have no power to make any grant, or authorize the making of any grant, of public money to any individual, association of individuals, municipal or other corporation whatsoever," except in the case of public calamity. This prohibition was amended in the 1890s to allow aid to Confederate soldiers and their widows. In the 1930s the constitution was amended to permit cash grants initially to the needy elderly and subsequently to other needy groups. Constitutional amendments in 1937 specified that cash grants were not to exceed $8 per month for one child or $12 per month for a family with more than one child. Limits on cash grant amounts to individuals were modified. In 1945 the constitution was amended to establish an appropriations limit of $35 million in cash grants to the needy: this limit was raised to $47 million in 1957, $52 million in 1962, and by 1969, $80 million.

Individualism, Hostility Toward Government and Ethnic Racial Diversity in a Decentralized Polity. As has been well documented by other analysts, the Elizabethan and subsequent Poor Law reforms were predicated on a conception of society and theories of individualism that inspired American individualism and antagonism toward governmental assistance. However, beginning with the 1930s, the national and many state governments began a process of expanding the scope of programs to assist the poor, unemployed, disabled, aged, and sick. Although these policy initiatives lagged behind most other advanced urban-industrial societies, enactment of these public assistance programs began at least to bring American national policies into greater harmony with those of other comparable nations.

However, as Wilensky (1965, 1975) noted, in decentralized polities—characterized by social heterogeneity and internal cleavages based on race, ethnicity, and language—the progress of welfare program development is often retarded. Nations, or their regions that are characterized by inequalities and internal divisions, tend to have greater difficulty initiating, sustaining, and expanding social policies that spring from notions of egalitarianism and collective responsibility (cf. Marshall 1964).

Such is the case of Texas. Many of its cultural ideals are hostile to egalitarianism and notions of collective responsibility. Also, Texas, in addition to being part of a decentralized, federal-state system of government, is divided into 254 counties that contain over 1,100 municipalities ranging in size from under 10 to nearly 2 million persons. Further, Texas encompasses many racial, ethnic, and linguistic groups. Despite the fact that since Stephen F. Austin's time, white Anglophones have dominated state government and other institutions, peoples of African ancestry and of Mexican and other Spanish-speaking cultures have formed sizeable proportions of the population. In particular regions or communities of the state, blacks or Spanish-speaking persons constitute the dominant group. Roughly one-third of the state's current population is made up of blacks, Hispanics, or other minority groups; over 20 percent of the state's population is Hispanic. Hence, compared to the United States as a whole, the population of Texas has a greater proportion of minority groups, especially Spanish-speaking peoples.

Following Wilensky's prediction, a polity so cleaved would encounter greater difficulty than more homogenous and centralized states in enacting egalitarian policies. Texas history is not inexplicable, rather it is intelligible in terms of broadly based theory and research on the political-institutional development of welfare policy, and its adoption and implementation.

TEXAS PARTICIPATION IN FEDERAL HEALTH AND WELFARE PROGRAMS

Texas is a state of extremes. In terms of personal wealth, the state has been the home of some of the world's most fabulously wealthy (and eccentric) individuals, for example, the late H. L. Hunt and Howard Hughes. Yet, Texas contains some of the nation's poorest residents. Per capita income figures document that Texas is a state of extremes. In 1983 its Midland Metropolitan Statistical Area (MSA) had the nation's third highest per capita income ($15,507), while Texas' three Rio Grande Valley MSAs had the nation's lowest per capita incomes. (The McAllen-Edinburg-Mission MSA had the nation's very lowest per capita income, $6,103 in 1983, Bureau of the Census, 1986.) Despite its concentrations of wealth and growth of an affluent professional and managerial class since World War II, Texas's public expenditures have not kept pace with its capacity to mitigate poverty. Despite the rhetoric of anti-taxing, anti-spending politicians of both parties, Texas is a relatively undertaxed state. In 1984 it ranked forty-third among states in per capita state tax burden and thirty-fourth in per capita tax burden, when both state and local taxes are considered (Texas Almanac 1985).

Reliance on Regressive Taxes. Further, the forms of taxation historically used in Texas are regressive, with the burden falling disproportionately on lower-income households. Texas relies heavily on regressive sales taxes and on property and oil severance taxes; unlike other urban-industrial states, Texas does not levy an individual or corporate income tax. An incantation uttered by most Texas politicians is that they will not enact such taxes because they would destroy the state's "good business" climate. With empirical evidence to the contrary (e.g., high taxing Massachusetts and California) and as the limit of sales tax expansion is being reached, Texas is being forced to consider alternative revenue sources. In any case, the ideological opponents of progressive income and corporate taxes have not found it in their interest to promote fiscal reforms that would enhance the state's ability to finance health, welfare, and education programs while reducing the inequalities in the tax system.

Underparticipation in Health and Welfare Spending. Texas is near the bottom of the league of states in terms of its participation in programs for the indigent. Unlike other urban states (e.g., New York and Wisconsin) Texas has not fully participated in public benefit programs for the indigent. Historically, Texas has had among the lowest payment schedules for families with dependent children under the AFDC system. In 1983 the state raised the average grant level

255

from only thirty-five dollars per person, per month to forty-six dollars. During the course of the indigent health care policy-making process, the Texas Department of Human Services raised the basic grant level to an average payment of about fifty-seven dollars per person. (Texas Almanac 1985; Task Force on Indigent Health Care 1984). However, Texas is still forty-sixth in the nation in the average grant amount for AFDC. In 1986, Texas provided AFDC benefits to only about 20 percent of the more than one million children living at or below the poverty level. The stringent eligibility guidelines continue to operate under a peculiar state constitutional mandate that limits AFDC spending to no more than 1 percent of the state budget. While that spending ceiling would have allowed an average grant of seventy-eight dollars per month in 1986, the Texas legislature has been spending considerably less than that amount.

In addition to the use of low AFDC financial standards, Texas was participating at a minimal level in the choice of eligibility groups that could be covered under Medicaid. Texas was covering the categorically eligible, primarily persons receiving AFDC or Supplemental Security Income (SSI) (a federal program that serves the aged, blind, and disabled), but it was not covering other optional coverage groups allowed under federal Medicaid regulations, such as children in two-parent families. While across the United States nearly half of the poverty population is covered by the Medicaid program, Texas's pattern of Medicaid coverage, like that of AFDC, was and still is far short of the national average. Only about 25 percent of the poverty population was being served under the program.

In sum, it would be hard to find a clearer case in the nation (or maybe even in any of the advanced industrial nations) of institutionalized hostility toward the poor than Texas. In the remainder of this paper I will explain how this antagonism was overcome and a new basis for enhancing public spending for the poor was made in the period from 1983 to 1985.

ASSEMBLING FORCES FAVORABLE FOR INDIGENT HEALTH CARE REFORM

As the history of public policy making reveals, the major turning points demarcating periods of incremental program growth from eras of innovative change are both a product of accidental developments and conscious planning and action. Texas public policy making for indigent health care was no exception to this rule. There were several accidents of history that made the early 1980s—an era of conservative ideological hegemony and governmental retrenchment led by the Reagan administration—auspicious for major public policy enactment in Texas.

Fiscal Crisis of a Petro-based Political Economy. First, the Texas economy was beginning to feel the effects of a leveling off in the demand for oil products, and though sharp declines in the world price for oil would occur several years in the future, public budgets were beginning to reveal their overdependence on and sensitivity to world oil price fluctuations. At this time of the twin national economic recessions of the early 1980s, Texas' economy was still relatively robust and the state was still the destination point for economic refugees from America's ailing industrial heartland. Also, migrants from an overpopulated and economically distressed Mexico, which was (and still is) unable to provide enough jobs for its people, flocked to a former province of Old Mexico.

Texas's nonunion, low-wage employers in construction and the service industries hired many of these migrants from north and south, but its underdeveloped state welfare services administered by the Texas Department of Human Services and local county welfare officials were overwhelmed with demands for public assistance benefits, food stamps, and medical services. Former residents of high-spending welfare states of the North and East were shocked when they encountered Texas's restrictive eligibility requirements, which prevented most applicants from receiving welfare benefits.

Private charities, soup kitchens, food banks, and shelters in Dallas, Ft. Worth, Houston, and San Antonio found themselves overwhelmed with demands for basic human needs of food, shelter, clothing, and transportation assistance—the spillover of persons unable to find work or to qualify for welfare benefits in Texas. Much to the chagrin of civic boosters in Houston and Dallas-Ft. Worth, homeless persons congregated in the shadows of gleaming, new downtown highrise office complexes. In short, even prior to the drop in oil prices beginning in 1985, the petroleum-dependent Texas political economy was grappling with a growing poverty population which was, among other privations, medically uninsured.

Public Hospitals in Crisis. The main recipients of the medically uninsured were (and are) the state's public community hospitals.

Past federal court orders had struck down county residency requirements that would have barred transients or new residents from hospital care. Hospitals like Dallas County's Parkland Memorial thus had to serve all persons who stated that they intended to reside in the area served by that public hospital.

Texas's underparticipation in Medicaid and its overreliance on public community hospitals to provide indigent health care is reflected in the fact that only about 6 percent of public hospital revenues come from Medicaid payments (Anderson et al. 1983). Public hospital administrators and their staffs were under such great strain that they formed their own statewide association in the early 1980s to bring their concerns to the legislature. By 1983 such lobbying efforts were beginning to pay off.

During the sixty-eighth Legislature public hospital lobbyists and their urban county representatives and senators introduced legislation (H.B. 565, H.B. 631, and H.B. 977) to enable hospital districts or public hospitals to bill counties for medical care rendered to their residents. Additional bills were introduced that would have expanded Medicaid to serve medically needy pregnant women and children. More ominous for counties making no indigent care effort was a proposal (H.B. 796) to fund tertiary care in the state's public hospitals by a per capita county assessment. State legislative leaders, under Lieutenant Governor William Hobby's direction, delayed full legislative enactment of these bills pending a statewide review of the indigent care crisis; but the county judges and commissioners realized that the days of doing nothing about indigent care, of dumping the problem on the public hospitals, were coming to an end.

Counties Confront Financial Liabilities. With its emphasis on individualism and local governmental responsibility for the problem of poverty, Texas continued to follow a course dating back to the seventeenth-century English Poor Laws' mode of regulating the underclass. One of the features of this tradition was granting to local authorities maximum discretion in determining who might be given public assistance and what benefits might be provided. Even by the early 1980s the definitions of "pauper" or "indigent" were not clearly established across the counties of Texas; almost complete local discretion in determining eligibility resided with the officials of the 254 commissioners' courts and their heads, the county judges, who directed local government affairs.

By the early 1980s the activities of public interest lawyers were placing county officials in over 125 Texas counties increasingly at risk. Counties that had neither established public hospital districts nor assisted in the construction of public hospitals, and had not allocated county funds to pay for their "paupers' " medical care, were facing a growing threat of lawsuits filed on behalf of poor residents. Some of these lawsuits had been decided in favor of the plaintiffs. While attorneys representing Texas counties were appealing these rulings, the county commissioners' courts realized that at some future date a judgment against counties might be sustained. Once that transpired, federal courts would be dictating the terms of and monitoring the compliance with a mandated method of providing and funding indigent health care services; this would severely constrain the Texas legislature's oversight and control. Texas's Department of Corrections and Department of Mental Health and Mental Retardation were already operating under federal court orders and no one in a position of power at the state or county level wanted to increase the number and level of state governmental entities operating under federal court direction.

Some oil rich counties of East Texas, South Texas, and West Texas had the ability to pay for medical care for at least some of their neediest residents; but most of the rural-agricultural counties were economically underdeveloped and had tens of thousands of medically indigent residents and few fiscal resources to provide for their care.

Shifting the Cost of Indigent Care From County to County. Historically, the more than 125 largely rural counties lacking public hospitals or indigent care programs shifted the burden of care to nearby urban public hospitals as patients migrated to urban areas with relatively liberal eligibility standards to receive services. Or, such patients were sent to the teaching and research hospitals of the University of Texas Medical Branch (UTMB) at Galveston, which in effect served as the state's only hospital for the medically indigent. The long trip for many ailing, indigent patients to see a doctor at UTMB's hospitals meant delays in treatment and unnecessary suffering for many, and even premature death for some, but other options did not exist. Mexican-American residents of Texas's medically underserved Rio Grande Valley counties, and blacks and poor whites of rural East Texas were the main groups utilizing the UTMB services. Some of these same people would make a difference in the 1982 gubernatorial election race, casting their votes for an unlikely co-initiator of health policy reforms in Texas, Mark White.

Hospital Districts Sue the Counties. The mainly urban public hospitals not receiving compensation for providing medical care for out-of-county residents were also suing their neighboring commissioners' courts, seeking payment for services rendered. The Dallas County Hospital District had sued eight counties for lack of compensation for care delivered to out-of-county residents. In 1983 Parkland Hospital won a judgment against Grayson County—the first time in the history of Texas that a public hospital had succeeded in litigation against a neighboring county for failing to pay the bill of one of its residents who used the services of a public hospital (Dallas Morning News, August 19, 1984; cf. Villanueva 1987). Hence, the counties were fighting on several fronts against public interest lawyers and lawyers representing hospital districts; they had lost and were fearful that they would continue to lose these court cases. Thus, the counties were willing to seek some kind of legislative solution, especially after the sixty-eighth Legislature, that would limit their liability in the provision of indigent care.

Federal Medicaid Options Create Opportunities. When the Reagan administration assumed office in 1981, its initial goals for the Medicaid program were to reduce the level of federal spending and to give states additional authority and flexibility to control costs in the administration of the program. Under the guise of serving only the "truly needy" and cracking down on welfare fraud and abuse, the Omnibus Budget Reconciliation Act of 1981 cut the number of persons eligible for Medicaid largely by making AFDC eligibility more restrictive and more cumbersome for states to administer. The administration also proposed a cap on the level of federal spending for Medicaid which was well below the projected rate of growth of the program. Along with this attempted transfer of fiscal responsibility to the states, the administration's agenda included substantial changes in the nature of the program. "Medicaid would have operated more like a fixed federal block grant to states rather than as a jointly underwritten entitlement for specific services" (Bovjberg and Holahan 1982). Congress rejected a fixed cap on federal Medicaid spending in 1981 and in subsequent years, as cap proposals were reintroduced by the administration. The 1981 Omnibus Budget Reconciliation Act did include a new set of options for state Medicaid programs, including new reimbursement requirements for providers, service alternatives to institutional care, and targeted eligibility expansions for the medically needy. Elsewhere Villanueva (1985, 1987) has summarized the process and impact of these federal legislative changes during 1984. It suffices to say that, through lobbying by Texas officials (including representatives of the governor, lieutenant governor, and the Texas Department of Human Services Board), Senator Lloyd Bentsen's efforts assured state officials that expansions of Medicaid would not penalize states like Texas. By late 1984 Senator Bentsen had also secured an amendment to the Maternal and Child Health Block Grant so that additional federal funds would be available to the states for services already being considered for enhancement by the Texas Task force on Indigent Health Care. Thus, by late 1984, it was possible to realize some of the task force's ultimate recommendations without securing formal approval of the often recalcitrant state legislature and without fear of losing federal funds.

THE 1982 ELECTIONS ASSIGN DANCING PARTNERS

On a rainy election day in November 1982 voters stood in long lines across the state and rejected the reelection bid of Governor William Clements, selecting instead Attorney General Mark White. White was actually the beneficiary of an extraordinary get-out-the-vote campaign orchestrated by United States Senator Lloyd Bentsen and Lieutenant Governor William Hobby; both of these men were facing well-financed Republican opponents and feared that the 1980 Reagan electoral tide would continue in an off-year election to sweep Texas's leading Democratic politicians from office.

The 1982 recession was responsible for the election of many Democrats, but Republicans continued to retain control of the United States Senate. In Texas, with its traditional electoral domination by conservative rural and small town Democrats and patrician Democrats (ranchers and bankers, oil company executives and lawyers), the results of this election were particularly distressing for conservatives. The 1982 Democratic Party nominations for all statewide offices (except for United States senator, governor, lieutenant governor, and comptroller) had been won by progressive candidates. The leader of this unofficial slate was a man whose parentage and initial political career marked him as a Tory Democrat. Yet, in recent years Lieutenant Governor William Hobby, occupant of the most powerful statewide office, became the defender of state spending for higher education, health, and welfare.

With Governor Clements' defeat, one of the most ideologically conservative states, with its institutionalized hostility toward egalitarian, collective welfare policies, was poised for welfare reform. Not only would indigent health care reform be placed on the policy agenda, but a number of other proposals were contemplated and many were indeed passed into law by the end of 1986. In short, after the November 1982 elections, Texas was unexpectedly set for innovations in public policy.

TASK FORCE ON INDIGENT HEALTH CARE: ASSEMBLING A COALITION FOR REFORM

Lieutenant Governor Hobby was convinced of the need to find solutions to the growing indigent care problem. Newly elected Governor White was willing to follow the Hobby lead, partly because his election was in large part due to efforts of groups with a vested interest in indigent care—poor whites, blacks, and Hispanics. With the cosponsorship of a newly chosen speaker of the House of Representatives, Gib Lewis from Ft. Worth (whose Tarrant County hospital district was struggling to cope with the rising demands for indigent care), the state's leadership began to tackle the indigent care crisis.

The creation of the Task Force on Indigent Health Care followed expectations for the formation and operation of coalitions for public policy making. The appointment of special investigative bodies whose charge is also to make public policy recommendations is a well-used device in liberal-democratic polities (Hanson 1969, Walls 1969, Brown 1972, Sinclair 1981, and Villanueva 1985). In the case of Texas, the critical elements of the public policy-making process—legislative staff experts, bureaucratically based policy specialists, and interest group advocates—were assembled under the leadership of department heads, key legislators, and the governor, lieutenant governor, and the speaker.

Membership on the task force was carefully chosen to reflect a variety of interests: public and university teaching hospitals (Dallas, Harris, and other urban counties hospital administrators; University of Texas Medical Branch at Galveston's President); the health professions (Texas Medical Association, Texas Nurses Association); health educators (members of the faculties of various state medical schools and universities); private, nonprofit, and for-profit hospital groups (Texas Hospital Association); community health clinics (directors of rural and urban community health centers); mental health services (directors of community mental health centers); county governments (Texas Association of Counties, both county judges, commissioners, and their lawyers); health and welfare advocates; insurance companies; legal services lawyers; and consumers.

Crafting a Reform Coalition. The staffing of the task force was critical and reflected the linkages between the policy-making triangle of legislative staffers, agency personnel, and lobbyists. The Texas Department of Human Services (TDHS) (the largest player in the indigent health care game and responsibile for administering the state Medicaid program) provided the staff director. TDHS played a key role in providing technical services to the task force. The other major agency player (the Texas Department of Health, which administers maternal and child health programs, crippled children's services and other community health programs) also provided staff; and TDH's board president, Dr. Ron Anderson (who was also Chief Administrative Officer of Parkland Memorial Hospital) was a member of the task force and served on its executive committee. Other state agencies concerned with health care were represented in staffing positions or by ex officio appointments, for example: The Texas Health Facilities Commission (which oversaw the soon-to-be-defunct certificate-of-need process), the Health and Human Services Coordinating Council (an interdepartmental planning agency), and the Texas Advisory Commission on Intergovernmental Relations. Further, the critical Legislative Budget Board (which oversees the development of the biannual state budget and is chaired by the lieutenant governor) provided staff, as did the Legislative Council.

Selecting a chair of the task force was a critical decision for the governors and speaker, but the choice turned out to be an obvious one: Helen Farabee. Wife of Democratic State Senator Ray Farabee, she had served as head of a successful task force on reforming Texas's mental health code and had chaired a Texas Senate special committee on human service delivery.

Finally, a notable and venerable figure from past critical watershed developments in American public policy making served as a consultant to the task force. Professor Wilbur J. Cohen, of the Lyndon B. Johnson School of Public Affairs, acted as a senior advisor and guide to Mrs. Farabee, the staff, and the task force as a whole. Now nearing the end of his academic career, Cohen made public policy again at this critical juncture in the history of a welfare laggard.[4] As a consultant to the task force, Cohen oversaw the creation of a Texas version of maternal and child health programs which echoed the 1960s War on Poverty health programs (Marmor 1973, Levitan and Taggart 1965, Davis and Schoen 1978, Levitan 1985, cf. Murray 1984).

TASK FORCE DELIBERATIONS AND RECOMMENDATIONS

The process of task force deliberations and recommendation formulation has been elsewhere analyzed (cf. Villanueva 1985). In December 1984 the task force delivered its final recommendations which were endorsed by nearly all of the diverse elements assembled to make policy recommendations. The proposals were in some cases predictable, for example, to expand Texas's Medicaid coverage so that by 1990 half of the poverty population would be covered. A late 1970s task force had previously called for an expansion of Medicaid, and this route was the easiest and surest way of enhancing Texas's coverage of the poor and relieving public and private hospitals of the growing burden of charity and uncompensated care. Yet, other recommendations could not have been so easily anticipated given the controversies surrounding issues of county responsibilities for patient care.

A plan for all counties not fully served by a public hospital to provide or purchase some minimal level of medical care for their eligible residents was recommended and supported by the counties. Liability limits were placed at 10 percent of the county's budget; counties could spend less, but if they spent any more than 10 percent to meet state mandated standards for indigent care, state financial assistance would be provided. Also, explicit eligibility standards tied to the state's AFDC financial eligibility guidelines would now be used under this plan so that counties would serve individuals who were not categorically eligible for AFDC or Medicaid, primarily medically indigent adults. Counties (such as Dallas, Harris, and Tarrant) who supported a public hospital directly or through local taxation levied by a hospital district were expected to maintain their existing

264

efforts and more liberal eligibility guidelines. In adopting this proposal the counties that historically had not provided indigent care
were willing to provide some services, as long as they could limit
their financial liability to relatively predictable amounts, rather than
face the uncertainties associated with a court imposed funding mechanism. The urban and generally more affluent counties that had been
supporting public hospitals were willing to accept lower standards for
public benefits provided by rural counties because of Medicaid expansions and other state program expansions that would benefit public
hospitals. The support by counties of this complex legislative proposal marked a turning point in the history of Texas institutionalized
antagonism toward the poor.

Women and Children First. The task force decided to put women and
their unborn children first by calling for maternal and child health
services to be made available to the medically indigent population.
With ninety-three counties lacking prenatal clinics, the Texas Department of Health estimated that forty clinics were needed to fill
gaps in the service delivery system. The placement of maternal and
children's service expansion headed the list of services to be enhanced, either with Medicaid dollars or with state funds; this was a
calculated means of targeting scarce resources where the payoff was
likely to be greatest and also a method of marketing major policy
reform in a state fundamentally hostile to welfare.

Proponents of change on the task force felt that they could wrap
their tradition-breaking proposals in the clothes of fiscal conservatism by placing the highest priority on maternal and child health
services. First, they could argue (with some justification) that preventative, prenatal services would save money from the start by reducing the risk of low-birth-weight or premature babies that cost thousands of dollars to treat in neonatal intensive care units (Institute of
Medicine 1985). The costs to public hospitals for such care were
mounting, as were the numbers of total births at indigent care hospitals.[5]

Second, the task force proponents felt they could market the
program as "fiscally conservative." Babies carried to term are more
likely to be healthy; premature, low-birth-weight infants run a much
greater risk of physical and mental birth abnormalities. Such infants
are often developmentally delayed and require expensive special educational services or institutional care. As adults they are less likely

to be fully productive (and tax paying) members of society. Hence, the cost effectiveness of targeted interventions for a vulnerable population and the long-term cost savings were linked in the debate and final proposals of the task force for initial expenditures on expansion of preventative maternal and child health services. In the legislative debate over the program, the argument would be explicitly made that the indigent health care program was fiscally conservative.

A comparable rationale was presented for proposals to permit the provision of primary health care services by the Texas Department of Health. Legal restrictions prevented TDH from flexibly using their funds to provide primary care, despite the fact that many low-income families used state health department clinics for various preventative services, such as immunizations. The task force proposed that these restrictions be removed and that TDH promote with grants or directly provide indigent care services. Again the fiscal-conservative rationale was emphasized: delays in seeking medical care lead to increased morbidity and mortality and increased health care costs. Someone must pay for these increases, and it is, first, local taxpayers supporting public hospitals and, second, all citizens whose health insurance premiums are higher than they otherwise would be if there was no cost shifting in hospital care.

In the recommendations about local government responsibility for the indigent and in the proposals for new programs of primary and maternity care, the task force findings and recommendations identified the need for minimum service standards established at the state level and service delivery systems designed at the community level. For county indigent health care programs this would take the form of legislative standards for application processes, financial eligibility standards and services to be provided, but few perspective elements as to how the county was to organize its new program. For primary care and maternity service programs, a competitive negotiation process conducted by the state with explicit requirements for community participation in the proposal development would be suggested and ultimately used.

Additional recommendations were made regarding hospital reporting requirements and the inappropriate transfer of patients. Still other recommendations dealt with mental health service needs of the medically indigent, medical education, the liability insurance crisis, Texas-Mexico health care issues, and emergency services for the indigent. The task force framed many of its recommendations in terms of intertwining responsibilities: the federal government should provide sufficient levels of Medicaid funds, the state should pursue a human investment strategy and undertake cost-effective maternity and primary care program expansions, counties should have explicit responsibility for a group of indigent adults, all hospitals should provide support for indigent care, and even indigent individuals should contribute to the costs of care if at all possible.

The task force completed its work by December 1984 and filed a report which was generally and enthusiastically subscribed to by almost all task force members. The question remained, which of the recommendations would be translated into bills to be introduced in the sixty-ninth Legislature's upcoming session? And, what would be the probability of these proposals' success, given the Texas record of hostility toward health and welfare reforms?

MEDICAID EXPANSION OPPORTUNITIES ARE PARLAYED

The advocates of indigent health care knew that passing innovative legislation would be difficult although Lieutenant Governor Hobby was committed to a solution and, under his leadership of the state senate, passage of some legislation by that body was virtually assured. House passage in the sixty-eighth legislative session of bills that prefigured task force recommendations suggested that there was a coalition of urban county and minority group representatives willing to support legislation that would benefit their constituents.

Because the Texas Department of Human Services had a budget surplus resulting from Medicaid cost containment initiatives and the statutory flexibility to expand Medicaid coverage as long as federal matching funds are available, TDHS could begin in October 1984, three months before the sixty-ninth legislative session, to add coverage groups to the state Medicaid program. Ultimately, TDHS would cover categories of persons never served under Medicaid in Texas: pregnant women who otherwise would not be eligible for AFDC until the child was born, children in two-parent households meeting AFDC financial eligibility standards, and medically needy children and pregnant women whose income is below 133.3 percent of the AFDC payment amount. These Texas initiatives exceeded federal minimum requirements at the time. Here the task force process and its ultimate recommendations lent important legitimacy to TDHS program expansions, marking a turning point in indigent care. The task force had achieved a major breakthrough by seizing opportunities provided by incremental policy initiatives at the federal level, but its job of reforming Texas's antiquated county responsibility laws and addressing its many other recommendations remained. Nevertheless, the action to expand Medicaid provided strong impetus to the resolution of the issue of county responsibility. The county governments' fears of being saddled with full responsibility for the medically indigent were reduced by the assumption of increased responsibility and spending by the state. And with the Medicaid expansions, the counties were ready to come to the bargaining table—the Legislature—in earnest.

TEXAS FISCAL CRISIS: CONSTRAINTS ON POLICY INNOVATIONS

When the Legislature convened on January 8, 1985 the prospects for major policy innovations were not auspicious. The drop in oil prices was already beginning to depress state revenue estimates Comptroller Bob Bullock, who had to certify the availability of revenues for biennium's budget, was projecting a shortfall which either had to be met with tax increases, spending cuts, or both. Even if the legislature passed bills proposed by the task force, would there be funds for new programs?

Enacting Indigent Health Legislation: Unlikely Heroes, Predictable Villains. Six bills were introduced in the regular, 140-day session of the legislature by three task force members, Senators John Traeger and Chet Brooks, and Representative Jesse Oliver. These bills included what was labeled Senate Bill 1 (S.B. 1) during the special session, the Indigent Health Care and Treatment Act. This bill reflected the task force recommendations that called for setting minimum county responsibilities for indigent care and for establishing limits on the financial liability of counties. Two other legislative proposals reflected other task force recommendations: H.B. 1023, the Maternal and Infant Health Improvement Act; and H.B. 1844, the Primary Health Care Services Act. Hospital reporting and the controversial hospital transfer requirements were contained in H.B. 2091 and H.B. 1963. A related assessment of hunger in Texas had resulted in a report entitled "Faces of Hunger in the Shadow of Plenty" by the

268

Senate Interim Committee on Hunger and Nutrition, chaired by Senator Hugh Parmer of Ft. Worth. Legislation embodying some of the report's recommendations were contained in S.B. 526, The Omnibus Hunger Act of 1985.

Governor White's Vacillation. At historic turning points both the unexpected and the predictable occur. This mix of the anticipated and unanticipated characterized the passage of the legislation package which followed from the task force's final report.

Governor White vacillated throughout the legislative process. A special session called by the governor in 1984 resulted in major educational reform legislation but also a state tax increase of $5.2 billion, the largest state tax increase in the nation's history. Already in trouble with the voters because of a broken campaign promise not to raise taxes, White backed the principles of the task force and supported legislation, yet wavered in his support of funding proposals for the legislation. This was predictable; Mark White continued througout the course of his one-term governorship to take varying positions on an issue depending on what his opinion polls were telling him voter sentiment was. Though White ultimately "found money" for indigent care financing, in part out of the governor's discretionary funds, he frustrated backers of the proposal by his "no tax increase to fund indigent care" position.

While the task force process had helped to energize and mobilize a lobby for health care reform, this lobbying effort could only try to force a reluctant Mark White to maintain his commitments. Lobbyists organized by the Maternal and Child Health Coalition (which brought together the Children's Defense Fund, the March of Dimes of Texas, and thirty other provider and community organizations) and groups led by the Industrial Areas Foundation had mounted direct appeal campaigns and held rallies at the Capitol in the effort to gain passage of the bills.

Structural Interest Group Opposition to Reform. The Texas Hospital Association was cool toward several task force recommendations, including hospital reporting requirements. THA and its representatives on the task force repeatedly claimed that all hospitals were providing indigent care, but THA's own survey could not sufficiently support this contention. The rapid growth of the for-profit sector among Texas hospitals and the growing rivalries among hospitals for paying patients led to strong differences among THA members. THA repeatedly claimed that indigent care was "a societal obligation," an assertion so broad as to be meaningless in the negotiations occurring throughout the task force process. Though the hospitals were not happy with the reporting requirements and patient transfer rules that were envisioned by two pieces of legislation, they reserved most of their lobbying muscle for blocking a funding proposal, a 1 percent tax on their net revenues (cf. Alford 1975).

Such a tax was enacted and implemented in Florida with hospital support. Yet THA labeled the task force and legislative sponsors proposal a "sick tax" and launched a massive statewide multimedia campaign to kill the proposal. While the legislative sponsors of the indigent care legislative package did ultimately drop the hospital revenue tax idea, the THA paid a price in credibility and integrity by their strident lobbying effort. In the end, when funds were found and the package enacted, the hospital association had alienated the coalition supporting the indigent care package that the task force had assembled.

Lieutenant Governor Hobby fulfilled expectations of the task force and coalition members that he could deliver support of nearly the entire senate for indigent care reforms. In both the regular and subsequent special session the legislative proposals had an easy time gaining near unanimous support. In this and many other proposals including tax increases necessary to maintain state services the Texas Senate emerged under Hobby's leadership as the deliberative body most receptive to pragmatic governmental expansion proposals, as compared to the House of Representatives with about one third of its membership Republican and often dominated by a bipartisan conservative coalition.

Republicans and conservative Democrats behaved as expected, seeking to block the legislative package. This coalition did succeed in blocking the reauthorization of the Texas Health Facilities Commission, and the use of the certificate-of-need approval process could therefore not be used as the task force report proposed to further indigent care goals. The new "religious right" members of this conservative caucus proposed limiting abortions and sought to tie anti-abortion measures to the reauthorization of the Texas Department of Health, which like the facilities commission had undergone a "sunset review" process and was up for legislative renewal. Nonetheless, the regular session was productive for proponents of indigent care legislation. Hospital reporting and patient transfer requirements were enacted, and new programs for maternal and child health and primary care were authorized. One last bill, the Indigent Health Care and Treatment Act, which defined local government responsibility and appropriated the funds necessary to implement the other pieces of legislation, tortuously made its way through the legislative process.

In the closing minutes of the sixty-ninth Legislature's regular session Republican House Representative Bill Ceverha, one of the conservative's most outspoken opponents of taxing and spending for the poor, filibustered the indigent legislation to death. After Governor White called a special session to enact the final bill of the indigent care package, United States Senator Phil Gramm sought to demonstrate his leadership of Texas Republicans and to embarrass Mark White and the Democratic legislative leadership. From his Washington, D.C., office, Senator Gramm lobbied the GOP representatives in House and Senate to vote *en masse* against the indigent care programs.

Thus, in contrast to a regular legislative session in which deals can be struck, vote trade-offs made (and hence ideology and party label count for less), in the special session party and ideology counted for everything. Supporting or opposing the indigent care package became a test of loyalty. The program's benefits, its essentially fiscally conservative features (spend state money "up front" in order to capture federal matching funds and to save money on expensive hospital care and, in the long run, on institutional care) could not be sold to Republicans and conservative Democrats being lobbied by Gramm.

S.B. 1, the unchanged Indigent Health Care and Treatment Act which had failed in the closing moments of the regular session, was passed quickly by the Senate and returned to the House. House Speaker Gib Lewis was the unlikely hero of health care reform. The business lobbyist's best friend cast the crucial, tie-breaking vote that permitted the programs condemned by anti-taxing, anti-welfare legislators to become law.

Ironically, without the lieutenant governor and the speaker—two of the most establishment figures in state government—and the Washington induced reforms facilitated by Senator Bentsen, the pro-indigent care lobby could not and would not realize its objectives in a state with so many well-entrenched ideological antagonists toward welfare reform.

PROGRAM IMPLEMENTATION

For fiscal years 1985–1987, $70 million was appropriated to fund the indigent care programs. More than $20 million in new spending by counties was anticipated once S.B. 1 was implemented, meaning that counties previously expending very little, if anything, would now contribute to support indigent care. Increased state Medicaid spending would capture new federal matching dollars, and for a suddenly cash starved Texas, recovery of every federal tax dollar shipped to Washington, D.C., was essential. These Medicaid expansions were estimated to cost over $110 million through fiscal year 1987. Thus, Texas was anticipated to directly or indirectly spend approximately $200 million on indigent care after the landmark bills passed.

While not enough to cover half of the Medicaid-eligible children on AFDC, not enough to assure access for all the poor to state funded services, not enough to pay for all of the medically underserved in Texas's counties without public hospitals, not enough to ensure the viability of public hospitals across the state, these funds nevertheless represented a down payment on the needed indigent care spending for poorest of the poor in the state.

CONCLUSION

Welfare reform may take many forms, reflecting the specific issues targeted for action, the institutional and ideological constraints that must be confronted, and the strategies and tactics adopted by advocates of change. In Texas, the prospects for the State Legislature raising AFDC benefit payments and coverage to levels comparable in other urban-industrial states are quite low. The very modest increases in AFDC in Texas approved in the early 1980s still leaves the vast majority of the state's poor children without cash benefits or Medicaid coverage. Beginning in late 1983, however, welfare reform advocates in Texas were able to successfully tackle one problem related to poverty—the deepening crisis in indigent health care.

This case study of indigent health care reform shows that even in a state where hostility toward taxing and spending for welfare is institutionalized, forces and processes working within and without the formal institutions of government can produce legislative and administrative changes resulting in an expansion of the welfare state. From a broad social control perspective (cf. Armour and Coughlin 1985), conservative members of the political elite (e.g., Speaker Lewis, Governor White) were able to realize that it was in their political interest to preside over program initiatives that did not just represent "payment" to their electoral allies (e.g., low-income black and Hispanic voters) but also yielded deeper and longer-term benefits, such as improving life expectancies at birth. Although these reforms were incremental and narrowly won in a difficult legislative struggle, they were comprehensive in scope and a precursor both to the efforts to enact indigent care legislation in other states and to the growing national interest in welfare reform. Texas was the second state (after Colorado) to create a special commission to study medical indigence, and it was the first of the states to enact a comprehensive package of reforms. By the end of 1985, ten states had established special study efforts on indigent care and another ten had adopted major policy changes (Desonia and Leuhrs 1985). As with national welfare reform efforts, the indigent care creation process in Texas was marked by an effort to define mutual responsibilities among levels of government, the public and private sector, and the indigent individual; and it placed a strong emphasis on investing in human resources, including the lives of poor people, to yield a more productive citizenry. Similarly, welfare reform and Texas's indigent care initiatives share an emphasis on the need for programs designed with local involvement. In this sense, the Texas story of enacting indigent care legislation is interpretable within the existing theoretical framework and empirical findings on the welfare state.

NOTES

1. Many people assisted in the research and writing of this chapter. Bryan P. Sperry, formerly director of Family Health Resources, Texas Department of Human Services, served as the chief of staff for the Task Force on Indigent Health Care. He provided much necessary information, made revisions, and enhanced the accuracy of this analysis. The doctoral dissertation and subsequent writings of Augusta M. (Toti) Villanueva provided the basis

for the descriptive narrative of policy making for indigent health care in Texas. Richard M. Coughlin made many editorial and substantive suggestions which have been incorporated in this work. Insights were gleaned from the following persons who were interviewed for this study: the Hon. William P. Hobby, the Hon. John Traeger, the Hon. Jesse Oliver, Jerry Chapman, and Buddy Jones. Helen Farabee was both interviewed and read an earlier version of this chapter. Dr. Ron Anderson made editorial suggestions and substantive comments as did Betsy Julian. In addition, I would like to thank Jorge Anchondo for his support in this project.

2. Hartz (1964; cf. 1955) conceived of the nations of the New World and the Antipodes as partaking of a fragment of European traditions, both ideological and institutional. The subsequent differing paths of development of these new societies (the nations studied included the United States, Australia, and various Latin American republics) were shaped by the particular fragment of the Old World civilization that was rooted in a new land.

3. The Northern and Central European democratic-corporatistic states (e.g., Sweden, The Netherlands, Austria), evidence a tradition in marked contrast with Texas and other societies holding to a comparable value-institutional constellation, which in its political manifestation takes the form of hostility to the welfare state (cf. Wilensky 1976).

4. Dr. Cohen had gone to Washington, D.C., in 1933 as a newly minted economics Ph.D. from the University of Wisconsin and had played a key role in the policy deliberations that yielded the 1935 Social Security Act. With its passage the United States began the slow process of joining the ranks of advanced nations with social insurance programs for the aged, unemployed, and other categories of dependent persons. During the next two decades Cohen helped oversee the implementation and expansion of Old Age Insurance and the enactment of Medicare and Medicaid as President Johnson's Secretary of Health, Education, and Welfare.

5. Dallas County's public indigent care facility, Parkland Hospital, ranks third nationwide in births, and to a large extent these are to women who have had little or no prenatal care. While about 80 percent of the county's low-income women were served by the twenty-two-year-old Maternal and Child Health clinic services, 18 percent of the women delivering babies had received no prenatal care. This group contributes about half of all newborns utilizing the neonatal intensive care unit at an average cost of $1000 per day (cf. Smith and Wait 1986).

BIBLIOGRAPHY

Alford, Robert. 1975. *Health Care Politics: Ideological and Interest Group Barriers to Reform.* Chicago: University of Chicago Press.

Anderson, Ron. J., R. G. Newman, and M. R. Zetzman. 1983. "Critical Issues

Confronting Public Teaching Hospitals in Texas." *Texas Medicine* 79 (April).

Armour, Philip K., and Richard M. Coughlin. 1985. "Social Control and Social Security: Theory and Research on Capitalist and Communist Nations." *Social Science Quarterly* 66 (December):770–88.

Bovjberg, Randall R., and John Holahan. 1982. *Medicaid in the Reagan Era: Federal Policy and State Choices*. Washington, D.C.: The Urban Institute.

Brown, David S. 1972. "The Management of Advisory Committees: An Assignment for the '70s." *Public Administration Review* 23 (August): 334–42.

Dallas Morning News. 1984. "Texas Indigent Health Care Crisis." 135 (August 19) 324:1 and 26–27.

Davis, Karen, and K. Schoen. 1978. *Health and the War on Poverty*. Washington, D.C.: Brookings Institution.

Desonia, Randy, and John Leuhrs. 1985. *Addressing Health Care for the Indigent: State Initiatives 1985*. Washington, D.C., National Governors' Association and Intergovernmental Health Policy Project.

Hanson, Hugh R. 1969. "Inside Royal Commissions." *Canadian Public Administration*. 12 (Fall):3.

Hartz, Louis. 1955. *The Liberal Tradition in America*. New York: Harcourt Brace.

———, ed. 1964. *The Founding of New Societies*. New York: Harcourt, Brace, and World.

Institute of Medicine. 1985. *Preventing Low Birthweight*. Washington, D.C.: National Academy Press.

Lanham, Leslie. 1985. *Understanding the Texas Indigent Health Legislation*. Austin: Children's Defense Fund, Maternal and Child Health Project.

Levitan, Sar. 1985. *Programs in Aid of the Poor*. Baltimore: Johns Hopkins University Press.

Levitan, Sar, and R. Taggart. 1976. *The Promise of Greatness*. Cambridge: Harvard University Press.

Marmor, Theodore. 1973. *The Politics of Medicare*. Chicago: Aldine.

Marshall, T.H. 1964. *Class, Citizenship, and Social Development*. Garden City: Doubleday.

Murray, Charles. 1984. *Losing Ground*. New York: Basic.

Sinclair, Barbara. 1981. "The Speaker's Task Force in the Post-Reform House of Representatives." *American Political Science Review*. 75 (July) 2:397–410.

Smith, Peggy B., and Raymond Wait. 1986. "Adolescent Fertility and Childbearing Trends among Hispanics in Texas." *Texas Medicine* 86 (November):29–32.

Task Force on Indigent Health Care. 1984. *Final Report.* Austin: State of Texas.

Texas Almanac. 1985. Dallas: Dallas Morning News.

U.S. Department of Commerce, Bureau of the Census. 1986. *State and Metropolitan Area Data Book, 1986.* Washington, D.C.: U.S. Government Printing Office.

Villanueva, Augusta M. 1985. *The Task Force on Indigent Health Care: 1983–85.* Ann Arbor: University of Michigan Microfilms and the University of Texas at Austin.

———. 1987. "Catching Up to the Seventies in the Eighties: The Politics of Indigent Health Care in Texas." Unpublished paper.

Walls, C.E.S. 1969. "Royal Commissions—Their Influence on Public Policy." *Canadian Public Administration.* 12 (Fall) 3:365–71.

Wilensky, Harold L. 1965. "Problems and Prospects of the Welfare State." In *Industrial Society and Social Welfare,* by H. L. Wilensky and C. N. Lebeaux. Glencoe: Free Press.

———. 1975. *The Welfare State and Equality.* Berkeley: University of California Press.

———. 1976. *The New Corporatism, Centralization, and the Welfare State.* Beverly Hills: Sage Publication.

List of
Contributors

PHILIP K. ARMOUR is Associate Professor of Political Economy at the University of Texas at Dallas. He is the author of *The Cycles of Social Reform* and has written on health and mental health policy, and the welfare state. He served as a member of the Texas Task Force on Indigent Health Care.

TOMÁS ATENCIO has worked for many years in the fields of mental health and community organization in northern New Mexico. Currently, he is Associate Director of the Southwest Hispanic Research Institute at the University of New Mexico.

GARY BURTLESS is a senior fellow in the Economic Studies Program at the Brookings Institution where he does research on labor markets, income redistribution, and the economic effects of taxes. He has written articles on applied econometrics and microeconomics, including recent papers on the effects of Social Security, welfare, unemployment insurance, and manpower training.

RICHARD M. COUGHLIN is Associate Professor and Chairman of the Department of Sociology at the University of New Mexico, where he has taught since 1978. He is the author of *Ideology, Public Opinion and Welfare Policy*. Besides welfare policy, his research interests include Social Security and the comparative political economy of industrialized societies.

JANE HOYT COTTER recently retired as director of the Income Support Division of the New Mexico Human Services Department. In a career of more than twenty years in the human services, she worked at every level of income support programs.

JOHN A. DAELEY is Regional Director, Region VI, of the U.S. Department of Health and Human Services, a post he has occupied since 1981. He has also served as chairman of the Southwest Federal Regional Council.

Prior to assuming his current position, he was Director of Project Review with the Texas Area-5 Health Systems Agency.

EDWARD J. HARPHAM is Associate Professor of Government and Political Economy at the University of Texas at Dallas. He is the author or editor of four books and numerous scholarly articles. His current research interests focus on the development of the American welfare state and the history of political economy.

A. SIDNEY JOHNSON, III, is executive director of the American Public Welfare Association, which represents the state and local human service departments and six thousand individuals in the social welfare field. He formerly served as a special assistant to Secretary of Health, Education and Welfare Wilbur Cohen, as a senior policy aide to then-Senator Walter F. Mondale, and as an outside consultant to Vice-President Mondale and HEW Secretary Joseph A. Califano.

CHARLES LOCKHART is Associate Professor of Political Science at Texas Christian University, where he has taught since 1974. He has done extensive work in the area of international relations and is the author of *Bargaining in International Conflicts*. His most recent book, *Tailoring Social Programs to American Values*, will be published by the University of California Press.

THE NATIONAL COALITION ON WOMEN, WORK, AND WELFARE REFORM was formed in 1985 to address the emergence of new state and federal welfare employment initiatives. The coalition represents over twenty national organizations concerned about the impact of AFDC work programs on women and their families.

THE NATIONAL GOVERNORS' ASSOCIATION, founded in 1908 as the National Governors' Conference, has as its membership the governors of the fifty states, U.S. commonwealths, and territories. The association works with the administration and Congress on state-federal policy issues, serving as a vehicle for sharing knowledge among the states and providing technical assistance and consultant services to the governors on a wide range of management and policy issues.

RICHARD K. SCOTCH is Assistant Professor of Sociology and Political Economy at the University of Texas at Dallas. His research interests include the role of ideological and organizational factors in public policy making and reform movements in social policy. He is currently completing a book on the disability rights movement.

DANIEL H. WEINBERG is an economist in the Office of Income Security Policy, U.S. Department of Health and Human Services. He is the coeditor of *Fighting Poverty: What Works and What Doesn't* and has published articles on the "poverty gap."

Index

LADYBIRD BOOKS, INC.
Auburn, Maine 04210 U.S.A.
© LADYBIRD BOOKS LTD 1990
Loughborough, Leicestershire, England
Printed in England

Bad Ben
and the Monster

By Joan Stimson
Illustrated by Diane Palmisciano

Ladybird Books

Ben was in trouble. He came home with a note from his teacher.

"Ben has cut Henry's hair, eaten Lucy's lunch, and let out the hamster," the note said.

Mom and Dad were furious. "You've behaved *very* badly," said Mom. "Tomorrow night, instead of coming to the movies with us, you will have to stay home."

But Ben didn't want to stay home. So that evening, he crept downstairs to say he was sorry.

He heard his parents talking in the kitchen.

"Mrs. Mason can babysit tomorrow night," Mom was saying. "But this time, she's bringing her monster."

Ben shot back upstairs. First he was puzzled. Then he was scared. The monster must be his punishment for misbehaving!

All night Ben tossed and turned. He kept seeing shadows in the curtains. Was Mrs. Mason's monster short and fat...or long and thin?

"I hope she keeps it on a leash!" he whispered.

At school the next day, Ben couldn't concentrate on math. All he could do was count. He counted monster arms, monster legs, monster horns, monster fangs....

"What if Mrs. Mason's monster has three eyes?" he wondered. "What if it has just *one*?"

After math, Ben's teacher got out the paints.
Ben shuddered as he picked up his paintbrush.

"Is Mrs. Mason's monster blue...or purple...
or *green*?" he wondered.

At recess, Ben stood in a corner of the schoolyard. He kept thinking about monster games—and about all his toys being trampled.

"I don't *want* to play hide-and-seek with a monster!" he thought.

That evening, Ben couldn't eat his dinner. His mind was on other meals. Did Mrs. Mason's monster eat cookies...or worms...or *worse*?

"Please don't go out," whispered Ben, as his parents were getting ready. But they didn't hear him.

"Mrs. Mason will be here soon," said Mom.

"*And* her monster," said Dad.

Ben flew upstairs. He hid his toys. Then he hid himself.

Ding-a-ling-a-ling! went the doorbell. Ben jumped into bed. He held the pillow over his ears, but he could still hear voices.

"Now, here's the coffee and here are the cookies," Mom was saying. "And you know what to do if Ben misbehaves."

"Don't worry," came the reply. "Just leave everything to me!"

Bang! The front door slammed shut.

Ben closed his eyes tight and pulled up the covers. But he could still see Mrs. Mason's monster!

And now he could *hear* the monster! It was coming up the stairs!

Ben didn't dare open his eyes. But he was too scared to keep them shut. He held his breath as the bedroom door opened.

"Hello, Ben," said Mrs. Mason. "This is Oliver."
Then she smiled. "*Awful* Oliver, his teacher calls him.
I'm afraid he's a bit of a...monster!"

Ben breathed again. He could hardly believe his eyes—the monster looked just like him!

Ben smiled.

Oliver smiled, too.

Ben and Oliver both behaved that evening. They ate cookies and played hide-and-seek. And when Mrs. Mason said it was bedtime, Ben went straight upstairs.

When Ben's parents came home, they went to Ben's room to tuck him in. They smiled as they bent down to kiss him good night.

"We love you, Ben," said Mom.

"Yes," said Dad, "even when you're a monster!"